Manzana
Publishing
Print - e-book

ManzanaPublishing@hotmail.com

Watch for other works
with
Jerry Appleton

The Letters
A Love Story
A Lifetime
*

Life Lessons
in a Collection of
Short Stories
*

Finally Home
The two-decade search
for a birth family
*

A Year in Quotes
Another day
Another quote

Book Two
*

Freddie Fuddle
from
Friendly Hollow
*

Once Upon A Rhyme
*Stories from the
Kingdom of Four Corners*

For more information visit our webpage:
JerryAppleton.com

A Year in Quotes
A quote a day
keeps the therapist away
Book One

with
Jerry Appleton

No part of this book may be used or reproduced in any manner whatsoever without the prior written permission of the author and the publisher, except in the case of reviews.

Manzana
Publishing
Print – e-books

ManzanaPublishing@hotmail.com

ISBN 978-0-9918478-2-2

CreateSpace Edition

A Year in Quotes
Book One

Copyright © 2013
Jerry Appleton

All rights reserved

Acknowledgements

Every writer will rapidly confess to a long list of individuals who encouraged him or her, directly or indirectly, to continue writing one project in particular or to pursuing writing in general.

This writer will humbly confess to a similar list. I wish to thank my many champions –

>To Lin (Caron) who never missed an opportunity to encourage my next writing day all the while totally immersed in her own writing project, *Onto The Next Lily Pad*.

>To my sons, Jeff, also a writer (*Henry Pride, Simon Fink* and *Eshu's Dream*) and Brad, totally dedicated to his career as a commercial pilot, for always being my beacon. Never have I forgotten the most important part of life – my reflection in your eyes. I love you.

>To Valery (Wint), another writer friend (*The Longer Run: A Daughter's Story of Arthur Wint*), and to my dear cousin, Jeannette Shirley, a retired educator, who patiently sat with *A Year in Quotes – Book One* and edited every single word. Thank you.

>To my many special friends dating back to my early days on Lefebvre Street in Cornwall and to my cherished university colleagues and life-long friends who have always inspired me to be a better person.

>And finally, to the great people I have had the pleasure of working along side over my four-plus decades in broadcasting. From the studio crews at CHCH-TV (Hamilton, Ontario), to the dedicated individuals during the early launch years at the Global Television Network, to my cherished friends at Venture Entertainment Group, to the special people I shared time with at Rogers Broadcasting Ltd/The Shopping Channel. All these kind patient people were, at one time or another, "prisoners" to my never-ending stories and quotes and, perhaps thinking it, never did one try to escape.

To all – a sincere thank you.

Introduction

Some writing projects are more emotionally draining than one might expect. Some test your discipline as a writer. Some challenge your endurance. Some prove to be a definite struggle to remaining at the keyboard in the face of any and all minor distractions.

A Year in Quotes – Book One was a pleasure – a pleasure to write from front cover to back cover. Spending the many months in the company of some of the most interesting minds of the centuries proved to be a fascinating journey. Each new piece of research from the countless sources led to yet another unknown personal fact about the authors of the quotes. The 366 mini-biographies offer but a mere glimpse into the personal lives of these interesting individuals. The hope is that the mini-bio's might trigger further curiosity on the part of the readers.

Over the past months I introduced myself to Confucius, Jean-Jacques Rousseau, Mark Twain, Moliere, Charles Dickens, Abraham Lincoln and countless other 'new' friends. Their wise and witty words made me smile, made me ponder life, made me deepen my admiration and respect for others, made me giggle out loud . . . and never, ever, failed to inspire me. I am a better person for having spent time with them.

Now – I wish to introduce you, the reader, to <u>your</u> new friends.

*"A good deed need not be paid back.
But should always be paid forward!"*

Jerry Appleton

January 1st

*I wish for you everything
you wish for yourself.*

Daniel Enright
Television Producer
(1917 - 1992)

Daniel Enright, born and raised in British Palestine, survived the atrocities of the Holocaust years as a young Jewish man. During the 1940's Enright moved to New York City to launch a career in broadcasting and became one of the most successful game show producers in American television. Within a short period of time, he teamed up with television personality, Jack Barry, and for over four decades they created and produced countless programs for network radio and television under the banner of Barry and Enright Productions. The company was responsible for such favorite game shows as *Concentration* and *Twenty-One.* Enright continued to operate the production company as Barry & Enright Productions after Barry's sudden death in 1984.

During his lifetime Dan served as devoted mentor and kind friend to a large number of aspiring young television producers and directors, including the author of this book of quotes. He shared the above quote, along with a tender hug, at the end of each lengthy get-together over a fine meal and great conversation. He was a hero to many and a sincere mentor to the fortunate few.

Dan Enright died of cancer on May 22, 1992, at age 74. The "wish" quote is carved on his headstone.

January 2nd

If you have a garden and a library, you have everything you need.

Marcus Tullius Cicero
Philosopher and Statesman
(106 BC – 43 BC)

Cicero was born into a wealthy Roman family. As a child he was encouraged by his parents to study and devote his life to the teachings of the ancient Greek philosophers, poets and historians. In time he mastered a full command of Latin and Greek – the sign of a cultured person at the time. Cicero became one of the great Roman orators.

Cicero, a talented lawyer, was involved in a number of high-profile criminal proceedings, including his successful defense of Sextus Roscius who had been charged with the heinous crime of patricide. Cicero's passion for public service led him to politics where his exceptional oratory skills made him a favorite of the people.

Cicero and Mark Antony became life-long political rivals. Eventually Cicero and his supporters were declared enemies of the state by Mark Antony. Cicero was hunted down by Antony's men with great difficulty because Cicero had the sympathy by a large segment of the Roman population and they refused to betray him.

Cicero was captured and history reports his last words to be - "There is nothing proper about what you are doing, soldier, but do try to kill me properly."

January 3rd

*In the depth of winter,
I finally learned that within me
lay an invincible summer.*

Albert Camus
Writer and Philosopher
(1913 - 1960)

Albert Camus was born in French Algeria into a poor and illiterate working-class family. Camus' farmer-father was killed during one of the great WWI battles. His partially deaf mother kept the family together in a ghetto-like part of Algiers.

As an active journalist, Camus was often called upon to defend his pacifism. He authored countless passionate articles and essays against the world-wide practice of capital punishment.

Camus became one of the most important philosophers of the 20th century. Camus' most famous was the novel *L'Étranger* (*The Stranger*). He was the second-youngest recipient of the Nobel Prize for Literature (1957), second to Rudyard Kipling.

Camus died in 1960 at the age of 46 in a car accident in France. At the last minute he had changed his travel plans and drove with his publisher. In his coat pocket lay an unused train ticket. He had originally planned to travel by train with his wife and children.

January 4th

Either that wallpaper goes or I go.

Oscar Wilde
Writer, Playwright and Poet
(1854 - 1900)

Oscar Wilde, was born in Dublin, Ireland, the second of three children born to Sir William Wilde, a surgeon, and Lady Jane Wilde, a devoted mother who was a poet in her own right. Lady Jane shared her love for poetry with the children. The household of intellects would influence young Oscar. He became an exceptional student and entered university at the age of seventeen. While at university Wilde developed a certain panache for fashion.

Wilde served as a journalist in London for four years. After trying his hand at several writing forms Wilde became one of London's most popular playwrights towards the end of the 19th century. His most notable play, *The Importance of Being Earnest*, remains an central piece of theatre to this day. Wilde wrote only one novel which has also withstood the test of time - *The Picture of Dorian Gray*.

Sadly he died destitute in Paris at the age of forty-six. Oscar Wilde, never at a loss for a memorable phrase, spoke the above quote on his death bed in Paris while holding the hand of a dear friend.

January 5th

Perfection is achieved, not when there's nothing more to add, but when there's nothing left to take away.

Antoine de Saint-Exupéry
Writer and Aviator
(1900 - 1944)

Antoine de Saint-Exupéry was born in Lyon, France, to an old established noble family. His father, the Viscount Jean de Saint-Exupéry, died when Antoine was shy of his fourth birthday.

Saint-Exupéry proved not to be an ideal student while at pre-university failing his preparatory exams. He eventually studied architecture at the famous École des Beaux-Arts. At the age of 21, he enlisted with a regiment of light cavalry (le 2e Régiment de Chasseurs à Cheval). The following year he earned his wings as a pilot and began a life-long love affair with aviation. Appropriately, his first published story in 1926 was entitled *L'Aviateur* (*The Aviator*).

Saint-Exupéry wrote a number of books with an aviation theme, including *Vol de Nuit* – 1931 (*Night Flight*) and his memoirs (*Wind, Sand and Stars*). But history remembers him best as the writer of the philosophical novella – *Le Petit Prince* (*The Little Prince*).

January 6th

***A candle loses nothing
by lighting another candle.***

Father James Keller
Spiritual Leader and broadcaster
(1900 - 1977)

James Keller was born James Kelleher in Oakland, California, in a devout Roman Catholic family. James' Irish-immigrant father changed the family name to avoid the anti-Irish sentiment of the early 20th-century.

James entered the seminary of the Maryknoll Order with the deep desire of serving in a foreign mission. In preparation for a life in the missions he devoted time observing surgical and medical procedures in order to better serve the needs of his third-world flocks.

Father James Keller was never assigned to a foreign mission. The young priest would go on to be a highly-respected spiritual leader in the North American Catholic church. In 1945, he founded *The Christophers*, a spiritual and inspirational organization. Over several decades he produced and hosted a weekly television network and syndicated series called *Christopher Close-up*.

Father Keller's teachings touched the lives of many individuals until his death in 1977.

January 7th

*I have learned that people
will forget what you said,
people will forget what you did,
but people will never forget
how you made them feel.*

Maya Angelou
Writer and Poet
(b. 1928)

Maya Angelou, born Marguerite Ann Johnson in Saint Louis, Missouri, during the depression, can trace her ancestry back to the Mende people of West Africa. Maya's father was a navy dietitian and her mother, a surgical nurse. Young Marguerite earned her nickname, Maya, from her older brother, Bailey Jr, as he attempted to pronounce "my-a sister".

Maya's early childhood was made more difficult by the fact that her parents separated and eventual divorced. After the family's break-up, Maya and her brother were sent to live with their paternal grandmother in Arkansas. Later, at the age of eight and under the care of her birth mother, Maya was abused by her mother's boyfriend. Maya told her brother about the abuse and eventually the man was charged but only spent one day in prison. He was beaten to death by her family. Maya was so traumatized by the events that she remained mute for five years. Maya Angelou overcame her challenges and became one of America's most notable black poets and autobiographers.

Maya went on to write a series of six autobiographical books starting with *I Know Why the Caged Bird Sings* in 1969 at the age of 41.

January 8th

Courage is the resistance to fear, mastery of fear – not absence of fear.

Mark Twain
Writer and Lecturer
(1835 - 1910)

Mark Twain, born in Florida, Missouri, as Samuel Clemens, moved with his parents at the age of four to Hannibal, Missouri, by the great Mississippi River. His early childhood on the shores of the river and later as a pilot on the majestic steamboats would prove to be the inspiration for the creation of a number of literature's greatest works and endearing characters.

Following a variety of jobs across the country, Clemens wrote a humorous story for a Virginia City newspaper in 1863 using for the first time the pen name, 'Mark Twain' – the term used by river boatmen to call out a safe depth of two fathoms ("by the mark twain"). Twain traveled extensively abroad as a reporter and earned his first acclaim as a writer with the release of the humorous tall tale, *The Celebrated Jumping Frog of Calaveras* (1865).

Mark Twain quickly earned a reputation as a gifted writer and lecturer. The *Adventures of Tom Sawyer* (1876) and *The Adventures of Huckleberry Finn* (1885) earned Clemens a place of honor in American literary history.

Twain is buried in Elmira, New York. The monument which stands at his grave is exactly twelve feet high – two fathoms or 'mark twain'.

January 9th

A politician is a man who will double cross that bridge when he comes to it.

Oscar Levant
Pianist, Composer and Humorist
(1906 - 1972)

Oscar Levant, was born in Pittsburgh, Pennsylvania, into a Russian Orthodox Jewish family. At the age of 16, young Levant moved to New York with his mother following the sudden death of his father.

After studying piano with the great Zygmunt Stojowski, Levant (22) transplanted himself to Hollywood where he met George Gershwin. The friendship proved to be life-changing. Levant became a popular composer for film sound tracks in the 30's and 40's. He also wrote a number of standard songs which made it to the pop 'Hit Parade'. During the same decades he was a frequent guest voice on radio.

Levant's career spanned the three main entertainment fields of the day – movies, radio and television. His quick and biting wit made him a popular guest on Jack Paar's late-night talk show.

The genius in Levant eventually haunted him. In his later years, he fell victim to his neurosis and self-confessed hypochondria. He became addicted to prescribed drugs and was admitted to mental institutions on several occasions by his devoted wife, actress June Gale.

Levant died of a heart attack at 65.

January 10th

*You got to be careful;
if you don't know where you're going,
because you might not get there.*

Yogi Berra
Baseball Player and Manager
(b. 1925)

Yogi Berra, born Lawrence Peter Berra, grew up in an Italian neighborhood of St. Louis. His childhood friend was another baseball great – Joe Garagiola.

The Baseball Hall of Famer (1972) was given his famous nickname, Yogi, by a friend, Bobby Hofman, after a character in a movie. Berra dropped out of school after grade eight, leading him to speak his own brand of English. His quaint sayings became very popular during his baseball years. At twenty-one (1946), the New York Yankees offered him a $500 signing bonus. Berra would go on to prove himself to be considered the greatest catcher in baseball history.

Berra's distinguished career as a player (MVP three times) was followed by an impressive second career as a manager for both the New York Yankees and the New York Mets. He is one of only six managers to take Americans and National league teams to the World Series.

January 11th

Laws should be like clothes.
They should be made
to fit the people they serve.

Clarence Darrow
Lawyer
(1857 - 1938)

Clarence Darrow came from well-established New England families in both his father and mother's lineage. His parents were activists – his father was a dedicated abolitionist and his mother, a woman's rights advocate.

Young Darrow attended Allegheny College and the University of Michigan. In 1878 at the age of 21, he was admitted to the Ohio bar. Darrow distinguished himself in three branches of law – corporate, labor and criminal. For a number of years Darrow represented the legal interests of various American railway companies and unions.

Throughout his life Darrow maintained a strong stand against capital punishment. He was involved in over one hundred murder cases and lost only one which ended in an execution. Darrow's two most famous cases (teen-agers Nathan Leopold and Richard Loeb accused of kidnapping and murder (1924) and the Scopes Monkey Trial) established him as an exceptional lawyer.

Darrow died at the age of 80 in Chicago.

January 12th

*Be amusing:
never tell unkind stories;
above all, never tell long ones.*

Benjamin Disraeli
Politician and Writer
(1804 - 1881)

Benjamin Disraeli was born of Jewish parents at the beginning of the 19th-century. His father, a literary critic and historian, had young Benjamin baptized at 13 years of age in the Christian faith after a feud with the local synagogue.

Disraeli's father wished Benjamin to enter law but he was drawn to a career in finance. After various business failures, most notably the failed attempt to launch a major newspaper, Disraeli turned his attention to writing. In 1826, he published his first novel – *Vivian Grey*. Only one of his novels, *Henrietta Temple*, proved to be a literary success.

In the 1830's Disraeli would find his true calling – politics. His command of the English language and his powers of persuasion allowed him to gain attention. Queen Victoria became his champion. Disraeli served as Prime Minister of Great Britain for two periods: 1868 (February – December) and 1874-1880 while acting as Leader of the Opposition between 1868 and 1874.

During his later years Queen Victoria elevated Benjamin Disraeli to Earl of Beaconsfield.

January 13th

Judge a man by his questions rather than by his answers.

Voltaire
Writer, Playwright and Philosopher
(1694 - 1778)

Voltaire was born François Marie Arouet in Paris one of five children – only two survived. His father, a successful notary, wished his son to follow in his footsteps but the young Francois' rebellious ways led him to a life in literature.

Arouet wrote under various names before settling on the pen name 'Voltaire' – an anagram of the Latin spelling of the family name. During his lifetime, Voltaire's defiant nature led to numerous confrontations with the French government and the Catholic Church. His wit and gift with the written word made him unpopular with the French aristocracy. Voltaire took every means to defend freedom of religion and speech.

During a three-year exile to Great Britain Voltaire developed a strong affinity for English literature, especially Shakespeare, and the British form of government. He was eventually banned from Paris in 1754.

The writings of Voltaire and other French writers, such as Jean-Jacques Rousseau, would prove to have a strong influence on the leaders of the American and French revolutions.

In 1778, Voltaire returned to Paris to attend a performance of his last play, *Irene*, where he was celebrated as a hero. He died within weeks.

January 14th

*Life is not measured
by the number of breaths we take,
but by the moments
that take our breath away.*

Unknown

Unknown is not a fitting tribute for such an inspirational quote but extensive research failed to produce a valid author.

The popular belief is that the quote was penned by a young Canadian gentleman who was hired by Carlton Cards to write greetings sometime in the 1970's.

Despite the popularity of the quote no one has stepped forward with proof they were the original writer.

The mystery continues.

January 15th

*Better to remain silent
and be thought a fool
than to speak out
and remove all doubt.*

Abraham Lincoln
Politician and Lawyer
(1809 - 1865)

Abraham Lincoln, the 16th President of the United States, was born in a one-room log cabin in Kentucky. Lincoln's only sibling, sister Sarah, died in early adulthood while giving birth. Lincoln's paternal grandfather who also carried the name, Abraham Lincoln, was killed during an Indian attack in 1786.

Lincoln began his political career at the age of 23 in a race for a seat in the Illinois General Assembly. He lost his first campaign. Two years later he won a seat in the state legislature. Lincoln had no formal education but nonetheless taught himself law and became a popular lawyer. Lincoln unsuccessfully ran for the U.S. Senate on two occasions but was defeated. He had an exceptional gift to deliver powerful and emotional speeches. His firm stand against slavery won him national attention. In 1860, at the age of 51, Lincoln won the Republican nomination and was elected President. He exercised great presidential powers and personally supervised the War Between the States. In 1863, the passage of the 13th Amendment put an official end to the practice of slavery.

Six days after the surrender of the Confederate Army, Abraham Lincoln was assassinated while attending a performance at the Ford Theatre.

January 16th

The timid are afraid before the danger,
the cowardly while in danger,
and the courageous after danger.

Jean Paul Richter
Writer
(1763 - 1825)

Jean Paul Richter *(*Johann Paul Friedrich) was born in Fichtel Gebirge, Germany. At the age of 18, he enrolled at the University of Leipzig (1781-1784) to study theology. The studious young Richter became a tutor to overcome some financial problems.

In his late twenties, Richter turned his full attention to a career as a writer. He took the name 'Jean Paul' in honor of the great French writer-philosopher, Jean-Jacques Rousseau. Both Rousseau and Johann Gottfried von Herder had a great influence on Jean Paul's philosophy and writings.

Jean Paul achieved his first success as a writer with the publishing of his novel, *Die Unsichtbare Loge* (*The Invisible Lodge*), in 1793. Jean Paul's novels touched on society, politics and education and would develop a following in the 20th century.

After the death of his beloved mother in 1797, Paul traveled extensively. He eventually married (Karoline Meyer) in 1801 and settled in Bayrouth, Germany. Blindness plagued his last years until his death at 62.

January 17th

***The pain passes,
but the beauty remains.***

Renoir
Artist and Painter
(1841 - 1919)

Renoir (Pierre-Auguste Renoir) was born into a working-class family in Limoges, France. His early years were devoted to earning a living drawing designs on porcelain figures and fine china. He would often visit the Louvre to study the great masters.

At 21, Renoir began studying art along with other painters, including Claude Monet. Like most artists poverty plagued his early years. In 1874, he gained the serious attention of the art world when six of his paintings were on display at the first Impressionist Exhibition.

During the 1880's Renoir traveled extensively studying the great masters – Eugene Delacroix in Algeria, Raphael in Rome and Velazquez in Madrid. In his late 40's, Renoir married Aline Charigot, one of his models and mother of his first child. Renoir had three sons. In his fifth decade he was stricken with rheumatoid arthritis which gradually restricted him to a wheelchair. In spite of his disabilities he continued his prolific creative output.

In 1919, Renoir, one of the best known painters of the Impressionist style, visited the Louvre one last time. His paintings hung along side the great masters he once studied. Renoir died later that same year.

January 18th

You know what makes a good loser?
Practice.

Ernest Hemingway
Writer and Journalist
(1899 - 1961)

Ernest Hemingway proved to be one of the most influential writers of the 20th century – as much for his writing as his adventurous lifestyle. The Nobel Prize-winner was born in Illinois to a physician (his father) and a musician (his mother).

At the age of 19, Hemingway enlisted and became an ambulance driver on the front lines in Italy. Despite serious wounds he carried an Italian soldier to safety and was decorated. His WWI experiences would serve as the basis for one of his greatest works – *A Farewell to Arms* (1929).

Following the war, young Hemingway began to hone his writing skills as a journalist, first for the Toronto Star in Canada and then as an editor for a monthly journal in Chicago. During his time as foreign correspondence for the Star, Hemingway met such writers as Gertrude Stein and James Joyce. Later he reported from the front lines during the Spanish Civil War and WWII. He was considered one of the writers known as 'The Lost Generation'. Hemingway added to his stature as a writer with such classic novels as – *The Sun Also Rises* (1924), *For Whom the Bell Tolls* (1940) and *The Old Man and the Sea* (1952).

In 1959, Hemingway moved from glamorous Cuba to take up residence in Ketchum, Idaho. Ernest Hemingway committed suicide at the age of 61.

January 19th

The oldest and shortest words, 'yes' and 'no' are those which require the most thought.

Pythagoras
Mathematician and Philosopher
(Circa 570 - 495 BC)

Pythagoras, a Greek philosopher of the 6th century BC, remains a mystery. The few details of his life carried forward over the centuries are sketchy at best.

Records show he was born on the island of Samos in or around the year 570 BC and was greatly influenced by a teacher named Themistoclea. During his forties he lived in Croton, a Greek community in the southern part of Italy. The mathematician-turned-philosopher created a religious movement called Pythagoreanism. The sect and Pythagoras were eventually forced to flee.

Modern academics often revere the man who gave the world the Pythagorean Theorem. His philosophy would later influence the great Plato and as such, Western philosophy.

The man of mystery is thought to have died at approximately 75 in Metapontum, Greece.

January 20th

To speak and to speak well,
are two things.
A fool may talk,
but a wise man speaks.

Ben Jonson
Dramatist, Poet and Actor
(1573 - 1637)

Ben Jonson, born in Westminster, London, England, was a contemporary of William Shakespeare. Jonson, son of a bricklayer, is believed to have attended the University of Cambridge. He managed to attract controversy most of his life.

Jonson married a lady whom history identifies as Ann Lewis before his 21st birthday. Church records list three children and that all died at an early age. The premature deaths had an impact on the marriage with Jonson and his wife living separate lives for some time.

In his late twenties, Jonson joined a theatre troupe called The Admiral's Men. Although he took on various roles as an actor he would prove to be a superior writer. Jonson's first encounter with the authorities was the result of a play he co-wrote. He was charged with lewd behavior. A year later he was charged with manslaughter in the death of a fellow actor in a duel (1598).

Jonson's greatest success was in his role as England's first Poet Laureate. He survived a number of strokes only to succumb on August 6, 1637. Ben Jonson is buried at Poet's Corner in Westminster Abbey.

January 21st

*To love another person
is to see the face of God.*

Les Miz
Musical
(Premiere 1980)

Les Miz, originally released as an album, debuted as a stage musical in Paris at a sports arena in 1980 for a three-month run. The musical was based on the classic French novel, *Les Misérables*, written by Victor Hugo in 1862. The original music was composed by Claude-Michel Schönberg with lyrics by Alain Boublil.

In 1985, British producer Cameron Mackintosh (*CATS*) introduced an English-language version at London's Barbican Arts Centre. The English adaptation was written by Herbert Kretzmer (lyrics) and the team of Trevor Nunn and John Caird (book). Theatre critics were very unkind with their first reviews and the literary world was appalled to witness a classic French novel translated to the stage as a musical. The general theatre going public had a much different reaction. The production was a sell-out and has remained so until this day.

Les Miz opened on Broadway on March 12, 1987. The musical earned eight Tony Awards, including Best Musical and Best Original Score. The main characters (Jean Valjean, police officer Javert and Fantime) rank among the most memorable in theatre history.

The quote is spoken by Jean Valjean at the end of Act II.

January 22nd

When I get a little money, I buy books; if there's any left, I buy food and clothes.

Desiderius Erasmus
Scholar and Priest
(1466 - 1536)

Desiderius Erasmus, the second son of a priest and a physician's daughter, was born in the Netherlands during the last period of the Christian unity movement. Erasmus became one of Europe's most controversial scholars.

Erasmus was educated by the Brethren of the Common Life between 1475 and 1487. The religious order had a great influence on young Erasmus. During his eighteenth year both his parents died of the plague. Three years later Erasmus entered a monastery run by the Augustine Order. He was ordained into the priesthood at 26.

In Paris, Erasmus discovered his greatest source of personal growth. He was inspired by John Colet and Sir Thomas Moore to expand his religious interests. Gradually his writings became more critical and confrontational. He openly wrote against the Catholic Church's involvement in war and the Church's accumulation of wealth. Erasmus was formally released from his religious vows in 1517 (51).

Erasmus continued his confrontational writings until his death at age 70. Despite his critical views he never left the Catholic Church.

January 23rd

*When I stand before God
at the end of my life,
I would hope that I would not have
a single bit of talent left,
and could say,
"I used everything you gave me."*

Erma Bombeck
Writer and Humorist
(1927 - 1996)

Erma Fiste became one of the most popular newspaper columnists from the mid-60's to the mid-90's. The Ohio native was born in a working-class family – her father was a crane operator for the city of Bellbrook.

During her early years, Fiste was an excellent student and always the avid reader. Fiste attended Catholic University of Dayton with the help of two part-time jobs. She graduated with a major in English. Her years at the university proved to be life-changing. Fiste converted to Catholicism the year she graduated.

Fiste married a former classmate, William Bombeck, and became a devoted mother (a daughter and two sons) and housewife for a decade (1954-1964). In 1964, Bombeck began writing a weekly column for a local newspaper for three dollars a column. Within a short period Bombeck's column, *At Wit's End*, was nationally syndicated. Her column reached over 30 million people in some 900 newspapers.

Bombeck died in 1996 at the age of 69 following a failed kidney transplant.

January 24th

***I praise loudly,
I blame softly.***

Catherine the Great
Russian Empress
(1729 - 1796)

Catherine the Great, the ruler of Russia (1762-1796), was born Sophia Augusta Frederica in Stettin, Germany. Her royal parents had wished for a son and as a result failed to demonstrate loving affection to their daughter.

Young Sophia was, for the most part, under the care of her caring governess, Babette, At fifteen Sophia was sent to Russia by her parents to meet Empress Elizabeth's sixteen-year-old son, Peter. The two were wed approximately a year later after Sophia converted to the Russian Orthodox faith. The unhappy arranged marriage led to numerous romantic affairs on both sides.

Empress Elizabeth died in 1761 leaving her son to become Emperor Peter III. Sophia became Empress Catherine. The new ruler proved to be extremely unpopular and soon a plot to overthrow the Emperor Peter surfaced. Empress Catherine gathered military support and succeeded in naming herself Catherine II. The Emperor was arrested and killed by the military during his incarceration. The well-educated Catherine II commanded great power during her 14 year reign. She led a reformation movement and was responsible for great changes in Russia's education system, arts and sciences and legal system. During her reign, St Petersburg became one of the worlds' leading capitals.

Catherine II died suddenly of a stroke (67) before completing her life's work. German-born Catherine the Great was a key figure in modern Russia.

January 25th

Choose a job you love, and you will never have to work a day in your life.

Confucius
Philosopher
(551 - 479BC)

Confucius was born Kong Qiu in the southern part of modern-day Shandong Province. His father had earned a reputation as a great warrior. Before Kong Qiu's third year his father died forcing his mother, a concubine, to flee their home with her young son and live in extreme poverty.

Confucius' mother encouraged his studies and his great thirst for knowledge. At 20, three years after the death of his mother, Confucius married. Shortly after Confucius set out in search of further knowledge. Over the following four decades he developed a social philosophy later known as Confucianism. History believes he authored five classics in the pursuit of his philosophy.

Confucius' China was a world of division and conflict. His philosophy aimed to unify a fragmented world by focusing on personal and social perfection. He emphasized family values, respect for elders and to lead by positive example. Confucius laid the ground work for the modern Golden Rule with his wise words: *"Never impose on others what you would not choose for yourself."*

Revered by Chinese scholars as the Greatest Master, Confucius died in his early 70's leaving a legacy which stands to this day.

January 26th

Whoever blushes confesses guilt, true innocence never feels shame.

Jean-Jacques Rousseau
Writer and Philosopher
(1712 - 1778)

Jean-Jacques Rousseau, the son of a watchmaker, became one of the most influential thinkers of the 18th century. His writings impacted political philosophy, education and music.

Rousseau was born in the then city-state of Geneva, losing his mother shortly after his birth. Rousseau's educated father introduced his two sons to literature and to a deep love of reading. Young Rousseau was sent to live with a Calvinist minister where his education in mathematics and art continued to flourish. Rousseau spent decades wandering through France and Italy.

Rousseau proved to be a prolific writer. His novels, especially *Julie, ou la nouvelle Heloise*, became an important influence on the Romanticism movement in fiction. Rousseau's *Confessions* gave birth to the modern autobiographical form of literature.

Rousseau's philosophy was based on the principle that man is basically good by nature but negatively influenced by the arts and sciences. His political writings greatly influenced the French Revolution and the American Revolution. Rousseau died suddenly during a nature walk. He is buried at the Pantheon in Paris.

January 27th

We can live without religion and meditation, but we cannot live without human affection.

Dalai Lama
Spiritual Leader
(b. 1935)

Dalai Lama, the 14th Dalai Lama, is the charismatic leader of a number of sects of Tibetan Buddhism. Tibetan Buddhism believes the Dalai Lama is a reincarnation of all the former Dalai Lamas. The Dalai Lama is also considered to be a manifestation of the Buddha of Compassion.

His Holiness, the 14th Dalai lama, was born Lhamo Döndrub in a large farming family in the eastern part of Tibet. Lhamo, one of seven children to survive, spoke a dialect of the Chinese language. In 1936, an official group of Tibetans were dispatched to seek out the new incarnation of the 13th Dalai Lama. The party was led by various omens directly to Lhamo's farm house.

The Dalai Lama's teen years were captured in the 1997 film *Seven Years in Tibet* starring Brad Pitt depicting the real-life experiences of Austrian mountaineer, Heinrich Harrer. Harrer became the Dalai Lama's tutor and introduced the impressionable young boy to the western world.

The 14th Dalai Lama continues his work and has become a spiritual leader known around the world.

January 28th

***Copy from one, it's plagiarism;
copy from two, it's research.***

Wilson Mizner
Playwright and Entrepreneur
(1876 - 1933)

Wilson Mizner was born in Benica, California, into a large family of seven brothers and one sister. His father, Lansing Bond Mizner, became President Benjamin Harrison's Envoy Extraordinaire in Central America. The Mizner family was relocated to Guatemala.

In the late 1890's, four of the Mizner brothers, including 21-year-old Wilson, were drawn to the Klondike to take advantage of the Gold Rush. But instead of mining gold for their wealth, the brothers created scam after scam to bilk the miners. Always one step ahead of the law, Wilson eventually fled to New York City.

Mizner wrote a number of Broadway plays at the turn of the century. His most popular stage plays included *The Deep Purple* (1910) and *The Greyhound* (1912). The charming rogue won the financial aid of Hollywood's Jack Warner and Gloria Swanson and purchased the famous Brown Derby.

Wilson Mizner's various colorful careers proved to be the basis of Stephen Sondheim's delightful and successful *Road Show*. Unfortunately Mizner's endeavors were often overshadowed his personal weaknesses.

He died at the age of 56 in Los Angeles, California.

January 29th

What you get by achieving your goals
is not as important
as what you become
by achieving your goals.

Zig Ziglar
Writer and Motivational Speaker
(b. 1926)

Zig Ziglar (Hilary Hilton Ziglar) grew up in a family of twelve children. Ziglar, born in Alabama and raised in Mississippi, lost his father at an early age leaving his mother responsible for the Ziglar family.

During the early 1970's, Ziglar left a successful career in sales to become a writer and motivational speaker. Within a short few years Ziglar established a strong reputation as an author of popular self-help books. Over the decades he wrote a total of 25 successful books on leadership and personal growth. His best-known work is called *See You at the Top* (1981). Many of his writings follow strong spiritual themes.

Zig Ziglar now lives in Dallas, Texas, and continues to be very active world wide.

January 30th

Treat employees like partners, and they act like partners.

Fred A. Allen
Entertainer and Humorist
(1894 - 1956)

Fred Allen, born in Cambridge, Massachusetts, as John Florence Sullivan, grew up to be an extremely popular and successful North American entertainer, Allen's Irish-Catholic mother died of pneumonia before his third birthday. His father struggled with the sudden death and turned to heavy drinking bouts. Allen's beloved Aunt Lizzie raised Allen and his younger brother, Robert.

An early job at the Boston Public Library introduced Allen to the fascinating world of comedy. In no time he had developed a bad juggling act combined with comedy and toured the Vaudeville circuit as Fred James for a large part of ten years. A marquee billing mistake led to the stage name we all remember him by. The billing accidentally interchanged the last names of Edgar Allen and Fred James creating "Fred Allen". Vaudeville success led to a popular career on Broadway followed by a long run on radio and eventually the early days of television. *Town Hall Tonight*, the longest-running comedy show in radio history, influenced such television iconic programs as *Rowan and Martin's Laugh-in, Saturday Night Live* and *The Tonight Show* starring Johnny Carson.

Fred Allen died from a heart attack while walking in New York City.

January 31st

Imagination is the highest kite one can fly.

Lauren Bacall
Film and Stage Actress
(b. 1924)

Lauren Bacall (Betty Joan Perske), the only child of William Perske and Natalie Weinstein-Bacall, is a native of New York City. Her parents divorced when she was five and she took her mother's last name. Bacall lost all contact with her father. Shimon Peres, President and former Prime Minister of Israel, is Bacall's first cousin.

During her teens Bacall studied acting at the American Academy of Dramatic Arts and worked as a fashion model. Her first acting job was as a walk-on in the 1942 Broadway play, *Johnny 2x4*. In 1943, film director, Howard Hawks' wife, Nancy, encouraged her husband to audition the 19-year-old model. As a result Bacall was cast in *To Have and To Have Not* (1944) opposite Humphrey Bogart. On March 21, 1945, Bacall married Bogart who was then 25 years her senior. They remained married until he lost his battle with cancer in 1957.

Bacall has worked with the great directors of Hollywood and starred along side major stars in such films as *The Big Sleep* (1946), *Key Largo* (1948) and *How To Marry a Millionaire* (1953). Her presence on Broadway is as memorable – *Goodbye Charlie* (1959), *Cactus Flower* (1965), her Tony-award winning performances in *Applause* (1970) and *Woman of the Year* (1981). In 1999, the American Film Institute named Lauren Bacall one of the top 25 actresses.

"Saved by the bell"

Between the 6th and 17th centuries the populations of cities throughout the world grew beyond the ability to service the masses. Sanitation and waste disposal became a serious problem. The situation led to various outbreaks of life-threatening diseases. Highly contagious diseases, such as measles and pulmonary infections, challenged the medical profession. Tuberculosis resulted in countless deaths. Smallpox devastated Europe and caused the deaths of over a half million people in a short period of time. The Bubonic Plague killed over 100 million people. The world population was reduced by as much as a third.

Space in existing and long-established cemeteries was at a premium. Authorities began to reclaim cemetery real estate by systematically digging up older gravesites only to discover a percentage of coffins had aggressive scratch marks on the inside. Because of the limited technology of the period, a percentage of the people were actually buried alive.

A new tradition was born. The relatives of a deceased loved one would tie a string to the wrist of the corpse, thread it through a hole in the coffin and up through the soil to a bell. For a number of days, a relative would sit by the grave day and night in case the bell would ring. The overnight hours in the cemetery became known as the "graveyard shift". If a buried person did wake up from a coma-like state, the movement would cause the above-ground bell to ring. Hence, the person ("a dead ringer") would be - *"saved by the bell"*.

February 1st

***Where there is charity and wisdom,
there is neither fear nor ignorance.***

Saint Francis of Assisi
Spiritual Leader
(1181 - 1226)

Saint Francis of Assisi (Giovanni Francesco di Bernardone) was born the son of a wealthy merchant in Assisi, Italy. Young Francesco, along with his six siblings, enjoyed all the trappings wealth could offer. His seemingly aimless life eventually led him to the military.

During a military expedition at Collestrada in 1201, Francesco (20) was captured and spent a full year as a prisoner. Before his 25th birthday the care-free young Francesco had a spiritual awakening leading him to turn his back on his family's wealth. Soon Francesco and a small group of devoted followers were wandering throughout Italy preaching to the people in the countryside and repairing old churches like the little chapel of St. Mary of the Angels.

A chance meeting in 1209 with Cardinal Giovanni di San Paolo led to a private audience with Pope Innocent III. Within a year the Pope officially blessed the Francescan Order. Francesco also met Cardinal Ugolilo of Segni.

In 1228, Pope Gregory IX, Francesco's friend and former Cardinal Ugolino, elevated him to sainthood. Saint Francis of Assisi has the distinction of being honored by numerous churches – Catholic, Anglican, Lutheran and the Church of England.

Saint Francis of Assisi died at 45 while praying at the little chapel of Mary of the Angels where his journey had begun.

February 2nd

The artist is nothing without the gift, but the gift is nothing without work.

Émile Zola
Playwright, Writer and Journalist
(1840 - 1902)

Émile Zola was born in Paris, the son of an Italian engineer. The family moved to Aix-en-Provence when Emile was three. His father died three years later leaving the family to struggle on a small pension. The Zola family returned to Paris. His childhood friend was the master artist, Paul Cézanne.

Young Zola supported his first love of writing by holding various jobs, including as a clerk and later as a salesman. He soon established himself as a harsh political journalist often taking aim at Napoleon III, the then President of France. Zola wrote a number of novels before gaining attention with his first major success, *Thérèse Raquin* in 1867. He was 27. He structured and wrote a 20-novel series, *Les Rougon Macquart*, capturing five generations of two branches of a fictitious French family during the Industrial Revolution.

On January 13, 1898, Zola, the journalist, risked his reputation and his life by taking up the cause of the falsely accused and wrongfully imprisoned Jewish military officer (Captain Alfred Dreyfus) in an open letter to the President of France. The Dreyfus Affair divided the country. Captain Dreyfus was eventually pardoned.

Émile Zola died mysteriously and was buried in the Panthéon in Paris along side Victor Hugo and Alexandre Dumas.

February 3rd

Never interrupt your enemy when he is making a mistake.

Napoléon Bonaparte
Military and Political Leader
(1769 - 1821)

Napoléon Bonaparte, the second of eight children, was born Napoléon di Bonaparte in Corsica, a French possession at the time. His father was a lawyer of Italian nobility and served as Corsica's representative to the court of Louis XVI. Young Napoléon and his siblings enjoyed the finest of education.

At the age of 15, Bonaparte was enrolled in the elite École Militaire in Paris, graduating with the commission of a Second Lieutenant. By 24, the natural strategist had earned the rank of Brigadier General. During his twenties he led French armies into a number of historic battles in Italy, Austria and Egypt.

In 1799 at 30, Bonaparte was part of a coup to over-throw the government and named himself First Consul. Five years later he proclaimed himself Emperor Bonaparte I. Napoléon I, a progressive ruler, created the Napoléonic Code of Justice which was later adopted throughout Europe. The ambitious young ruler spear-headed a series of successful conquests across Europe. In 1813, Napoléon I took his expansionist ambitions to Russia only to be defeated at the famous Battle of Waterloo (1815).

Napoléon spent his last six years a prisoner on the Island of Saint Helena. His death at 51 has led to a series of investigations and debates as to whether he died of natural causes or was slowly poisoned with arsenic.

February 4th

***When you do the common things in life
in an uncommon way,
you will command
the attention of the world.***

George Washington Carver
Agricultural Chemist
(1864 - 1943)

George Washington Carver was born on the farm of Moses Carver in Missouri. Confederation night-raiders kidnapped baby George and his mother. After the Civil War ended Moses Carver found young George but his mother was lost forever. The Carvers raised George as their own child.

Young Carver struggled against all odds in the segregated South to get an education graduating at 33 with a Master of Science degree. Farmland in much of the South had been devastated by the war years and decades of cotton and tobacco planting. Carver developed new farming methods which revolutionized agriculture and saved the farming industry. He introduced the new concept of "crop rotation" to replenish the land. Carver also introduced new soil-enriching crops such as peanuts, soybeans and potatoes.

In his lifetime Carver developed a number of industrial applications from various agricultural products such as the peanut but only patented three of his many inventions believing they were gifts from God and belonged to the people. In 1943, President Roosevelt dedicated a national monument to honor his accomplishments. In 1940, three years before his death at 79, Carver donated his money to the Carver Research Foundation for continuing work in agriculture.

February 5th

*Blessed is the man,
who having nothing to say,
abstains from giving
wordy evidence of the fact.*

George Eliot
Writer and Journalist
(1819 - 1880)

George Eliot, born Mary Anne Evans, was the daughter of a farmer who managed an estate in Warwickshire, England. Young Mary Anne enjoyed full access to the extensive library on the estate and developed a strong interest in novels.

After her mother's death when Mary Anne was 16, the family moved to Foleshill near Coventry. She became a member of a group who encouraged radical thinking and life styles. Mary Anne turned her back on her faith and eventually lived with a married man (philosopher-writer George Henry Lewes) for twenty years until his death.

Mary Anne's father recognized his young daughter's intelligence and the fact that, because "she likely would never marry because of her lack of physical beauty," encouraged her education. Mary Anne's classical education greatly influenced her writing style and her subject matter. Her seven novels shared the familiar themes of Greek tragedies. At 39, Mary Anne wrote her first critically-acclaimed novel, *Adam Bede*, under the pen name George Eliot in order to be taken more seriously as an author.

Eliot wrote her seventh and last novel, *Daniel Deronda*, was written in 1876 at 57. She died four years later as the result of complications from a liver disease.

February 6th

***Not everything that is faced
can be changed,
but nothing can be changed
until it is faced.***

James Baldwin
Writer and Civil Rights Activist
(1924 - 1987)

James Baldwin grew up in Harlem, New York, after his single mother married a minister named David Baldwin. Young James' relationship with his adoptive father deteriorated as the years passed. Eventually James turned his back on the Pentecostal Church and at 17 moved to New York City's Greenwich Village's artist community.

By the time James Baldwin was in his mid-20's, he left his native U.S.A. to take up permanent residence in Paris. He moved to the more liberal city of artists to further develop his writing skills and to escape the prejudices against blacks and homosexuals. Baldwin's first major success was his 1953 novel, *Go Tell it on the Mountain*, where he begins to explore the themes of homosexuality and bisexuality.

During the tumultuous 1960's in the U.S., Baldwin often joined his friends, including Sidney Poitier, Harry Belafonte and Marlon Brando, in one of numerous Civil Rights non-violent protests.

James Baldwin lost his battle with cancer in 1987 at the age of 63 in his adopted France.

February 7th

*An inconvenience is only an adventure wrongly considered;
an adventure is an inconvenience rightly considered.*

G. K. Chesterton
Writer and Journalist
(1874 - 1936)

G. K. Chesterton was born Gilbert Keith in the Kensington area of London, England, in a devoted Anglican family. His early years were spent at St. Paul's School where he studied art with the intention of becoming an illustrator.

During the first six years of his working life, Chesterton was employed at a publishing firm while also working as a freelance journalist. In 1902, he began writing a weekly column for The Illustrated London News which he continued for thirty years. Chesterton and George Bernard Shaw shared a devoted friendship which frequently included great heated debates. Chesterton (6'4" and near 300 pounds) proved to be an exceptionally prolific writer, producing 80 books, hundreds of short stories, poems and essays and several plays. He skillfully made use of his clever wit and cunning sense of humor to challenge the conventional thinking of his day.

Chesterton's beloved wife, Frances, was often called upon to reply to one of his many telegrams declaring himself lost in the city. It is believed he suffered from developmental dyspraxia. He died at 61.

February 8th

Kind words can be short and easy to speak, but their echoes are truly endless.

Mother Teresa
Spiritual Leader
(1910 - 1997)

Mother Teresa (Agnes Gonxha Bojaxhiu) was born in what is modern day Skopje, the capital of Macedonia. Agnes, the youngest in the family, lost her politician father when she was eight. By the time she was 12 Agnes had committed herself to a religious life.

At 18, she joined the Sisters of Loreto and was sent to Ireland to study English. The following year she began her novitiate near the Himalayan Mountains in India. Agnes took her final vows in 1937 as Sister Teresa in honor of St. Thérèse de Lisieux, the patron saint of missionaries. By 1950, the Vatican recognized her work in the area of Calcutta and granted permission to establish a new religious order - the Missionaries of Charity.

By the beginning of the 21st century Mother Teresa had become a household name in many parts of the world for her work. During her lifetime the Missionaries of Charity had over 5,000 nuns operating some 600 missions, hospitals and schools in 120 countries.

Mother Teresa died in 1997 at 87. She was beatified by Pope John Paul II for her devoted service to the needy throughout the world.

February 9th

***Be nice to people on your way up
because you meet them
on your way down.***

Jimmy Durante
Entertainer
(1893 - 1980)

Jimmy Durante, born James Francis into an Italian-American family, dropped out of school in the eighth grade to become a full-time ragtime piano player at the turn of the century. The Brooklyn-born Durante is considered one of the most popular and admired performers in American history.

Durante's career covered all the entertainment avenues with radio following a very successful run as a Vaudeville star. The song-and-dance trio (Clayton, Jackson and Durante) featured his closest friends, Lou Clayton and Eddie Jackson. Durante brought the two along with him even when the industry only wished his talents. Soon he was starring in a string highly-popular Broadway hits and winning the hearts of Las Vegas audiences. In the early 50's, the Durante magic conquered television. The soft-hearted entertainer who had his own endearing brand of English devoted himself to raising dollars for needy children. His never-ending selfless support of one of the charities eventually led them to adopt a new name. The Jimmy Durante Children's Fund has raised well over 20 million dollars.

Jimmy Durante suffered a debilitating stroke in 1972 confining him to a wheelchair for his remaining years. He died at 87.

February 10th

Comedy is simply a funny way of being serious.

Peter Ustinov
Actor and Writer
(1921 - 2004)

Peter Ustinov was born Peter Alexander Baron Von Ustivow in London, England. His father, a journalist of Russian-German noble decent, served as a spy for the British MI5.

Young Ustinov enjoyed the finest education at London's Westminster School. During his late teens he changed his family name and embarked on an acting career. WWII interrupted his performing career while the young private served as Batman to a British Intelligence Officer later turned actor named David Niven.

Peter Ustinov changed his family name slightly (a 'v' replacing the 'w') and soon established himself to be a true Renaissance man of the arts with successes as an actor, writer, columnist and a film, theatre and opera director. He also served as an Ambassador for UNICEF. Ustinov had full command of six languages – English, French, Spanish, Italian, German and Russian. In 1977, he wrote a highly-acclaimed and entertaining autobiography called *Dear Me*.

The trice-married Ustinov won two Oscars (*Spartacus* and *Topkapi*), a Golden Globe (*Quo Vadis*), three Emmys, a Grammy and nominated twice for Tony Awards. Sir Peter Ustinov died at 82 of heart failure.

February 11th

We are here to change the world with small acts of thoughtfulness done daily rather than with one great breakthrough.

Rabbi Harold Kushner
Spiritual Leader and Writer
(b. 1935)

Rabbi Harold Kushner was born and raised in Brooklyn. He has become an influential spiritual leader within progressive Conservative Judaism.

Young Harold studied at Columbia University before being ordained a rabbi at the Jewish Theological Seminary in 1960. A decade later, Rabbi Kushner was awarded a PhD in Bible Study. Rabbi Kushner has served the congregation of Natick, Massachusetts Temple Israel for more than a quarter century.

The death of his son, Aaron, from progeria, commonly known as 'the aging disease', prompted Rabbi Kushner to write the best-selling book *When Bad Things Happen to Good People* in 1981. Rabbi Kushner, author of a number of additional theological books, has been translated in a dozen languages.

In 2004, Rabbi Kushner was invited to do a reading at President Ronald Reagan's state funeral at the Washington National Cathedral.

February 12th

The time will come when, with elation, you will greet yourself arriving at your own door, in your own mirror, and each will smile at the other's welcome.

Derek Walcott
Playwright
(b. 1930)

Derek Walcott was born in the West Indies. Walcott studied painting before turning his attention to writing. The young man from Saint Lucia eventually became one of the influential writers from the West Indies.

Walcott studied at the University of the West Indies in Jamaica. In 1959, Walcott founded the Trinidad Theatre Workshop and later the prestigious Boston Playwright's Theatre at Boston University. Over his career Walcott has penned two dozen plays many dealing with the hardships in post-colonial West Indies.

Derek Walcott was awarded the Nobel Prize for Literature in 1992.

February 13th

A ship is safe in harbor, but that's not what ships are for.

William Shedd
Theologian
(1820 - 1894)

William Shedd, the son of a pastor, was born in Massachusetts. He proved to be a bright and curious student at an early age.

Young William enrolled at the University of Vermont at 15 (1835). Following graduation in 1839, William taught school for a year before deciding to study theology at the Presbyterian Church's Andover Theological Seminary. He returned to teaching (English) at his two alma maters – English at the University of Vermont (1845-1852) and Theological History at Andover. Dr. Shedd spent the last near two decades of his teaching life at Union Theological Seminary.

Dr. Shedd established himself as one of the most celebrated systematic theologians of the Presbyterian Church of America. His theological writings are contained in the three volumes of *Dogmatic Theology* published in 1888.

Dr. Shedd died in New York City at the age of 74.

February 14th

*The cruelest lies
are often told in silence.*

Robert Louis Stevenson
Writer
(1850 - 1894)

Robert Louis Stevenson, the only child of a lighthouse engineer, was born in Edinburgh, Scotland. Lighthouse designing and building was a family business going back to young Robert's grandfather. The Stevensons were devoted Presbyterians.

The frail and often sickly young Stevenson was sent away to a school at the age of six. His frequent bouts with various illnesses prevented him from attending school and had private tutors. Stevenson escaped within his imagination, creating wild tales for the enjoyment of his parents. As expected he enrolled in the engineering faculty of the University of Edinburgh. He soon announced his wishes to pursue the life of a writer. Stevenson reached a compromise with his parents and earned a degree in law as a back-up to a writing career.

During a writing career which barely spanned two decades, Stevenson became one of the most popular writers of his time. His works, including *Treasure Island*, *Kidnapped* and *The Strange Case of Dr. Jekyll and Mr. Hyde*, would contribute to making him one of the most translated authors in the world.

Stevenson, financially very successful in his living years, settled in the Samoan Islands for health reasons. In December of 1894, Robert Louis Stevenson died. He was 44.

February 15th

*Absence is to love
what the wind is to fire;
it extinguishes the small,
it kindles the great.*

Comte Roger De Bussy-Rabutin
Military Leader and Writer
(1618 - 1693)

Comte Roger De Bussy-Rabutin was born into a distinguish family in the Burgundy area of France. Young Roger spent his early school years at a Jesuit school.

At the age of 16, Roger enlisted in the French army and enjoyed a very honorable military career for the most part. He participated in a number of important military campaigns. In 1641, Roger (23) was found guilty of neglect of duties and confined to the Bastille for a full year. Eventually he managed to further alienate many of his colleagues in the army and in the French court.

Comte Roger De Bussy-Rabutin became a celebrated writer following his military career and was a member of the prestigious Académie Française for the last 28 years of his life. The Comte is responsible for several notable literary works, including *Histoires Amoureuses des Gaules* (1660). His *Mémoires Secrets de m. le Comte De Bussy-Rabutin* (1769) were published after his death.

The Comte De Bussy-Rabutin spent the final seventeen years of his life in Burgandy where he died at 75.

February 16th

I was brought up to believe that how I saw myself was more important than how others saw me.

Anwar El-Sadat
Statesman
(1918 - 1981)

Anwar El-Sadat was born in Mit Abu Al Kim, Egypt, in a large family of 13 brothers and sisters. Anwar's early childhood was spent in the loving care of his grandmother.

Anwar graduated from Egypt's Royal Military Academy at the age of 20 as a Second Lieutenant. He had the greatest of respect for Mahatma Gandhi and his non-violent philosophy. During his early military career Anwar met Gamal Abdel Nasser and formed the Free Officers Movement. The Movement took an active part in the Egyptian Revolution of 1952 which led to Nasser's 18-year role as President of Egypt.

In 1970, following Nasser's death then Vice President Sadat assumed the role of President. The new President's term was widely believed to be short-lived but Sadat proved he was an active and wise politician. During his eleven years as president he influenced numerous important political and economic changes. Sadat was instrumental in the signing of the Egyptian-Israeli Peace Treaty of 1979. The treaty stands to this day as a testimony of both Anwar Sadat and Israeli Prime Minister Menachem Begin. They were both awarded the Nobel Peace Prize.

Anwar Sadat was assassinated on October 6, 1981.

February 17th

Excess on occasion is exhilarating. It prevents moderation from acquiring the deadening effect of a habit.

W. Somerset Maugham
Playwright and Writer
(1874 - 1965)

W. Somerset Maugham spent his childhood at the British Embassy in Paris. His father was a lawyer in charge of embassy legal affairs. In order to circumvent the French conscription laws, the elder Maugham arranged to have his son born inside the embassy which was technically British soil.

Young Maugham's life changed dramatically when his mother died. He was eight years old. Two years later tragedy struck a second time when his father lost his battle to cancer. Maugham was placed in the care of a paternal uncle in England. At 16, he was sent to Heidelburg University in Germany where he had his first sexual encounter with a man ten years his senior.

Maugham had little interest in following in his father and grandfather's legal profession. He pursued a career in medicine. While a medical student Maugham wrote a novel, *Liza of Lambeth*, which became very popular. Armed with a medical degree he set out to establish himself as a serious writer. Somerset Maugham became an extremely successful author earning the greatest income among writers of his time.

Maugham was one of the first writers to profit from film adaptations of his works. W.S. Maugham died at 91 at his villa in France.

February 18th

There is a time for departure even when there's no certain place to go.

Tennessee Williams
Playwright
(1911 - 1983)

Tennessee Williams (Thomas Lanier Williams) was born in Columbus, Mississippi, at the home of his maternal grandparents. Williams' father became an alcoholic while his mother suffered from emotional issues.

Williams' writing career began at 16 with the publishing of his first essay. He earned a degree from the University of Iowa followed by studies at the Dramatic Workshop at New York City's New School. From that moment on he began a life-long love affair with the theatre. At 28, he changed his first name to Tennessee in honor of his father's birth place. Williams's sister, Rose, spent much of her adult life in institutions battling schizophrenia. His dysfunctional family and his own struggles with alcohol and severe bouts of depression served as a basis for many of his characters. Williams and his partner, Frank Merlo, shared a long-lasting relationship.

Tennessee Williams gave the theatre world a series of memorable plays and unforgettable characters, including *The Glass Menagerie* and *Suddenly Last Summer*. He was twice awarded the Pulitzer Prize for Drama for *A Streetcar Named Desire* (1948) and *Cat on a Hot Tin Roof* (1955).

Williams suffered through numerous nervous breakdowns in his later life. He died at 71 from the prolonged use of drugs and alcohol.

February 19th

You can be pleased with nothing when you are not pleased with yourself.

Lady Mary Wortley Montagu
Writer
(1689 - 1762)

Lady Mary Wortley Montagu, the daughter of the Earl of Kingston-upon-Hull, was born Mary Pierremount in London. She was a bright and studious child learning Latin as a youngster.

The Pierremount family estate featured extensive private libraries which would shape young Mary's life. Mary fell in love with Edward Wortley Montagu but her father refused to give his blessing wishing his daughter to marry another suitor. Mary and Edward responded by eloping when she was 23. She is reportedly part of the Montegu family made famous by Shakespears' *Romeo and Juliet*. Three years after her marriage Lady Mary was partially disfigured by a bout of smallpox. During her husband's posting as British Ambassador to Turkey she became aware of an inoculation against smallpox. She promoted the practice in England.

Lady Montagu established herself as one of the most important woman writers. After years abroad Lady Montagu returned to London in 1762. She died within months.

February 20th

If you want to be happy, be.

Leo Tolstoy
Writer
(1828 - 1910)

Leo Tolstoy, born Lyev Nikolavich Tolstoy in Russia, is considered by many scholars to be one of the world's greatest writers. His writings influenced many of the great minds of the 19th and 20th centuries.

Young Leo, the fourth child of five in an old Russian aristocratic family, lost both his parents at an early age. He and his siblings were raised by various relatives. A bright but restless student, Leo abandoned his legal studies and traveled throughout Europe of the early 19th century. The political and social unrest in Europe had a direct impact on his literary endeavors. Tolstoy's greatest contribution to the world of literature came in the form of two classics – *War and Peace* (1869) and *Anna Karenina* (1873-77). Both novels are considered among the greatest literary works ever written.

In 1862, at 23, Tolstoy married 17-year-old Sophia Bers. The marriage produced thirteen children. Sophia became involved in her husband's literary career as his proof-reader and financial manager. Their relationship grew to be very difficult as Tolstoy aged. He gradually turned his back on his wealth often giving large sums of money away to total strangers.

The great Leo Tolstoy died of pneumonia at the age of 82.

February 21st

***Many a man's reputation
would not know his character
if they met on the street.***

Elbert Hubbard
Philosopher and Writer
(1856 - 1915)

Elbert Hubbard, was born in Bloomington, Illinois, but raised in Hudson, Illinois. Hubbard became a very successful sales person creating the foundation for some of modern-day sales tactics.

In his late 30's, Hubbard founded the Roycroft Press, named after the 17th century London printers, Samuel and Thomas Roycroft, and published two whimsical magazines. The Roycroft Press became a platform for Hubbard's homespun philosophy. The Roycroft Press and Roycroft Shops proved to be highly successful. Hubbard became a popular lecturer on the North American circuit. The romantic in Hubbard led him to praise in print the decision of Mrs. Ida Straus to remain on board the Titanic with her husband as the famous liner sank in the North Atlantic in 1912.

Three years later, in 1915, the Hubbards took a sailing vacation to Europe on the Lusitania. A short distance off the coast of Ireland the Lusitania was torpedoed by a German submarine. Elbert and his wife, Alice, decided to remain in their cabins as the ship slipped in the icy waters of the North Atlantic. Elbert was 58.

February 22nd

Once a woman has forgiven her man she must not reheat his sins for breakfast.

Marlene Dietrich
Actress and Singer
(1901 - 1992)

Marlene Dietrich was born Maria Magdalene Dietrich in Berlin. Her father, a police officer, died when she was 10. Marlene's maternal grandparents owned and operated a successful clock-making enterprise.

At a young age, Marlene studied the violin but her dreams as a concert violinist were dashed after a serious wrist injury. In 1922, she launched what would establish her as one of the greatest female stars of all times. Over the decades the beautiful lady of mystery conquered the film, stage and recording industries. Her roles in such films as *Shanghai Express* and *Desire* were memorable.

In 1924, Marlene (23) married the love of her life – Rudolf Sieber. They had a daughter (Maria). Marlene and Rudolf enjoyed a beautiful relationship until his death in 1976. She never remarried.

Marlene spent her final years to some degree in seclusion in her Paris apartment. She died at 90.

February 23rd

***Do something for somebody
every day for which
you do not get paid.***

Albert Schweitzer
Philosopher, Physician and Missionary
(1875 - 1965)

Albert Schweitzer was born in the Alsace-Lorraine region of France in the later part of the 19th century. As a child Albert spoke both German and French. Over the centuries the region had been a German or French possession at different times.

The village of Gunsbach where Albert grew up benefitted from a near-perfect Protestant-Catholic relationship. Albert's father was the town Lutheran-Evangelical pastor. The two congregations actually shared one place of worship. This harmonious balance had a great influence on Albert during his formative years. In 1899, he earned his degree in Theology and published his PhD thesis. After graduation, Schweitzer became a deacon at the Saint Nicholas Church of Strasbourg.

Albert Schweitzer had dedicated himself at a young age to serving the greater good of people of all walks of life. Schweitzer through his writings challenged the academic and secular communities of his day on the historical validity of Jesus of Nazareth. In 1952, he was awarded the Nobel Peace Prize for his philosophy captured in *Reverence of Life* and for establishing the Albert Schweitzer Hospital.

Albert Schweitzer enjoyed a long and relatively healthy life. He died at 90.

February 24th

Life is not about waiting
for the storm to pass,
it is about learning
to dance in the rain.

> Anonymous

Anonymous. The author of this beautiful, optimistic inspirational quote has not been identified.

There are those who walk among us who allow a day, a week, a year to slip away without fully savoring what each moment has to offer. These individuals are forever promising themselves and others around them, to be a better friend, a better spouse, a better parent, a better person . . . tomorrow. Obstacles, real and imaginary, appear to always be preventing them to fulfill that basic promise of happiness and forever preventing them to fully enjoy the day. Sadly, such habitual behavior encourages a year to become a decade and a decade to turn into a lifetime.

The anonymous quote has been repeated by many individuals over the years. The most likely authorship scenario is that the quote was created for a motivational poster or a greeting card by a staff writer.

We salute the anonymous author.

February 25th

In the end, we will remember not the words of our enemies, but the silence of our friends.

Martin Luther King Jr.
Spiritual Leader and Activist
(1829 - 1968)

Martin Luther King Jr. became a symbolic figure of the Civil Rights movement in the United States during the 1960's.

King was born Michael Luther King Jr. in Atlanta, Georgia, the son of Reverend Michael Luther King Sr. When young King was five, the family traveled to Germany his father changed both their first names to Martin in honor of Martin Luther, the German Protestant leader. Young Martin advanced through high school by skipping grades. By 26, he earned a PhD in Philosophy.

In 1959, Martin Luther King Jr. visited Mahatma Gandhi's birth place in India. The trip had a great impact on King as he learned to appreciate Gandhi's non-violent philosophy. The non-violent philosophy proved to move mountains on King's historic journey towards an end to racial segregation in the U.S. In 1964, King was awarded the Nobel Peace Prize for his leadership.

Martin Luther King Jr. was assassinated on April 4, 1968.

February 26th

If you want to sacrifice the admiration of many men for the criticism of one go ahead, get married.

Katharine Hepburn
Actress
(1907 - 2003)

Katherine Hepburn, born and raised in Connecticut, was the second of six children of Dr. Thomas Hepburn and suffragette Katherine Houghton. The Hepburns challenged their children to compete at the highest of physical and intellectual levels possible. Katherine and her siblings enjoyed the best in life and offered the finest educations. Young 14-year-old Katherine fell into a deep depression after she discovered her oldest brother, Tom (16), who had committed suicide at their summer retreat. She was home-schooled for a number of years following the tragic incident.

The strong-willed Katherine graduated from Bryn Mawr College in Connecticut with a degree in History and Philosophy in 1928. After a number of summer stock years, Hepburn caught Hollywood's attention in a Broadway play called *The Warrior's Husband* in 1932. In a short period Katherine was recognized as a serious and, at times, non-conforming actress. In 1999, the American Film Institute named her 'the greatest film actress of all times'.

Katherine Hepburn and Spencer Tracy co-starred in nine films together. They also shared a relationship for more than a quarter century until his death in 1967.

Katherine died at 96 in her beloved Connecticut.

February 27th

Imagination was given to man to compensate him for what he is not, a sense of humor to console him for what he is.

Francis Bacon
Philosopher, Politician and Writer
(1561 - 1626)

Francis Bacon was born in London into a noble family. His father was Sir Nicholas Bacon. Young Francis suffered poor health as a child, a condition which followed him throughout his life.

Francis was an exceptionally bright and curious student and was enrolled at Trinity College in Cambridge at the age of twelve. With the assistance from his influential uncle, William Cecil, the Baron of Bughley, he was admitted to the bar in 1582 at 21. Two years later Bacon earned a seat in parliament and soon ascended to the prestigious position as the Queen's Counsel. Francis struggled with various financial set-backs and eventually his political career was tarnished in 1598 when he was arrested as a debtor. The new king, James I, was a great champion of Bacon and he was called upon to fill the important roles of Solicitor General (1607) and Attorney General (1613) and finally in 1618 as Lord Chancellor. In 1603, King James I knighted Bacon.

As he reached his sixties, Bacon was found guilty of corruption, fined and sentenced to the Tower of London. Within days, King James came to his rescue and forgave the fine and released him from prison.

Sir Francis Bacon married late in life at 45 and died without heirs. His titles were not passed on after his death.

February 28th

*Honesty is the first chapter
of the book of wisdom.*

Thomas Jefferson
Statesman
(1743 - 1826)

Thomas Jefferson was born in Virginia, the third of ten children of Peter Jefferson, a successful planter and surveyor, and Jane Randolph. Jane was a descendant of one of the most prominent Virginia families.

Young Thomas proved at an early age to be a gifted and keen student. He enthusiastically studied languages (Greek, French and Latin) as well as history and science. Thomas' classical education led him to enroll at William and Mary College at 16, graduating with the highest of honors. He was admitted to the bar at 24. In addition, to a successful law practice, Jefferson (26) launched his political career as a county representative in 1769.

In 1776, Jefferson (33) was called upon, because of his known writing abilities, to produce a first draft of the *Declaration of Independence*. Over the span of a three-decade political career, Jefferson served his country as the first Secretary of State (1790-93), the second Vice-President (1797-1801) and the third President (1801-09). Under his presidency the United States doubled in size through the Louisiana Purchase (1803). President Jefferson is considered by historians as one of the U.S.'s greatest presidents.

Thomas Jefferson, a man of many talents, founded the University of Virginia. He died at 83 in Charlottesville, Virginia.

February 29th

*If you talk to a man
in a language he understands,
that goes to his head.
If you talk to him
in his language, that goes to his heart.*

Nelson Mandela
Politician and Activist
(b. 1918)

Nelson Mandela, the young boy born and raised in the district of Umtata, South Africa, grew up to be the first democratically-elected president of his country. His journey to the presidency proved to be long and dramatic.

Mandela's great grandfather ruled as King of the Themby people of South Africa in the early 19th century. He lost his father, the chief of the village of Mvezo when he was nine. Mandela became the first in his family to attend school. While he worked as a clerk at a law office he earned a Bachelor of Arts degree and began his law studies. In 1961, Mandela became leader of the African National Congress' armed wing in charge of sabotage campaigns in the battle against apartheid. A year later, Mandela was arrested and sent to the infamous prison on Robben Island where black prisoners were segregated and given fewer food rations and privileges. During his years in prison, Mandela studied and earned his degree in law.

Nelson Mandela was released from prison in 1990 at the age of 72 after twenty-seven years behind bars. In 1993, the world recognized his valiant efforts for equality for his people by awarding him the Nobel Peace Prize.

> **"A red letter day."**

During medieval times, the power struggle between church and state survived through a number of historical stages. The ongoing balance of power between kings and popes prior to the tenth century shaped history.

Monarchs took advantage of the early century belief that kings ruled by divine right. The belief allowed royalty to hold domain over people and church. The 5th century was witness to a shift in power as a result of the fall of the Roman Empire. The power and wealth of the Catholic Church grew as did the importance of Rome as the centre of the church. Royalty and peasants paid homage to the church and to church leaders.

The church, both the Catholic Church and the Church of England, exercised tremendous control over the followers of the faith by preaching the power of heaven and hell. The church's wealth grew by the fact it was exempt from any tax and by the privilege of collecting "tithes", representing 10% of total annual earnings in the form of money or goods. Peasants were also obligated to work for the church without compensation. Cathedrals in large cities towered over any of the other structures and could be seen for miles, reinforcing the power and importance of the church.

Sundays and other holy days throughout the year were expected to be honored. The First Council of Nicaea in the year 325 decreed that all such days be marked in red in church calendars. Centuries later, calendars in general frequently mark special event days in red. Hence, an event day was referred to as "*a red letter day*".

March 1st

*I am not what I want to be,
I am not what I hope to be in another world;
but still I am not what I once used to be,
and by the grace of God I am what I am.*

John Newton
Sailor and Clergyman
(1725 - 1807)

John Newton, the son of a shipmaster, was born and raised in London. Young Newton lost his mother to tuberculosis while still in his teens. His father introduced John to a life at sea when he was eleven years old.

At 18, Newton was forced to serve with the Royal Navy but found himself often at odds with officers and crew. He was finally dropped off in the West Indies where he became one of many slaves owned by the tribal princess. Newton was mistreated by his fellow slaves and eventually rescued by a ship's captain. Between 1748 and 1754, Newton served as first mate and then captain of various slave-trading ships. A severe stroke caused him to end his career at sea. In 1757, Newton began his theological studies and was ordained in the Church of England. Newton began repenting for his involvement in the slave trade and lobbied to outlaw the practice. He formed an alliance with a Member of Parliament named William Wilberforce which eventually led to the passing of the Slave Trade Act of 1807.

During his later years, Newton co-wrote a number of hymns which have survived the centuries, including *Amazing Grace*. John Newton died at 82 blind and still trapped in the guilt of his youth.

March 2nd

Being deeply loved by someone gives you strength; while loving someone deeply gives you courage.

Lao Tzu
Philosopher
(106BC? - 43BC?)

Lao Tzu is a central historical figure in the Chinese culture whose exact dates of birth and death are unknown. He is the founder of Taoism, often referred to as "Daoism". The literal translation of his name means "Venerable" (Lao) and "Master" (Tzu).

History scholars offer various explanations for Lao Tzu's origins. Some sources suggest Lao Tzu is a Chinese mythical figure while others describe him as a spiritual leader from the 4th century BC. Certain historians report that Lao Tzu was a contemporary of Confucius. Chinese tradition records him as the author of the Daodejing, the mystical source of all existence. During the Tang Dynasty, Lao Tzu was considered an ancestor of the dynasty.

Traditional tales suggest Lao Tzu was the "Keeper of the Archives" for the royal court. He developed a large following of disciples, including possibly Confucius himself. Lao Tzu was claimed by both the nobility and the common people.

March 3rd

What a grand thing, to be loved!
What a grander thing still, to love!
Victor Hugo
Writer and Political Activist
(1802 - 1885)

Victor Hugo was born in France at a period when great historic events were shaping the country. Hugo became an important literary figure during the 19th century and exercised great influence over future writers.

During young Hugo's childhood Napoleon proclaimed himself Emperor. The event set in motion a century of political and religious conflict between the classes which would influence Hugo's writings. The conflict unfolding in the country was mirrored by the differences between Hugo's own parents. His father, an officer in Napoleon's army, was an atheist who favored a strong Republic. Sophie, Hugo's mother, was a devout Catholic and a Royalist. Hugo's own politics shifted from Royalist in his youth to a passionate republican in his adult years.

In 1822, Hugo (20) married his childhood friend, Adèle Foucher, against his mother's wishes. The Hugo's had five children. The tragic death of his oldest daughter and her young husband devastated Hugo. Literary scholars suggest Hugo never recovered from the tragedy.

The author of such masterpieces as 1831's *Notre Dame de Paris* (*The Hunchback of Paris*) and *Les Misérables* (1862) was buried in the Panthéon in Paris.

March 4th

Growing old is like being increasingly penalized for a crime you have not committed.

Anthony Powell
Writer
(1905 - 2000)

Anthony Powell, born in Westminster, England, is considered by many scholars as one of the 50 greatest British writers of the second half of the 20th century. His best-known works have remained in print.

Powell grew up the son of a military officer who was frequently absent on various assignments. Powell studied at Eton where his aptitude for the arts led him to become a founding member of the Eton Society of Arts. Powell tried his hand at various writing employments, including a stint in Hollywood in the late 1930's as a scriptwriter.

The war years interrupted his writing career while he served in his mid-30's with the British Military Intelligence unit. Following WWII Powell devoted himself to what would prove to be a very productive career. Between 1951 and 1975, Powell wrote a twelve-volume fiction masterpiece under the umbrella title *A Dance to the Music of Time*.

Anthony Powell was appointed Commander of the Order of the British Empire in 1956. Powell also turned down a knighthood in 1973. He died at the advanced age of 95 in 2000.

March 5th

Genius is one percent inspiration, ninety-nine percent perspiration.

Thomas Edison
Scientist
(1847 - 1931)

Thomas Edison, born in Ohio and raised in Michigan, grew up to become one of the most successful inventor/businessman combinations in modern times. Edison was the seventh child of Canadian-born Samuel and Nancy Edison.

Young Edison had three months formal schooling. An ear infection caused by scarlet fever resulted in a serious hearing problem. By the age of seven, Edison was riding the Michigan trains selling his candy and newspapers, launching his entrepreneurial career. Edison began his career as an inventor at the age of 30 with various devices improving the telegraph system. His early financial successes led him to create the first industrial research laboratory in New Jersey. Over the years the Edison lab was responsible for the invention of the phonograph player, the motion picture camera and the long-lasting light bulb to name but a few.

Edison is still considered to be one of the most prolific inventors in modern history. At one point he held over a thousand U.S. patents. Edison created 14 companies in his lifetime, including the still-operating General Electric. He married twice (Mary Stilwell died at 29) and fathered six children, including Charles Edison who was elected the 42nd Governor of New Jersey (1941-44).

Thomas Edison suffered from diabetes and died at the age of 83.

March 6th

Why not go out on a limb?
Isn't that where the fruit is?

Frank Scully
Writer and Journalist
(1892 - 1964)

Frank Scully was born in Massachusetts, at the end of the 19th century.

Scully was associated as a writer with the entertainment weekly publication, *Variety*, for a good number of years. In the late 1940's, his *Variety* column reported an extraterrestrial event which drew a great deal of attention from the general public. The column reported the tale of mysterious flying saucers crashing in various parts of the U.S. south west. Two "sources" described celestial beings recovered from the crash sites. A 1950 Frank Scully book, *Behind the Flying Saucers*, offered more details of additional saucer crashes.

The 1993-2002 television series, *The X-files*, featured a character called Dana Scully portrayed by actress Gillian Anderson. The character was named after Frank Scully.

In 1952, the U.S. sensational publication, *True Magazine*, exposed the reports as a hoax concocted by two conmen on a rather gullible Frank Scully. In June of 1964, Scully suffered a heart attack while working at his typewriter at his home in Palm Springs, California. He was 72.

March 7th

***Friends are the family
we choose for ourselves.***

Edna Buchanan
Journalist and Writer
(b. 1939)

Edna Buchanan was born in Paterson, New Jersey, and attended Montclair State College.

Buchanan became one of the first female crime reporters in south Florida. Over the years she wrote for two daily publications – the Miami Herald and the Miami Beach Daily Sun. She also made a name for herself writing more than a dozen crime mystery novels, including *Nobody Lives Forever* (1990), *Pulse* (1998) and *Cold Case Squad* (2004). Buchanan's crime novel, *Miami, It's Murder*, was nominated for the Edgar Award in 1995.

Buchanan became involved in an awkward situation in 1990 when she was quoted extensively in the Thomas Burdick/Charles Mitchell book about the murder of speedboat designer Donald Aranow. The highly respected journalist possessed a great insight into crime and police affairs in the greater Miami area. The published book caused Buchanan great embarrassment.

Edna Buchanan was awarded the Pulitzer Prize in 1986 and in 2001 she was honored with the George Polk Award for Career Achievement in Journalism. She continues to live in the Miami area.

March 8th

We become just by performing just actions, temperate by performing temperate actions, brave by performing brave actions.

Aristotle
Philosopher
(384 – 322 BC)

Aristotle, was born near modern-day Thessaloniki, Greece. Aristotle is often referred to as the last person to know everything there was to know in his time.

Young Aristotle grew up in the privileged world of an aristocratic environment. Aristotle's father, Nicomachus, was the personal physician of the king of Macedon. Aristotle's family status allowed him to be educated at the exclusive Plato's Academy for over twenty years. Aristotle became head of the royal school in Macedon where one of his students was Alexander, the future king of Macedon.

Aristotle mastered every academic subject of the day. His profound knowledge covered everything from anatomy to zoology, from ethics to theology. His numerous writings, not all of which have survived the ages, are considered a thorough encyclopedia unto themselves.

Following Alexander the Great's death, Aristotle retreated from Athens and died within the year. He was approximately 62.

March 9th

*If a person gives you his time,
he can give you no more precious gift.*

Frank Tyger
Cartoonist
(b. 1929)

Frank Tyger, born the eldest of three brothers, demonstrated a natural talent to draw at an early age. Young Frank would often entertain visitors with sketches of family members.

Frank Tyger's first introduction to newspaper life and published cartoons was on the school paper at Tilden High School. Following his years at City College in New York City, Tyger enrolled at the Cartoonists and Illustrators School. He served as an account executive at an advertising agency in New Jersey where he further perfected his drawing skills.

In his early thirties, Tyger began the job of a lifetime as the editorial cartoonist for the Trenton Times. Over the next three-plus decades, Tyger lived out his dreams. In his late 60's, Tyger was forced into retirement due to a diagnosis of early Parkinson's disease.

Frank Tyger settled into a New Jersey retirement home in 2002.

March 10th

The value of a sentiment is the amount of sacrifice you are prepared to make for it.

John Galsworthy
Writer
(1867 - 1933)

John Galsworthy was born and raised in a wealthy Surrey, England, family. Young Galsworthy studied law at Oxford and was admitted to the bar in 1890. He traveled extensively for the family's shipping business.

Between 1897 and 1904, Galsworthy published various works under the pen name of John Sinjohn, hiding his budding writing career from his father. His first novel authored under his own name, *The Island of Pharisees*, was released in 1904 following the death of his father. The first part of his career was built on a successful number of plays dealing with England's social issues, including *The Skin Game* (1920).

In later years his fame as a writer resulted from the release of several of his novels. His novels were the basis of a number of films – *The Forsyth Saga*, Alfred Hitchcock's adaptation of *The Skin Game* (1931) and Joseph Mankiewick's *Escape* (1948) starring Rex Harrison.

John Galsworthy was awarded the Nobel Prize for Literature in 1933, six weeks before he succumbed to a stroke.

March 11th

A day without laughter is a day wasted.

Charlie Chaplin
Director, Writer and Actor
(1889 - 1977)

Charlie Chaplin was born Charles Spencer Chaplin in Walworth, England, to entertainer parents. His parents separated when young Charles was three. Charles Chaplin Sr. died of alcohol poisoning while his mother, Hannah, suffered from a mental illness.

Chaplin first toured the U.S. in his early 30's with a troupe which included a young performer named Arthur Stanley Jefferson who later found fame under the name Stan Laurel, the rather thin half of the comedy duo, Laurel and Hardy, of the 1920's and 1930's. By 1913, the head of Keystone Film, Mack Sennett, hired Chaplin. Within a year Chaplin created his endearing on-screen character, The Tramp, by borrowing the various trade-mark pieces of clothing from fellow performers, including actor Ford Sterling's size 14 shoes which Chaplin wore on the wrong feet to keep them from falling off. The Tramp was featured in dozens of popular films with Chaplin retiring the character in the 1936 movie, *Modern Times*, considered to be the last silent film produced.

Chaplin created a great deal of controversy towards the end of his 75-year career with his association with left-wing politics. The McCarthy investigations forced Chaplin to relocate to England. In 1975, Queen Elizabeth II knighted 85-year-old Chaplin.

March 12th

***The best way to make
your dreams come true
is to wake up.***

Paul Valéry
Philosopher and Poet
(1871 - 1945)

Paul Valéry was born in Sète, France, on the shores of the Mediterranean. The bright and curious student earned a degree in law in his early twenties.

Following graduation from his law studies, Valery settled in Paris where he befriended the older master poet, Stéphane Mallarme. In 1900, at the age of 29, Valéry married Jeannie Gobillard, a friend of the Mallarme family. The Valérys had three children. Valery did not launch a full-time writing career until he was 49. Within five years Valery was elected to the prestigious Academie Française. He became a popular speaker on the French lecture tour and a favorite within Paris society circles.

Paul Valéry is best remembered for his poetry despite the fact he published less than 100 poems. *La Jeune Parque*, written in the first person, was released in 1917 and firmly secured his place in French literature.

During WWII Valery made every attempt not to cooperate with the Germans. He spent the final years of his life writing under the difficult cloak of the war. Paul Valéry died as the European conflict ended.

March 13th

You can only lose something that you have, but you cannot lose something that you are.

Eckhart Tolle
Writer and Spiritual Teacher
(b. 1948)

Eckhart Tolle was born Ulrich Tolle in Lunen, Germany. His dysfunctional family caused young Tolle to retreat into a deep depression which would follow him into his twenties.

At the age of 13, after his parents separated, Tolle moved to Spain to live with his father. Tolle was not encouraged to attend high school. His mid-20's were devoted to a methodical search for answers to his persisting depression. The search led him to earn a degree at the University of London which, in turn, led him to do post-graduate work at Cambridge.

During the 1970's, Tolle worked as a student counselor and spiritual teacher. In 1997, Tolle wrote *The Power of Now* which had an original printing of 3,000. Three years later the book was featured on the Oprah Winfrey Show and immediately placed on the New York Times Best Seller list. The book and Tolle's next book, *A New Earth*, sold a combined eight million copies.

Tolle's writings have been both praised and criticized by the reading public and the critics. He and his wife live in Vancouver, British Columbia, Canada.

March 14th

Man is not the sum of what he has already, but rather the sum of what he does not yet have, of what he could have.

Jean-Paul Sartre
Philosopher and Writer
(1905 - 1980)

Jean-Paul Sartre, born in Paris, lost his father, a naval officer in the French Navy, when he was an infant. Young Jean-Paul was raised in his maternal grandparents' home in Meudon, France, and then when his mother remarried twelve years later, in LaRochelle. Jean-Paul's mother, Anne-Marie, was a first cousin of Albert Schweitzer.

Sartre was introduced to classical literature by his maternal grandfather. He studied the great philosophers such as Kant and Hegel and graduated from L'École Normale Supérieure in Paris with a PhD in philosophy. During WWII Sartre (mid-30's) served as a meteorologist with the French Army. While he was a German prisoner of war, Sartre wrote his first play, *Bariona, Fils du Tonnerre*.

After the war years, Sartre became an important member of the literary and social scene in Paris. Sartre's philosophy of existentialism is captured in *The Transcendence of the Ego*. Sartre was awarded the Noble Prize in Literature in 1964 but declined the recognition.

Jean-Paul Sartre endured poor health during his last years eventually becoming blind in 1973. He died in 1980 at 75.

March 15th

Live your questions now, and perhaps even without knowing it, you will live along some distant day into your answers.

Rainer Maria Rilke
Writer and Poet
(1875 - 1926)

Rainer Maria Rilke was born in Prague. The Rilke family had lost a daughter in infancy and Rainer's mother dressed the young boy in girl's clothing. Rainer was forced against his wishes to attend a military school between the ages of 11 and 16. The experience marked him for life. He studied philosophy, literature and art history at university.

Rilke traveled extensively in his early 20's to Russia and Italy. In 1900, he married the sculptor, Clara Westhoff, and they had a daughter, Maria (1901-1972). They settled in his beloved Paris where he wrote most of his works. Rilke was caught off-guard by the outbreak of WWI while visiting Germany and forced into military service. The experience caused him to retreat from writing for several years. Rilke's endless output of poems established him as one of the most important German poets. He also wrote two significant prose works – *The Notebook of Malte Laurids Brigge* (1910) and Letters to a Young Poet (published in 1929).

During his final three years Rilke became increasingly ill resulting in long periods in a sanatorium in Switzerland. On December 29, 1926, Rainer Maria Rilke died from what was determined to be leukemia.

March 16th

Genuine poetry can communicate before it is understood.

T. S. Eliot
Playwright and Poet
(1888 - 1965)

T.S. Eliot, born Thomas Stearns Eliot in St. Louis, Missouri, is considered by most scholars as the most important English-language poet of the 20th century. Eliot was awarded the Nobel Prize in Literature in 1948.

Eliot, the product of a well-to-do family transplanted from New England, enjoyed the advantages of a fine education. He was subjected to the classics as a young student and studied philosophy, first at Harvard, and then at the Sorbonne in Paris. Eliot married in 1915 and settled in London, becoming a British citizen in 1927.

At 37, T.S. Eliot joined the prestigious publishing firm, Faber and Faber, a relationship he maintained until his death in 1965. During his 40 years of employment with the firm, Eliot wrote some of his most memorable poems, including The Hollow Man (1925), Ash Wednesday (1930) and Four Quartets (1945). He also wrote seven plays such as Murder in the Cathedral (1935). Eliot's first marriage ended in separation after 17 years. At the age of 68, Eliot married his former Faber and Faber secretary. Esme Fletcher was 36 years his junior.

T.S. Eliot struggled with poor health during his last years. He died in London of emphysema at the age of 76.

March 17th

Golf is a good walk spoiled.

Mark Twain
Writer and Lecturer
(1835 - 1910)

Mark Twain (born Samuel Clemens), the writer William Faulkner called "the father of American literature", relied on his gift for intelligent wit and satire to author some of the world's classic novels.

Twain acquired valuable first hand experiences as a boy on the shores of the Mississippi River, and later as a riverboat pilot, which became the rich background and the source for interesting characters in his writings and lectures. The Mississippi River served Samuel Clemens well and gave the world his alter ego, Mark Twain.

The main character in *The Adventures of Tom Sawyer* (1876) is based on young Clemens' own childhood along the Mississippi. The novel swept Twain to the heights of the literary world. In 1885, Twain published yet another classic and what has repeatedly been called The Great American Novel – *The Adventures of Huckleberry Finn*.

Mark Twain's literary crown is adorned with many gems, the envy of many novelists. In fact, Twain was so prolific that no complete catalogue of his writings exists because of the great volume of projects he either wrote under other pen names or were lost. Researchers continue to uncover new material – as recently as 1995.

March 18th

I told my psychiatrist that everyone hates me. He said I was being ridiculous – everyone hasn't met me yet.

Rodney Dangerfield
Comedian and Actor
(1921 - 2004)

Rodney Dangerfield (Jacob Cohen) was born on Long Island, New York, of Jewish-Hungarian parents. His father, Philip Cohen, performed on the Vaudeville circuit as Phil Roy.

Dangerfield began his show business career as a teenager writing comedy routines for various stand-up comics of the day. He wrote and also performed under the name, Jack Roy. In the 1940's he gave up on his career as a comic and sold aluminum siding to support his growing family. In the early 60's, he returned to stand-up comedy. He took the stage name, Rodney Dangerfield, after one of Jack Benny's radio characters. Dangerfield's career took off following a last-minute fill-in appearance on *The Ed Sullivan Show* which led to *The Tonight Show* (over 30 appearances) and a regular spot on *The Dean Martin Show*. During the 80's, Dangerfield became a hit on the big screen in such classic comedies as *Caddyshack* (1980), *Easy Money* (1983) and *Back to School* (1986). He also won a Grammy for his comedy album, *No Respect*.

In his 82nd year, Dangerfield underwent heart surgery. He slipped into a coma and died two months later. As per his request, his headstone reads – "There goes the neighborhood!"

March 19th

*Marriage is a mistake
every man should make.*

George Jessel
Actor and Producer
(1898 - 1981)

George Jessel was born in the Bronx into a rather poor family. At 10, he was obligated to leave school and work to help support the family after his father died. His mother worked in the ticket booth of the Imperial Theatre where young Jessel performed as part of the Imperial Trio which included Walter Winchell. Winchell became a celebrated newspaper columnist.

Between the ages of 11 and 16, Jessel worked on stage with Eddie Cantor. During his twenties, Jessel became a Broadway star with the help of his leading role in *The Jazz Singer* (1925). Warner Bros. failed to negotiate an acceptable salary with Jessel, allowing young Al Jolson to step into the role of a career. Jessel's performing career was over-shadowed by Jolson's well-managed career.

During the 1940's and 50's, Jessel produced some two dozen musicals for the 20th Century Fox studios. Jessel also was a very popular member of the USO performing company entertaining troops in various parts of the world. Jessel frequently stepped outside his role as a performer to speak out on political issues. He became an outspoken supporter in favor of the Vietnam War.

George Jessel died of a heart attack in 1981.

March 20th

***It's a poor sort of memory
that only works backwards.***

Lewis Carroll
Writer
(1832 - 1898)

Lewis Carroll, born Charles Lutwidge Dodgson, grew up in a very conservative family. Carroll's great-grandfather was a bishop in the High Anglican Church and his father was also a clergyman in the Anglican Church. Carroll, whose mother died at 47, was the eldest son of eleven children.

During his early years the bright but precocious young Carroll was educated at home. He became deaf in one ear and developed a stammer which followed him throughout his life. He was also prone to whooping cough which left him with respiratory problems. Despite his afflictions, Carroll was comfortable entertaining family and friends with songs and mimicry. In 1856, Carroll (24) published his first poem (*Solitude*) under the name Lewis Carroll which was a clever play on the Latin translation of his real name.

While a student at Christ Church Oxford, Carroll met the young daughter of the Dean – Alice Liddell. In 1864, Carroll (32) presented young Alice with a manuscript entitled *Alice's Adventures Under Ground*. A year later the work was published with a new title – *Alice's Adventures in Wonderland*. The fantasy was hugely popular throughout the world and made Carroll a wealthy writer in his lifetime. A sequel, *Through the Looking Glass*, was darker in style but equally successful.

Lewis Carroll died of pneumonia just shy of his 66th birthday.

March 21st

The very best proof that something can be done is that someone has already done it.

Bertrand Russell
Philosopher and Social Critic
(1872 - 1970)

Bertrand Russell was born into a British family with a long aristocratic history. Bertrand's paternal grandfather, John Russell, became Prime Minister of England twice in his lifetime (1840's and 1860's). His maternal grandfather was Edward Stanley, the Baron of Alderley.

Russell's childhood was dotted with tragic losses. At 2, he lost his mother followed by the death of his older sister. Within two years, young Russell and his older brother, Frank, became orphans with the death of their father. The two brothers, 4 and 11, were sent to live with the paternal grandparents. His grandfather died when Russell was 6. The following decade proved difficult for Russell as he faced bouts of depression often contemplating suicide.

The bright student excelled in mathematics and philosophy at Cambridge. At 24, while teaching at the London School of Economics, Russell published his first work – *German Social Democracy* (1896). Over his long productive life he authored major works on mathematics, including three volumes of the *Principles of Mathematics* (1905-1910). In 1945, he wrote a best-seller, *A History of Western Philosophy*, which created a stream of royalties for the remainder of his life.

Bertrand Russell was awarded the Nobel Prize in Literature for his body of works. Russell died at 97 in Wales.

March 22nd

I care not so much what I am to others as what I am to myself.

Michel de Montaigne
Writer and Politician
(1533 - 1592)

Michel de Montaigne was born in a wealthy French family on the Montaigne estate in the area near Bordeaux, France. Young Michel was placed in the care of a peasant family in order for the child to grow up with the knowledge and appreciation of the life of the poor people.

Montaigne was raised with Latin as a first language. He studied law in Toulouse before beginning life as a public servant. Montaigne served in various roles, including legal counsel to the parliament in Bordeaux and as a member of the court of King Charles IX. Under the pressure of his family he reluctantly gave in to the prearranged marriage to Françoise de la Cassaigne.

In 1571, Montaigne (38) retired from public life to devote himself to writing a collection of essays under the umbrella title *Essais* (*Essays*) published in 1580. *Essays* is considered to have established the essay as a legitimate literary form. Montaigne's writings influenced many writers to follow, including Jean-Jacques Rousseau, Isaac Asimov and William Shakespeare.

Michel de Montaigne suffered from a generic condition related to kidney stones. In 1592, Michel de Montaigne died at the ancestral Chateau de Montaigne.

March 23rd

Wanting to be someone you're not is a waste of the person you are.

Kurt Cobain
Singer and Songwriter
(1967 - 1994)

    Kurt Cobain's Irish ancestors migrated from Ireland in 1875 and settled in Cornwall. Ontario, Canada. The Cobane family (original spelling) then transplanted themselves to Washington State where Kurt was born.
    After his parents divorced young Cobain's (8) life took a turn for the worse. He became confrontational towards adult figures and aggressive towards his schoolmates. Kurt continued his rebellious behavior well into his teens. He often enjoyed antagonizing those around him by deliberately allowing them to believe he was gay when he was, in fact, heterosexual.
    Cobain came from a very artistic family. His maternal uncle was a member of the band The Beachcombers and his great-uncle an Irish tenor and starred in the 1930 film *King of Jazz*. In 1985, Kurt (18) formed the band (Nirvana) which would propel him to fame and fortune. The name of the popular 1980's band came from Kurt's fascination with Buddhist philosophy.
    Cobain suffered from depression most of his life and struggled with drug addiction. He was married to musician-singer, Courtney Love.
    Kurt's 12-year career ended in 1994 in what was officially determined a suicide. He was 27.

March 24th

O peace!
how many wars were waged in thy name.

Alexander Pope
Poet
(1688 - 1744)

Alexander Pope was born into a Catholic family in London. Within a decade the family was forced to distance itself from the city limits since it became unlawful for Catholics to live within ten miles from London. The persecution also forbade them to vote, hold public office or attend university.

Young Pope developed various health issues as a child. The form of tuberculosis followed him throughout his life leaving him deformed and rather slight in stature – 4'6'. At 21 (1709), Pope published *Pastorals* which quickly established him as an important literary figure. Three years later his most popular poem, *The Rape of the Lock*, was published. In 1713, the first of six volumes of Pope's famous translation of Homer's *Iliad* was published with the remaining volumes released one per twelve months. The translation proved to be a huge economic success for Pope. Alexander Pope is one of the most quoted English writers along with William Shakespeare and Lord Tennyson.

Pope never married but had a supposedly romantic relationship with the writer, Martha Blount. His poor health eventually led to serious respiratory problems and an exaggerated hunchback. In the spring of 1744 Pope's health took still another turn. He called for a priest and received the Last Rites of the Catholic Church. The following day Alexander Pope died at 56.

March 25th

Computers make it easier to do a lot of things, but most of the things they make it easier to do don't need to be done.

Andy Rooney
Broadcaster and Humorist
(1919 - 2011)

Andy Rooney was an iconic figure on the CBS Television Network for the past six decades. Rooney's broadcasting career encountered turbulence a number of times because of his gift for sarcasm.

Rooney was born in Albany, New York, and graduated from Colgate University. He served in the U.S. Army where he was first introduced to the world of journalism with regular contributions to Stars and Stripes. Rooney flew on the first U.S. bombing raid over Germany and was one of the first journalists to report on the Nazi concentration camps. In 1949, Rooney became a regular writer for CBS radio's *Arthur Godfrey's Talent Scouts*. The assignment triggered a deep friendship until Godfrey's death. By 1978, Rooney became an established feature on the network's long-running *60 Minutes* with an end-of-program segment called *A Few Minutes with Andy Rooney*. The tongue-in-cheek few minutes did not escape controversy. In 1990, Rooney was given a three-month suspension without pay for an anti-gay remark. During the first month of suspension the program lost 20% of its audience and Rooney was reinstated. The beloved Andy Rooney continued to fill the popular "few minutes" on CBS to the delight of his many loyal fans until his death in 2011.

March 26th

A successful marriage requires falling in love many times, always with the same person.

Mignon McLaughlin
Writer and Journalist
(1913 - 1983)

Mignon McLaughlin was born in Baltimore, Maryland, but grew up in New York City. Her mother, Joyce Neuhaus, was a very successful New York City lawyer.

Young McLaughlin was encouraged by her mother to achieve the highest of standards in her education. McLaughlin enrolled at the prestigious Smith College in Northampton, Massachusetts, and graduated in 1933 at twenty years of age. Her well-developed writing skills led her to launch a career in journalism. Over the years McLaughlin proved to be in great demand as a writer of very sensitive and powerful short stories which appeared in a large number of major women's magazines, including Cosmopolitan.

During her thirties, McLaughlin was a staff writer for Vogue magazine and later served as Managing Editor of Glamour. Her husband, Robert McLaughlin, was an editor for Time Magazine. Mignon McLaughlin died in her 71st year in Coral Gables, Florida.

March 27th

***Flattery won't hurt you
if you don't swallow it.***

Kin Hubbard
Cartoonist
(1868 - 1930)

Kin Hubbard was born Frank McKinney Hubbard in Bellefontaine, Ohio, a mere few years after the end of the American Civil War. His mother always called him Kinney. Thomas Hubbard, Kin's father, was publisher of the Bellefontaine Examiner.

Hubbard, the last of six children, was forever entertaining his family with his drawings as a child. He dropped out of school during his seventh grade to take a job in a paint shop. Hubbard's first love was the entertainment world of the circus and the theatre. His natural drawing skills led him to a career as a newspaper cartoonist. In 1901, Hubbard (33) accepted a full-time position for fifteen dollars a week with the Mansfield News in Ohio where he remained until his death. A few years after he launched his career he created the country philosopher character, *Abe Martin*. The loveable character became an immediate hit and was syndicated to over 300 newspapers across the U.S. for 25 years.

In 1930, Hubbard and his family enjoyed a perfect Christmas celebration in their new home. The next morning he collapsed and died instantly of a heart attack. Kin Hubbard was 62.

March 28th

The first step to getting the things you want out of life is this: decide what you want.

Ben Stein
Economist and Actor
(b. 1944)

Ben Stein was born in Washington, D.C., the son of economist and political adviser, Herbert Stein. Young Ben attended Montgomery Blair High School along with schoolmates Sylvester Stallone, Goldie Hawn and journalist, Carl Bernstein. Stein earned an economics degree from Columbia University and studied law at Yale.

Stein devoted a number of years teaching economics and law at various universities in the U.S. During his thirties, he spent time as a speechwriter for both President Nixon and President Ford. An unexpected acting career was launched with the memorable role of the monatomic high school teacher in the 1986 movie, *Ferris Buller's Day Off*. He repeated a similar character in television's *The Wonder Years* (1988-93). The two roles led to a number of movie and television appearances, including the John Candy-Steve Martin movie, *Planes, Trains and Automobiles* (1987). His distinct voice and delivery have also been featured in countless commercials.

Ben Stein continues to contribute articles, television commentary appearances and lectures on economic and political issues. Stein and his wife, entertainment lawyer Alexandra Denman, live in California.

March 29th

When you judge another,
you do not define them,
you define yourself.

Wayne Dyer
Author and Lecturer
(b. 1940)

Wayne Dyer, was born in Detroit, Michigan. After the premature death of his alcoholic father, Dyer's mother placed both of her children, Wayne and his brother, Jim, in an orphanage. Following high school, he served in the U.S. Navy for a four-year period.

Despite a difficult childhood, Dyer earned his doctorate in counseling from Wayne State University. He also served as a high school guidance counselor and later taught counseling at one of the leading Catholic universities - St. John's University in New York City. After years managing his own successful therapy practice, Dyer wrote the popular best-selling self-help book, *Your Erroneous Zones*. His reputation was further established with a series of successful books, audio tapes and lectures. Dyer is also a supporter and regular contributor during PBS's annual pledge drives.

In 2009, Dyer was diagnosed with chronic lymphocytic leukemia. Dyer and his third wife, Marcelene, live in Maui, Hawaii. Wayne Dyer has six grown children.

March 30th

***It's a shallow life
that doesn't give a person a few scars.***

Garrison Keillor
Author and Radio Personality
(b. 1942)

Garrison Keillor, was born Gary Edward Keillor in Anoka, Minnesota, of Scottish-Norwegian ancestry. Keillor launched his radio career at the University of Minnesota where he graduated with an Honors B.A. in English.

Keillor launched his professional broadcasting career in radio at the now Minnesota Public Radio system in 1969. In October of 1971, he began a unique radio format under the title *A Prairie Home Companion.* The variety format included live musicians, comedy sketches, mini-dramas and weekly home-spun commentaries. An interesting side fact is that the world-wide syndicated show never mentions Keillor by name. The radio program has been on the air for four decades except for a 6-year hiatus in the late 1980's. The program boasts of a loyal fan base of over four million listeners on nearly 600 radio stations.

Garrison Keillor, the public radio raconteur par excellence, was inducted into the Radio Hall of Fame in 1994 and was recognized with the 2007 John Steinbeck Award. The dusty voiced radio host underwent open-heart surgery in 2009 and hints at retirement. Keillor and his wife, violinist Jenny Lind Nilsson, live on the Upper West Side of New York City.

March 31st

***Money is a terrible master
but an excellent servant.***

P. T. Barnum
Showman and Businessman
(1810 - 1891)

P.T. Barnum (Phineus Taylor) is reputed to be the first millionaire in the entertainment business. He also has been erroneously labeled as the author of a famous quote – "There's a sucker born every minute." The quote actually belonged to a Barnum rival named David Hannum.

Barnum was born in Bethel, Connecticut, at the end of the first decade of the 19th century. As a child, Barnum proved to be adept at mathematics, a talent which led him to eventually be involved in the launch of lotteries in the U.S. Barnum married his "sweetheart", Charity Hallett, at 19 and they remained together for 44 years until her death in 1873. As a young man Barnum launched several businesses, including a weekly newspaper. In 1841, Barnum (31) created the Barnum American Museum where he put a 4-year-old dwarf named Charles Stratton on display as an 11-year-old Tom Thumb. By 1846, the museum was attracting an astounding near half million visitors per year.

Oddly enough, Barnum began his circus career late in life. In 1871, at 61, he launched the P.T. Barnum Circus which would later become known as The Greatest Show on Earth. Barnum was the first to make use of the train to criss-cross his circus through the U.S.

P.T. Barnum died peacefully in his sleep in Bridgeport, Connecticut, in his 80th year.

> **"Your name is mud!"**

During the mid-19th century, the United States of America found itself in the midst of a constitutional and moral crisis surrounding slavery. A soft-spoken gentleman lawyer from Kentucky named Abraham Lincoln became the 16th President of the United States on March 4th, 1861. Within weeks, the Confederate Army launched the American Civil War with an unprovoked attack on Fort Sumter. President Lincoln's hands-on approach to the war eventually led to the Thirteenth Amendment to the U.S. Constitution outlawing slavery.

On April 14th, 1865, President Lincoln and his wife, Mary Todd Lincoln, attended a play at the Ford Theatre – *Our American Cousin* by Thomas Taylor. At approximately 10:15pm, John Wilkes Booth shot the president at close range and stabbed 28-year-old Major Henry Rathbone, the president's guest. The president died at 7:22am the following morning. During his leap onto the stage, Booth fractured his left fibula but managed to escape. Booth sought medical help at the farm house of Dr. Samuel Mudd, an acquaintance he had met. Dr. Mudd set the leg and, after a period of rest, Booth and his accomplice continued their escape. Booth was pursued by the Union Army and shot and killed on April 26th. Four of the eight conspirators were executed in early July while the others were imprisoned at Fort Jefferson. During late 1867, an outbreak of yellow fever took the life of the fort's only doctor and Dr. Mudd was crucial in controlling the disease. In 1869, Dr. Mudd was pardoned by President Andrew Johnson.

Dr. Mudd never escaped the stigma of his accidental connection with the man who killed President Lincoln. The less-than-flattering *"Your name is mud!"* phrase has sadly been his legacy.

April 1st

*Life is a big canvas,
throw all the paint on it you can.*

Danny Kaye
Entertainer
(1913 - 1987)

Danny Kaye was born David Daniel Kaminsky in Brooklyn, New York. Kaye's Russian Jewish parents immigrated to the U.S. with two older sons. Young Kaye learned to entertain family and friends with his natural singing talents and clever impressions.

During his early years Kaye expressed desires to pursue a life as a surgeon but he lacked the financial support. Kaye developed his performing skills during his teen years in the Catskills. Kaye's gift at pantomime and facial expression landed him a role in the 1935 comedy film, *Moon Over Manhattan* followed by a series of Broadway and Off-Broadway productions. In 1944, the film *Up in Arms* established Kaye as a motion picture star. Over the next number of decades Kaye became a loveable and popular performer on radio, television and films. Kaye earned two Academy Awards while his never-ending charity work was recognized with the Jean Hersholt Humanitarian Award in 1981. Kaye was the first Ambassador at Large for UNESCO. Kaye developed other passions in his life. He was an accomplished multi-engine pilot and was also the original owner of baseball's Seattle Mariners.

At 70, Kaye underwent a quadruple heart bypass operation where he contracted hepatitis from the blood transfusion. He struggled with his health until his death in 1987.

April 2nd

Nothing strengthens the judgment and quickens the conscience like individual responsibility.

Elizabeth Stanton
Social Activist
(1815 - 1902)

Elizabeth Stanton, born into a family of eleven children in Johnstown, New York, was not allowed the same education privileges as a male. Stanton became one of the strongest voices in the fight for women's rights.

Stanton's father, Daniel Cady, was a successful lawyer who later served as a member of the New York State Supreme Court. Her father introduced young Stanton to the power of law which launched her interest in social activism. She was determined to improve the status of women who as recently as the mid-19th century, not only did not have the right to vote but had limited rights to owning property, an education and employment. Stanton set out to change the way the world treated women. In 1848, at 33, Stanton joined forces with feminist Lucretia Mott to organize the first convention focused on women's rights in Seneca Falls, New York. Stanton wrote and presented the convention with a draft document entitled, *Declaration of Sentiments* which many believe advanced the fight for women's rights. In 1864, Stanton and fellow activist, Susan B. Anthony, founded the National Women Suffrage Association with Stanton serving as President for 21 years.

Elizabeth Cady Stanton died of a heart attack at 86. Eighteen years after her death women in the U.S. were given the right to vote.

April 3rd

***What lies behind us
and what lies before us
are tiny matters compared
to what lies within us.***

Ralph Waldo Emerson
Poet and Philosopher
(1803 - 1882)

Ralph Waldo Emerson, the son of a Unitarian minister, was born in Boston, Massachusetts. When Emerson was eight, his father died of cancer leaving him to be raised by his Aunt Mary who had a great influence on him.

Emerson's education began at the Boston Latin School. Later the young Emerson managed to juggle a few side jobs as he attended Harvard. By the time he reached his early twenties there were signs of health issues. At 26, he married Ellen Louisa Tucker (18) who had died within two years. Emerson eventually lost two brothers to tuberculosis – Edward in 1834 and Charles in 1836. He resigned from the church's clergy a year following his wife's death and traveled to Italy, Malta, Switzerland and France. His journeys helped him uncover a new direction for his life and his talents. In 1833, he gave the first of over 1,500 lifetime lectures and launched a career as an important essayist and lecturer.

Emerson's philosophy was at times considered radical but his writings influenced some of the great minds of the next two centuries. During his last decade the great thinker of the 19th century began to develop serious memory problems. At times he would forget his own name and find it impossible to find the correct words. In 1879, he stopped his lectures. During the spring of 1882, Ralph Waldo Emerson died of pneumonia.

April 4th

You don't have to be great to start but you have to start to be great.

John C. Maxwell
Pastor and Motivational Speaker
(b. 1947)

John Maxwell was born and raised in Garden City, Michigan. His father was a pastor and young Maxwell eventually earned a Doctor of Ministry degree at Fuller Theology Seminary where Robert Fuller became his mentor.

Maxwell served as a pastor for over thirty years before he turned his full-time attention to writing and lecturing. He became an internationally-recognized expert in leadership with his lectures in great demand amongst the Fortune 500 corporations throughout the world. Maxwell has authored more than fifty inspirational books which have sold well over 12 million copies in fifty languages. Two of his best-selling books were *The 21 Irrefutable Laws of Leadership* and *Developing the Leader Within You.*

In 2004, Maxwell returned to the ministry and became a teaching pastor at Christ Fellowship in Palm Beach Gardens, Florida. He also proudly serves as a guest pastor at his mentor's world-famous Crystal Cathedral in Orange County, California. Maxwell and his wife live in South Florida.

April 5th

***A curious paradox is that
I accept myself just as I am,
then I change.***

Carl Rogers
Psychologist
(1902 - 1987)

Carl Rogers, born in Oak Park, Illinois, in the mid 19th century, became one of the most influential psychologists of his time. Rogers is considered by many in his field as one of the important founding fathers of psychotherapy.

Rogers' parents were well educated. His father was a civil engineer and his mother raised the children in a devout Pentecostal Christian household. Young Rogers, the fourth of six children, grew up in a strict religious environment. By the time he was in his early twenties, Rogers dropped out of the seminary and returned to university. In 1931, Rogers (29) earned a PhD. Over his lifetime, he was a devoted professor of clinical psychology at various U.S. universities. Rogers developed the all-important 'Person-centered' approach to therapy. A founding father of psychotherapy, he wrote sixteen books on the subject. The importance of his work in therapy was recognized in 1972 when he was given the Award for Distinguished Professional Contribution to Psychology. He was also a nominee for a Nobel Peace Prize for his tireless work in resolving social conflict in Northern Ireland and in Africa.

Carl Rogers, considered the second most important clinician (Sigmund Freud being the first), suffered a debilitating fall in his 85th year. He died a few days later after his pancreas failed.

April 6th

Retirement is waking up every day and realizing you have nothing to do all day, then ending the day realizing you only did half of it!

Unknown wisdom

Unknown wisdom eloquently captured the essence of retirement which, by definition, is the age when an individual is placed in a position to end a working life for various reasons. In some cultures government legislation forces the issue at a pre-determined age marker. In other cases retirement is the result of illness or sudden physical limitations.

During the early centuries retirement did not exist for a number of reasons, notably life expectancy. Life expectancy has changed over the centuries – Bronze Age (3300 BC-1200BC): 26 years; Medieval Britain (880-1599): 40 and in the 20th century: 77.5. The concept of government-supported pension funds to military personnel can be traced back to colonial days in the U.S. while government employee pensions began in the 20th century. The introduction of Social Security programs encouraged employers to participate.

But retirement does bring its own angst for certain people. Suddenly an individual can face a loss of identity. For decades the person was identified by a title or a job function and over-night that identity is unceremoniously removed. For most retirees there is a period of adjustment before they can finally relax and enjoy their new-found freedom.

April 7th

*Spread love everywhere you go.
Let no one ever come to you
without leaving happier.*

Mother Teresa
Spiritual Leader
(1910 - 1997)

Mother Teresa founded the Missionaries of Charity order in 1950 with the blessing of the Vatican. For 47 years, Mother Teresa and her followers cared for the poor, orphaned, sick and dying beginning in her native India.

By the 1970's, the Missionaries of Charity had reached well beyond India and Mother Teresa had gained an international reputation. In 1979, Mother Teresa was awarded the Nobel Peace Prize for her endless and selfless humanitarian efforts around the world. A year later India honored her with the Bharat Ratna.

The world found numerous reasons to praise Mother Teresa during her lifetime. But despite her tireless humanitarian work she was criticized by certain medical circles for offering below standard medical care in the order's hospices. What was never in question was Mother Teresa's passion to help the needy of the world.

In 1991, after suffering several heart attacks, Mother Teresa offered to resign as head of the order but the nuns, in a dramatic show of support and respect, voted not to accept her resignation. Mother Teresa remained in her position until months before her death in 1997 at 87.

At the time of her death the Missionaries of Charity had a presence in 123 countries.

April 8th

I am not young enough to know everything.

James M. Barrie
Playwright and Writer
(1860 - 1937)

James M. Barrie (the 'M' for Matthew) was born in Scotland of working-class parents. His father, David Barrie, became a successful weaver. Barrie, the ninth of ten siblings, was well educated as were his brothers and sisters.

Young Barrie, a slight of stature child (5'3" as an adult), was blessed with an unusual gift for storytelling. He attended school where his two eldest siblings were teachers. His parents encouraged him to become a Calvinist minister but he enrolled and graduated (1882) from the University of Edinburgh with a Master's degree in literature. After a few years as a journalist, Barrie wrote his first novel – *Auld Licht Idylls* (1888). The next string of novels were not well received by literary critics but were embraced by the reading public. In 1897, a chance meeting in Kensington Gardens where Barrie would walk his Saint Bernard, led to a lifetime friendship and his greatest works. He met the Davies children, initially three and then five. Barrie would delight in entertaining the young boys with countless made-up stories. The regular encounters eventually set the stage for Barrie to create Neverland, the fantasy setting for *Peter Pan*, undoubtedly Barrie's most memorable work. The play instantly struck a chord with audiences around the world and made Barrie a wealthy man.

Sir James M. Barrie died in 1937 of pneumonia. His last will left his estate to his secretary and the rights to *Peter Pan* in perpetuity to the Great Ormond Street Hospital for Children in London.

April 9th

The possible's slow fuse is lit by the imagination.

Emily Dickinson
Poet
(1830 - 1886)

Emily Dickinson came from a prominent Massachusetts family. Dickinson's paternal grandfather was key to the founding of Amherst College. Edward Dickinson, Emily's beloved father, was a lifelong treasurer of Amherst College. Edward also served numerous terms as a State Legislator and a member of the U.S. Congress.

Young Dickinson was born in the family's homestead which had been built by her grandfather in 1813. Emily was the precocious middle child between her brother, Austin, and sister, Lavinia. At 10, Emily and younger Lavinia were enrolled at Amherst Academy and exposed to a classical education. Emily suffered an emotional set-back when, at 14, she lost her dear friend, Sophia, to typhus. Gradually Dickinson withdrew from all social activities, relying more and more on correspondence as a means of communication. During her rather eccentric and secluded life, Dickinson wrote hundreds of unorthodox poems with a mere dozen published in her lifetime. As the years passed Dickinson became more withdrawn and was often referred to by the locals as "the eccentric lady in white".

After Dickinson's death in 1886 at 56, her sister, Lavinia, uncovered a number of hand-bound manuscripts holding hundreds of unique poems – unique in style, content and form. Emily Dickinson is now recognized as one of the most important poets in American history.

April 10th

***It is not flesh and blood
but the heart which makes us
fathers and sons.***

Johann Schiller
Playwright, Poet and Historian
(1754 - 1805)

Johann Schiller was born Johann Christoph Friedrich Schiller in Marbach, Germany, the only son of a military doctor. Young Schiller, named after Frederick II, the King of Prussia, had five sisters. He struggled with illness most of his life.

As a child, Schiller would dress up and play the role of a pastor complete with made-up sermons. But he eventually followed in his father's footsteps and studied medicine. While at school Schiller wrote his first play, *The Robbers*. The play and the playwright became overnight sensations. The play's challenging content about social corruption resulted in Schiller being imprisoned for two weeks and forbidden to write any more such plays. He fled to Weimar, Germany, where he became a professor and devoted the last two decades of his life to writing poetry and historical works.

In 1790, Schiller (31) married Charlotte von Lengefeld. The couple had two sons and two daughters. Schiller returned to the theatre and, together with Johann Wolfgang von Goethe, one of the key figures in German literature, founded the Weimar Theater which revolutionized theater in Germany.

Johann Schiller's poor health left him vulnerable and at 45 he died of tuberculosis.

April 11th

***Death ends a life,
not a relationship***

Jack Lemmon
Actor
(1925 - 2001)

Jack Lemmon, born John Uhler Lemmon III, became one of Hollywood's most beloved actors. Over the period of an impressive five-decade acting career, Jack Lemmon gathered a large collection of industry friends.

One of Lemmon's claims to fame is that he was born in an elevator at a hospital in Newton, Massachusetts. He was the only child of Mildred and John Uhler Lemmon II, the president of a successful doughnut company. After graduating from Harvard (1947), Lemmon served as an ensign in the U.S. Navy, launching an acting career immediately after his release. He honed his performing skills with numerous radio and television appearances. In 1949, Lemmon had a small non- credited part in his first movie – *The Lady Takes a Sailor* starring Jane Wyman and Dennis Morgan. Five years later he starred opposite Judy Holliday in a 1954 comedy entitled *It Should Happen to You* and a star was born. Lemmon won Oscar's Best Supporting Actor for his endearing performance in *Mister Roberts* (1955) and Best Actor in 1973's *Save the Tiger*. He also earned two Best Actor awards at the Cannes Film Festival for *The China Syndrome* (1979) and *Missing* (1982). The talented actor has worked with many of Hollywood's great, including eleven films (*Grumpy Old Men*) with his lifelong friend, Walter Matthau.

Jack Lemmon died on June 27, 2001, almost to the year after the death of Walter Matthau. Lemmon was buried in the Westwood, California, cemetery, near his friend.

April 12th

***A poem begins in delight
and ends in wisdom.***

Robert Frost
Poet and Playwright
(1874 - 1963)

Robert Frost, who so eloquently and vividly captured American early 20th century rural life, was actually born and raised in the city. Frost could trace his lineage to the early British settlers to America in 1634.

Frost held various jobs following his graduation from high school in 1892, including delivering newspapers and working in a factory. In 1894, he published his first poem for $15 in the New York Independent and realized poetry was his calling. In order to support a growing family, Frost toiled on his farm during the day and wrote poetry at night. When farming proved not to be financially viable, he took a teaching position in New Hampshire. Following the war Frost turned his attention to the life of a full-time writer and lecturer and eventually became one of the most quoted poets. Frost did not escape the pain associated with the loss of loved ones. His life was dotted with grief. His father died when Frost was merely 11 and he lost his mother to cancer sixteen years later. Frost's mother, wife and daughter battled depression and his sister, Jeanie, died in a mental hospital. Three of his six children died of various illnesses while one son committed suicide in his late 30's. Frost was awarded the Pulitzer Prize for Poetry on four occasions in his lifetime.

In January of 1961, Frost read one of his poems at the inauguration of President John F. Kennedy. Robert Frost died two years later.

April 13th

He who loses wealth loses much.
He who loses a friend loses more.
But he who loses
his courage loses all.

Miguel de Cervantes
Playwright and Poet
(1547 - 1616)

Miguel de Cervantes was born in Spain to a family of intellectuals. His father was a surgeon and his grandfather a very influential lawyer. His uncle was a mayor.

At the age of 23, Cervantes became a member of the Spanish naval elite corps. He fought bravely in a battle in which he was shot three times in the chest and arm. Cervantes was taken prisoner and spent five years as a slave in Algiers. His military exploits contributed the ground work for his writings.

His classic masterpiece, *Don Quixote*, is considered the first modern novel and ranks as one of the most important works in literature. Centuries later his classic novel served as the basis for an extremely popular stage musical called *Man of La Mancha*.

Cervantes died in Madrid on April 23, 1616.

April 14th

The only thing necessary for the triumph of evil is for good men to do nothing.

Edmund Burke
Statesman and Philosopher
(1729 - 1797)

Edmund Burke, one of Great Britain's most celebrated statesmen of the 18th century, was actually born in Dublin, Ireland, to a very successful Anglican lawyer for the Church of Ireland. Burke's mother was a devout Catholic but young Burke was raised an Anglican. Burke and his sister enjoyed a somewhat perfect childhood for the time.

Burke attended Trinity College in Dublin graduating in 1748 at 19. His father encouraged young Burke to pursue a career in law and enrolled him at Middle Temple in London. But he soon gave up law in an attempt to become a writer. A few years later Burke published *A Vindication of Natural Society*. The work attracted a great deal of attention from scholars who were exceptionally impressed with the writing style. Burke continued to draw attention with his thought-provoking and, at times, challenging writings. In 1757, Burke married Jane Mary Nugeat and the year following he launched a publication called *Annual Register* which would invite commentary about current political events from various authors.

Burke developed health issues relating to his stomach. Edmund Burke died in Buckinghamshire, England, at the age of 68. The above quote has been spoken in various combinations by several great minds, including Burke.

April 15th

There may be times when we are powerless to prevent injustice, but there must never be a time when we fail to protest.

Elie Wiesel
Political Activist and Writer
(b. 1928)

Elie Wiesel grew up in a loving family with a desirer to be a teacher. His father, Shlomo, wished his young son to be fluent in Hebrew and study literature while his mother, Sarah, encouraged their faith as an answer to all. By the time Wiesel was 12 WWII and its horrors were becoming a reality.

Wiesel was born in what is now Sighetu in Romania. In 1944, the entire population of Wiesel's native town was placed in various ghettos of Sighetu (then Sighet). Within months the Nazis moved everyone to the infamous Auschwitz camp. The Wiesel family was separated. Young Wiesel (then 16) never saw his parents and youngest sister again. His two older sisters survived the Holocaust. Following the war Wiesel became a journalist but refused to talk about the concentration camps. Eventually he wrote a book entitled *La Nuit* (*Night*) but sales were slow. Oprah Winfrey featured *Night* on her book club and the book hit the New York Times best seller list. *Night* has been translated into 30 languages and has sold millions of copies.

Wiesel, founder of the Elie Wiesel Foundation for Humanity, is responsible for some of the most valuable literature about the Holocaust. In 1986, 58-year-old Elie Wiesel was awarded the Nobel Peace Prize.

April 16th

The most beautiful things in the world are not seen nor touched. They are felt with the heart.

Helen Keller
Author, Lecturer and Activist
(1880 - 1968)

Helen Keller was born a healthy child in Tuscumbia, Alabama, on a homestead called Ivy Green. Her father, Arthur Keller, served as the editor for the town newspaper. Kate Adams Keller, her devoted mother, was the daughter of Brigadier-General Charles Adams of the Confederate Army.

Young Keller became ill before her second birthday with what modern medicine believes was either scarlet fever or meningitis. She never recovered her sight or her hearing. At the age of 6, a specialist introduced her to Alexander Graham Bell who was working with deaf children. The life-changing meeting led her parents to the Perkins Institute for the Blind and to meet a 20-year-old partially blind student named Anne Sullivan. In 1887, Sullivan began to teach Helen how to communicate with the use of her hands. Young Keller became ferociously eager to learn and attended school with other children. She eventually was accepted at Radcliff in 1900. In 1904, Helen Keller (24) became the first blind-deaf person to earn a B.A. Sullivan remained Helen's constant companion for 49 years until Anne's death in 1936. Helen became a successful author (12 books) and highly respected lecturer world wide. She is also remembered as a tireless advocate for people with physical disabilities.

Helen Keller died in 1968. She was 87.

April 17th

Good judgment comes from experience, and a lot of that comes from bad judgment.

Will Rogers
Actor and Humorist
(1874 - 1935)

Will Rogers, born William Penn Adair Rogers in Oklahoma, grew up to be one of America's most popular and highest paid performers of the 1930's and 40's. He won the hearts of the common folks as well as high-placed politicians.

Rogers, the youngest of eight children, would boast that both his parents were part Cherokee. His father, Clement Rogers, was a leader within the Cherokee nation. Rogers, a professional cowboy, began his show business career in a series of circuses in the U.S. and Australia followed by years on the vaudeville circuit. In 1918, he signed a three-year contract with Samuel Goldwyn and headlined his first silent movie. His stardom accelerated with the introduction of sound. In total Rogers made 48 silent movies and 21 talkies. The high-energy Rogers also penned weekly and then daily newspaper columns reaching an incredible forty million readers. In the thirties, he also conquered a new medium – radio. Will Rogers and his wife, Betty Blake, had four children who made their marks, including a member of Congress (Bill), a Broadway actress (Mary) and a journalist (Jim). The youngest child died at two.

Will Rogers died tragically at the age of 55 in a plane crash in Alaska which also took the life of his friend and pilot, Wiley Post.

April 18th

***If you can dream it,
you can do it.***

Walt Disney
Producer and Entrepreneur
(1901 - 1966)

Walt Disney developed a love for drawing at a very young age and later attended the Kansas City Art Institute. He grew up to become one of the most popular and admired producers in the world of animation. The Walt Disney Company, founded by Walt and his brother, Roy, is valued well over 30 billion dollars with theme parks in the U.S., Tokyo, Paris and Hong Kong.

In 1878, Elias Disney, Walt's father, moved from Ontario, Canada, to California and eventually to Chicago where Walter was born. At the outbreak of WWI, Walter (16) attempted to enlist in the U.S. Army but was turned away because of his age. He eventually became a Red Cross ambulance driver in France as the war ended. Following a number of business disappointments after the war, Walt and his brother, Roy, opened the Disney Brothers Studio in Hollywood to produce animated cartoons. One of the young artists hired was Lillian Bounds later to become Mrs. Walt Disney. In the late 1920's the Disney studio created a new character – a mouse named Mortimer. Lillian later convinced everyone to change the mouse's name to Mickey. Mickey Mouse ruled for decades. The studio released its first animation feature, *Snow White*, in 1937, and its first live-action film, *Treasure Island*, in 1950.

As a leader in family entertainment, Disney Productions has won 22 Academy Awards and Walt Disney has been given four honorary Oscars for his endless contributions. In late 1966, Walt Disney died of complications caused by lung cancer.

April 19th

We can easily forgive a child who is afraid of the dark; the real tragedy of life is when men are afraid of the light.

Plato
Philosopher
(Circa 427 BC - 347 BC)

Plato's precise dates of birth and death are details lost through the ages. History does record that Plato was likely born in Athens into an aristocratic and wealthy family. His father, Ariston, died during Plato's early years. The family also consisted of two brothers and one sister. Plato's mother, Perictone, remarried and had another son.

Plato is reported to have been a bright child with a great thirst for knowledge. The belief is that Plato and his siblings were exposed to the finest educators and instructed in the basics as young children. Plato went on to study the notable Greek philosopher, Heraclitus. History also suggests Plato likely traveled throughout the known world, including Italy and Egypt. Soon after Plato's return to Athens, he founded the earliest known school for advanced learning in the Western world. A number of Greek intellectuals, including Aristotle, were educated at Plato's Academy in Athens. Plato, along with his mentor, Socrates, and his student, Aristotle, is credited with laying the foundations for Western philosophy.

Plato is known to have died in Athens but the precise date unknown. The belief is Plato died in his 80th year.

April 20th

Never close your lips to those whom you have opened your heart.

Charles Dickens
Writer
(1812 - 1870)

Charles Dickens, the author of the great English novel, *A Tale of Two Cities*, was born in Portsmouth, Hampshire, to Elizabeth and John Dickens. The first years of his life appeared to be somewhat idyllic until misfortune struck the Dickens family. Charles' father, then a clerk with the British Naval office, was imprisoned in a debtors' prison. Young Dickens began to work long ten-hour days in a rat-infested warehouse. The theme of social injustice of the working class surfaces in many of his writings.

Young Dickens, a physically small boy, spent long periods devouring the popular early 19th century novels. His near-perfect photographic memory served him well in his later writings capturing the social conditions of his early childhood and of his visits to the debtors' prison to spend time with his father. In 1834, Dickens (22) became a political journalist for the Morning Chronicle in London. At 24, he married Catherine Hogarth, the 20-year-old daughter of the newspaper's editor. The couple had ten children with two of them becoming writers. Dickens traveled to the U.S. and Canada during his early thirties to encourage support for copyright laws for intellectual properties. He also took the opportunity to offer his voice in favor of the abolition of slavery. In his later years, Dickens became a philanthropist.

Charles Dickens suffered a fatal stroke in June, 1870, and died in his home in Kent.

April 21st

Dancing can reveal all the mystery that music conceals.

Charles Baudelaire
Poet
(1854 - 1900)

Charles Baudelaire was born in Paris to François Baudelaire, a senior civil servant and Caroline who was 34 years younger than her husband. François died in his sixtieth year when Charles turned six. Caroline remarried a military officer who later became an ambassador. The loss of the full attention of his mother proved to be traumatic for young Charles.

Baudelaire was a bright but easily distracted student. He studied law at the Lycée Louis-le-Grand in Paris and graduated in 1839 at 18. He turned his back on a career in law and diplomacy to pursue the more care-free life of a writer. Baudelaire became acquainted with a circle of prostitutes and was exposed to syphilis in his early twenties. He became all too easily swayed by the excesses in life and his literary output suffered. By the time he reached his late twenties, Baudelaire faced other obstacles as he struggled with poor health and mounting personal debts. Finally in 1857, Baudelaire (36) published his first and most famous collection of poems under the title *Les Fleurs du mal* (*The Flowers of Evil*). The themes of his poems proved to be scandalous and he was charged with creating an offense against public morals. His fine was reduced but six of the poems were banned.

Baudelaire continued a life of drug and alcohol abuse. He spent the last years of his short life in a nursing home in Paris where he died at the age of 46.

April 22nd

Death is not the greatest loss in life.
The greatest loss is what dies inside us
while we live.

Norman Cousins
Journalist
(1915 - 1990)

Norman Cousins, born in Union City, New Jersey, was diagnosed at age 11 (1926) with tuberculosis and placed in a sanatorium. Eventually the diagnosis proved to be incorrect. Young Cousins went on to enjoy a healthy and athletic youth.

After graduating from Columbia University with a Bachelor of Arts degree, Cousins launched a career in journalism in 1934 at the New York Post (then the Evening Post). He joined the staff of Saturday Review in 1940 and was named editor-in-chief two years later. Over a thirty year period, Cousins was responsible for overseeing the circulation increase from 60,000 to 650,000. During his lifetime, Cousins was a relentless champion of liberal causes. He took every opportunity to use the power of the word to promote nuclear disarmament. Cousins wrote a number of best-selling books on the subject, including the 1953 *Who Speaks for Man?* He was recognized by President John F. Kennedy and Pope John XXIII for his leadership leading up to the Soviet-American nuclear test ban agreement. Cousins received the United Nations Peace Medal in 1971 and the Albert Schweitzer Prize in 1990.

Cousins was diagnosed with heart disease in his mid-30's and suffered his first heart attack at 65. Norman Cousins died of heart failure in late 1990.

April 23rd

*What you believe has more power
than what you dream
or wish or hope for.
You become what you believe.*

Oprah Winfrey
Broadcaster and Actress
(b. 1954)

Oprah Winfrey was born in rural Mississippi and raised for most of her childhood in a poor district of Milwaukee. Her mother, Vernita Lee, was an unwed 19-year-old housemaid and her father, Vernon Winfrey, a barber who later became a city councilman. Oprah was under the care of her maternal grandmother until she entered school. The rebellious young girl was sent to live with her father in Tennessee.

Winfrey won the 1971 Miss Black Tennessee which opened the path into broadcasting. During her final high school year and her time at college, Winfrey worked in the news department of WVOL radio. After a number of years in various radio and television stations, she moved to Chicago in 1984 and took over the WFL-TV's AM Chicago morning talk show. Within two seasons the show became a rating success, expanded to one hour with a new name – *The Oprah Winfrey Show*. In 1985, Winfrey was nominated for a Best Supporting Actress Oscar for her memorable role as Sofia in Steven Spielberg's *The Color Purple*. And Oprah's life changed forever.

After twenty-five years on *The Oprah Winfrey Show* she stepped down to begin a new chapter in her life. On January 1, 2011, she teamed up with Discovery Communications to launch OWN: the Oprah Winfrey Network.

April 24th

***If you want to improve,
be content to be thought
foolish and stupid.***

Epictetus
Philosopher
(50 – 135)

Epictetus was born a slave in Pherrapolis, Phrygia (now Pamukkale, Turkey). He was shipped to Rome where he became the slave of a wealthy Roman who, against tradition, allowed Epictetus to study philosophy. During this period his leg was crippled in some fashion never recorded.

Epictetus was freed from his life as a slave and began to teach philosophy until he was forced to flee Rome in his late thirties when all philosophers were banished. He continued to teach philosophy in Greece. History assumes Epictetus never wrote his philosophy in book form but in his fifties a gifted student named Arrian kept detailed lecture notes and compiled an eight-volume record of Epictetus' teachings under the title *The Discoveries*. Only four volumes have survived the ages. Arrian also translated his professor's lectures in digest form called *The Handbook* (*Enchiridion*). Epictetus' extensive teachings distinguish between what man can control (opinions, desires and impulses) from what cannot be controlled – our bodies, material possessions, glory and power. His theory states that man has no control over external things and the goal of our lives can only be found within us.

Epictetus, the slave turned wise philosopher, has not only influenced the great minds over the centuries but has also had an impact on the common man. Epictetus died in Nicopolis, Greece, in approximately 135AD in his 80th year.

April 25th

Men are more moral than they think and far more immoral than they can imagine.

Sigmund Freud
Physician and Founder of Psychoanalysis
(1856 - 1939)

Sigmund Freud (Sigismund Schlomo Freud) was born in Freiburg, Austria (now the Czech Republic), when his father was in his forties. Freud was the first of eight children. Despite the family's poverty after Jacob Freud lost his business, young Sigmund received an excellent education.

Freud's intentions were to enter law but decided to earn a medical degree and eventually became a neurologist. In his late twenties Freud traveled to Paris to study with the renown neurologist, Jean-Martin Charcot, who was conducting research in hypnosis Freud immediately pursued the fascinating field of psychopathology. During the early years of his private practice, Freud began experimenting by assisting patients talk through their problems. Freud faced many critics and endless skepticism but held to his beliefs. The "talk cure", as it was labeled, grew to be accepted worldwide as the basis of psychoanalysis. At the turn of the century a small group of his followers, called the Wednesday Psychological Society, would meet in his apartment in Vienna to discuss psychoanalytic theories. In the late 30's, the anti-Semitism movement spread through Austria and the Freud family fled with the help of a Nazi official named Anton Sauerwald. Freud's four sisters died in the concentration camps. The father of psychoanalysis also carried out invaluable research in other diseases, notably Cerebral Palsy.

April 26th

Look at everything as though you were seeing it either for the first or last time.

Betty Smith
Writer
(1896 - 1972)

Betty Smith's parents emigrated from Germany to Brooklyn, New York, where Elizabeth Wehner was born. Her early childhood was spent in poverty but her parents were determined to give their daughter a proper education.

After attending Brooklyn's Girls' High School Betty had every intention of going to university. She married George Smith and moved with him to Ann Arbor while he earned a law degree at the University of Michigan. By the time her two daughters were in school she decided to study journalism and writing. In 1938, she and her husband divorced and Betty transplanted herself to North Carolina. Five years later she married Joseph Jones. Later that same year a book she had been working on for some time was released. Smith drew on her childhood in Brooklyn and the various people to write *A Tree Grows in Brooklyn*. The semi-autobiographical novel shot up to the top of the best-sellers list. Director Elia Kazan created a memorable motion picture based on the popular novel in 1945.

Smith also wrote *Tomorrow Will be Better* (1947), *Maggie Now* (1958) and *Joy in the Morning* (1963). Betty Smith died of pneumonia in 1972 in Shelton, Connecticut.

April 27th

A successful man is one who can lay a firm foundation with the bricks others have thrown at him.

David Brinkley
Broadcast Journalist
(1920 - 2003)

David Brinkley, the man who humbly considered himself merely a reporter, became one of the most admired network broadcast journalists. Brinkley's dry wit made him a favorite with both viewers and politicians.

Brinkley, the youngest of five children born to William and Mary Brinkley, grew up in his native Wilmington, North Carolina. Following his WWII service in the U.S. Army, Brinkley joined NBC's Washington bureau as a White House correspondent. He remained with NBC for 38 years. On October 29, 1956, the network launched the nightly newscast, *The Huntley-Brinkley Report*, teaming up a 38-year-old Brinkley and the 47-year-old Chet Huntley. The half-hour NBC newscast out-rated both ABC and CBS news programs. In 1970, Chet Huntley retired only to die four years later from a battle with lung cancer. Brinkley left NBC and joined ABC to host what became an extremely popular Sunday morning news program title *This Week with David Brinkley*.

Over a 53-year broadcast career, Brinkley won ten Emmy Awards and three Peabody Awards. In 1992, he was honored with the Presidential Medal of Freedom. David Brinkley died in 2003 at 92.

April 28th

I do not think much of a man who is not wiser today than he was yesterday.

Abraham Lincoln
Politician and Lawyer
(1809 - 1865)

Abraham Lincoln is considered by many scholars as one of the greatest Presidents in U.S. history. His short years in the White House (1961-1965) changed the course of history.

Lincoln's formal education spanned less than two years. Following his school years he became an avid reader and educated himself. In his mid-twenties he decided to study law on his own and was admitted to the Illinois bar in 1837. Lincoln became an exceptional lawyer and practiced law in Springfield, Illinois. But he never forgot his roots and every year over a sixteen year period, he would tour the state counties on horseback representing people. At 6'4", his very presence in a court room intimidated his opponents.

Lincoln had two failed relationships in his twenties before meeting Mary Todd. In 1840, they announced their wedding for that December but the couple ended their engagement. They later rekindled their relationship and were married on November 4, 1841.

The Lincolns were very affectionate with one another and shared a love for the theatre. Four sons were born but only the eldest (Robert) reached adulthood. The loss of three children devastated both parents.

April 29th

*It is every man's obligation
to put back into the world
at least the equivalent
of what he takes out of it.*

Albert Einstein
Physicist
(1879 - 1955)

Albert Einstein was born in Ulm, Germany, to Hermann, an engineer, and Pauline Einstein. When Albert was one-year-old the family moved to Munich where his father and his uncle established a company manufacturing direct current electrical equipment.

At a young age, Albert demonstrated an unusual talent for mathematics. By the time he reached the age of ten, Albert was exposed to serious studies in mathematics, science and philosophy. In the mid-1890's, his father's manufacturing business failed because alternative current (AC) proved to be more favored than DC current. The family settled in Pavia while young Einstein, then 16, remained in Munich to finish school. A year later he joined his family and completed his high school. At 17, Einstein began advanced studies in physics and mathematics with the intention of teaching. Einstein met a student at the Zurich Polytechnic named Mileva Maric. A daughter was reportedly born in 1902 but the child's fate was never documented. Einstein and Mileva did marry in 1903 and two sons were born in 1904 and 1910. After five years of separation they divorced in 1919. Einstein later married Elsa Lowenthal and they remained together until her death in 1936. Einstein was 57. Hours before his death at 76, Albert Einstein was busy writing about quantum physics.

April 30th

It is the province of knowledge to speak, and it is the privilege of wisdom to listen.

Oliver Wendell Holmes
Jurist
(1841 - 1935)

Oliver Wendell Holmes was born into a privileged Boston family. His father, Oliver Wendell Holmes Sr, was a prominent physician and his mother, Amelia, a dedicated abolitionist.

Holmes' last year at Harvard Law School was interrupted by the outbreak of the American Civil War. Holmes (20) enlisted as a first lieutenant with the Massachusetts Volunteer Infantry. He was wounded three times in three different campaigns. Following the end of the Civil War, Holmes returned to Harvard to complete his law degree and was admitted to the bar in 1866. Later that year 25-year-old Holmes married a childhood friend named Fanny Dixwell and settled in Boston. During their 63 years of married life they had one adopted daughter named Dorothy. Fanny died in 1929. At 40, Holmes wrote a highly-respected book, *The Common Law*, which influenced American jurisprudence for decades. The following year Holmes (41) was appointed to the Massachusetts Supreme Court.

President Theodore Roosevelt called upon Holmes in 1902 to serve on the U.S. Supreme Court. His exceptionally distinguished career extended over three decades with Holmes retiring at 90. Oliver Wendell Holmes died of pneumonia a few days before his 94th birthday. He was buried in Arlington National Cemetery.

> **"To hold a wake."**

Fresh drinking water during the Middle Ages was not always trust-worthy. People relied on two main sources for drinking water - rivers or streams and man-made wells or canals. In some areas close to oceans, the rivers or man-made canals actually contained salt water which caused several illnesses. Fresh inland rivers were frequently contaminated by the careless disposal of human waste products or decomposing animal carcasses.

The search for ways to quench a thirst led the lower classes to favor a more popular beverage – home-grown ale. Ale was made from a combination of barley, oats and wheat (and later hops) with a touch of honey to sweeten the taste. The most common method to enjoy ale was from a lead cup. The combination of lead and alcohol would sometimes render the drinker unconscious for a couple of days. They were often mistaken for dead and the families would prepare them for burial. Since the practice of embalming was popularized in the 19th century, there was a fear of burying a person alive. For that reason the "deceased person" was often laid out in the family home for a number of days and all would gather around and eat and drink and wait and see if their loved one would wake up.

Over time the event took on a more social character, where family and friends of the deceased would gather to bid him farewell and enjoy some food and drink in the process.

The potentially life-saving custom was called - *"to hold a wake"*.

May 1st

***God loves each of us
as if there were only one of us.***

Saint Augustine
Theologian and Philosopher
(354 - 430)

Saint Augustine's journey to sainthood was paved with dramatic personal challenges and discoveries during the early part of his life. The journey would contribute to developing an individual whose writings would endure the ages and would have a tremendous influence on Western Christianity.

Saint Augustine, whose mother language was Latin, was born in Thagaste, North Africa (now Souk Ahras, Algeria). His father, Patricius, was a pagan and his mother, Monica, a Christian. When he was 11, he was sent to school in a neighboring town steeped in pagan beliefs and practices which would have a great impact on the young boy for decades. For a period Augustine followed the teaching of Manichaeism, a religion where astrology played an important role. Over the next decade he took a lover who would give birth to a son who died in his teen years. After being influenced by the life of Saint Anthony of the Desert (251-356) Augustine converted to Christianity and entered the priesthood. Augustine was named Bishop of Hippo (modern day Annaba, Algeria). Over his thirty years as bishop, Augustine, through his writings (*Confessions* and *On the Trinity*) became an influential religious leader.

The Bishop of Hippo died at the age of 75. Augustine was elevated to sainthood in 1298 by Pope Boniface VIII. Augustine had great influence on Saint Thomas Aquinas (1225-1274).

May 2nd

Three things in human life are important.
The first is to be kind.
The second is to be kind.
The third is to be kind.

Henry James
Writer and Playwright
(1843 - 1916)

Henry James, who spent over 53 years of his life in England, was actually born in New York City into a wealthy mid-19th century American family. Henry James Sr. was a clergyman and intellectual. William, his brother, became an important psychologist while his sister, Alice, a writer.

Young James enjoyed the privileges of wealth by studying abroad in Paris, London, Geneva and other European cities. During his twenties, James wrote for American journals in order to cover his traveling expenses. In 1876, at the age of 33, James moved permanently to England, becoming a British citizen in 1915. James wrote a number of classic novels while living in Europe – *Daisy Miller* (1879), *Portrait of a Lady* (1881) and *The Wings of the Dove* (1902). Many of his novels were serialized in monthly editions of popular magazines. Since he wrote the installments to meet the deadlines, he released the work in novel form later. During the last decade of his late, he wrote a three-part autobiography. The prolific writer was responsible for 22 novels, 15 theatrical plays and countless essays. During his five decades in England , James visited the U.S. once for a lecture tour in 1904.

In early 1916, he died as the result of a stroke he suffered some three months earlier. Henry James's ashes were buried in Cambridge, Massachusetts.

May 3rd

Your task is not to seek love, but merely to seek and find all the barriers within yourself that you have built against it.

Rumi
Philosopher, Poet and Theologian
(1207 - 1273)

Rumi, born in a small town what is now Tajikistan, became one of the most influential philosophers and theologians of the 13th century. Rumi's teachings survived long after his death and enjoy popularity worldwide to this day.

Rumi was born into a family boasting seven generations of Hanafi Jurists. Rumi's father, Baha ud-Din Walad, was himself a famous theologian and jurist known as the "Sultan of Scholars". When his father died Rumi (25) inherited the highly-regarded position as head of the religious school. Rumi traveled extensively throughout the Middle East.

Rumi devoted the last dozen years of his life capturing all his teachings in the six-volume *Masnavi*. He believed and preached that the path to God was through poetry, music and dance. Rumi's son, the Sultan Walad, organized his father's philosophy into the Order of the *Mawlawi*.

Rumi was buried in Konya what is present-day Turkey.

May 4th

***The big print giveth,
and the fine print taketh away.***
Bishop Fulton J. Sheen
Religious Leader
(1895 - 1979)

Bishop Sheen, the oldest of four sons, was born Peter John Sheen, in El Paso, Illinois, to Newton and Delia Sheen. His devoted mother's maiden name was Fulton. Young Sheen was diagnosed with tuberculosis as a child.

Sheen attended St. Viator College in Bourbonnais, Illinois, before studying theology at Saint Paul Seminary in Minnesota. He was ordained into the priesthood in 1919 and later earned a PhD in Philosophy at the Catholic University of Leuven in Belgium. After some 25 years teaching philosophy, Bishop Sheen (56) was consecrated a bishop in 1951 and served as Bishop of the Archdiocese of New York until 1959. His weekly radio program, *The Catholic Hour*, reached an impressive four million people per week and his winning style was also featured on television (1951-1968) up against programs hosted by Milton Berle and Frank Sinatra, gathering a viewership of 30 million at one point. The program won an Emmy. The television program reportedly had a great influence on the conversions of such people as Henry Ford II, actress Virginia Mayo and Clare Boothe Luce. Bishop Sheen took strong, and at times, unpopular stands such as his lectures against the Vietnam War.

Bishop Sheen's health became an issue during his last years. In December of 1979, Archbishop Fulton J. Sheen died at 84 of heart disease. He is buried in the crypt of St. Patrick's Cathedral in New York City.

May 5th

***It is not the answer that enlightens,
but the question.***

Eugene Ionesco
Playwright and Poet
(1909 - 1994)

Eugene Ionesco was born in Slatina, Romania, but lived in France for a great part of his childhood. Growing up in the Ionesco family offered him diversity. His father, from an Orthodox religion, brought a Romanian flavor to the family while his Protestant mother was from a French-Greek background.

After his parents divorced, Ionesco (16) returned to Romania to attend school, including studying French literature at the University of Bucharest. Ionesco married Rodica Burileanu in 1936 and, with their young daughter, the family moved to France so he could work on his doctorate. After WWII, the Ionescos settled in Paris. His first entry into the world of literature was by way of his inventive and rather satirical poetry. He reached the age of 41 (1950) before turning his attention to the theatre with his first and most famous play – *La Cantatrice chauve*. The one-act play is still being performed more than six decades later. Ionesco followed up with a collection of innovative plays – *The Lesson* (1951), *The Chairs* (1952) and *The Submission* (1955). His last play (*Voyage chez les morts*) was written in 1981.

Ionesco, one of the great playwrights of the Theatre of the Absurd, was made a member of L'Académie française in 1969. Eugene Ionesco died at the age of 84 in Paris.

May 6th

*People seldom see
the halting and painful steps
by which the most
insignificant success is achieved.*

Anne Sullivan
Teacher
(1866 - 1936)

Anne Sullivan was born Johanna Mansfield Sullivan in Feeding Hills, Massachusetts, to poor illiterate Irish immigrants. Her mother died of tuberculosis and her abusive alcoholic father left the family. Anne (8) and her frail younger brother were sent to a government shelter where Jimmie died.

Young Anne was partially blind as the result of an untreated trachoma. After four years at the shelter, Anne was sent to the Perkins School for the Blind in Boston where her life changed dramatically. She discovered reading and writing and was taught how to use the manual alphabet to communicate with the blind-deaf. After graduation, Anne's life changed once again with the introduction to a blind-deaf six-year-old named Helen Keller. Anne moved into the Keller home to become Helen's full-time tutor. Over time she broke through to the rebellious child and eventually taught Helen how to communicate with the manual alphabet. Young Helen went on to graduate from Radcliffe College with Anne by her side in every lecture.

Anne Bancroft won an Oscar for her portrayal of Anne Sullivan in the 1962 movie *The Miracle Worker* with Patty Duke in the role of Helen Keller. Anne Sullivan died at 76 in 1936. Helen Keller died in 1968 and her ashes were placed next to Anne's in the Washington National Cathedral.

May 7th

Silence may be golden, but can you think of a better way to entertain someone than to listen to him?

Brigham Young
Playwright and Poet
(1801 - 1877)

Brigham Young, one of the pioneers of Mormonism, was born into a Vermont farming family in the first year of the 19th century. During his young adult years, he worked at various jobs, including as a carpenter. In 1823, Young converted to the Methodist faith and married Miriam Angeline Works.

When Young turned 30, he joined the Mormon Church as a missionary in Upper Canada. Young rose quickly within the ranks of the church's leadership. He led the movement in introducing Mormonism to Europe. The president of the Mormon Church was killed in 1844 and within a few years Young was ordained to the role of president. In 1847, Young led his followers to an area which was part of Mexico and is now Utah. Young founded a new community called Salt Lake City. Over the 29 years of his presidency the church expanded and the community grew. His presidency was not without conflict with the U.S. government and the wagon trains of settlers traveling through the Utah area. The infamous Mountain Meadows massacre of 1857 resulted in over 120 men, women and children killed by the Mormons.

Young practiced polygamy for more than three decades. He reportedly had a total of 55 wives and 56 children. At the time of his death, he had 16 wives living with him. Brigham Young died at the age of 76.

May 8th

Those who dance are considered insane by those who cannot hear the music.

George Carlin
Entertainer
(1937 - 2008)

George Carlin was raised in a Roman catholic home by his mother, Mary. Carlin's parents separated when he was merely months old. He lived with his mother in Manhattan. Carlin's relationship with his mother deteriorated through his rebellious teen years.

After attending Bishop Dubois High School in Harlem, Carlin joined the U.S. Air Force and was introduced to the radio disc jockey world. Carlin's first post-service years were spent on-air at a Fort Worth radio station where he met Jack Burns. The Burns and Carlin comedy team performed together in the California clubs. In 1960, Jack Burns teamed up with funny man Avery Schreiber (1935-2002) while Carlin set out as a solo stand-up comedy act. Carlin became a popular performer on such television programs as *The Ed Sullivan Show* and *The Tonight Show* first with Jack Paar and later with Johnny Carson. During the 1970's, Carlin's appearance changed to the defiant blue jeans, long hair and beard and distanced himself from his fans. An appearance on *The Ed Sullivan Show* gave him an opportunity to reclaim his audience. Over his career Carlin won five Grammy Awards for Best Comedy recordings. Carlin was married to Brenda Hosbrook for 16 years until her death in 1997. They had a daughter named Kelly. In 1998, Carlin married Sally Wade.

After struggling with heart disease (first heart attack in 1978), George Carlin died in Santa Monica, California, two days before his tenth wedding anniversary.

May 9th

If we all worked on the assumption that what is accepted as true is really true, there would be little hope of advance.

Orville Wright
Inventor
(1871 - 1948)

Orville Wright, born in Dayton, Ohio, grew up to become half of the historic team responsible for the first fixed-wing aircraft. A second member of the Wright family, older brother, Wilbur, completed the team.

The Wright brothers were two of seven children born to Susan and Milton Wright and part of the Church of the United Brethren. Orville left high school before earning a diploma. When Orville was seven years old his father bought the brothers a toy helicopter which triggered a lifetime fascination with aviation. The brothers tried their hand at various business enterprises, including publishing a weekly newspaper (*The Westside News*) and during the early 1890's, they manufactured a new brand of bicycles. The brothers were convinced that control was as vital to flight as wings and engines. Their persistence led to the crucial invention of the three-axis control device which is still part of modern-day aircrafts. During the early years of the 20th century, Orville and Wilbur conducted a series of historical flights at Kitty Hawk, North Carolina. A great deal of controversy surrounded the first flight claim but the Wright brothers were granted a patent in 1906.

Orville Wright suffered a second heart attack in early 1948 and died shortly after at 46. Wilbur, four years his senior, died of typhoid fever in 1912.

May 10th

People who work sitting down get paid more than people who work standing up.

Ogden Nash
Writer and Poet
(1902 - 1971)

Ogden Nash was born in Rye, New York, and because his father, Edmund, managed his own successful import-export business the Nash family moved frequently. His early high school years appear to be those of a middle-class family.

After graduating from high school at St. George School in Middletown, Rhode Island, young Nash enrolled at Harvard University in 1920 at the age of eighteen. At the end of his first year he returned to St. George School as a teacher. Nash also served as an editor at Doubleday Publishers. In 1931, Nash (29) published his first collection of poems under the title, *Hard Lines*.

The distinct Ogden Nash humorous and unconventional writing style soon gained him world-wide attention. Nash's quick wit and communications skills made him a popular figure on the lecture circuit. He was also drawn to writing lyrics for stage musicals, including the popular tune, *Speak Low*, from *One Touch of Venus*.

Ogden Nash died of Crohn's disease in 1971 at the age of 68.

May 11th

***There is no greater hell
than to be a prisoner of fear.***

Ben Jonson
Dramatist, Poet and Actor
(1572 - 1637)

Ben Jonson (Benjamin) made Westminster, London, home for a large part of the 65 years of his life. His father died before Benjamin's birth and his mother remarried two years later. Jonson, of proud Scottish descent, attended Westminster School followed by an apprenticeship as a bricklayer, his step-father's trade, before serving in the military.

At the age of 22, Jonson married a lady history believes was named Ann Lewis. Church documents record that the couple's only daughter (Mary) died when she was an infant while their first son (Benjamin) died in his tenth year. A second son died a few years before Ben Jonson. In his mid-twenties, Jonson became a regular member of London's famous Admiral's Men theatre group. He served the company as both an actor and a writer. Jonson's first writing success was a comedy performed in 1598 with a cast which included a 34-year-old actor named William Shakespeare. When King James I was crowned in 1603, Jonson (31) became a favorite of the court with a pension granted when he reached his mid-fifties. Jonson is believed to be England's first Poet Laureate. His greatest achievements as a playwright are found in two plays – *Volpone* (1605) and *The Alchemist* (1610).

Jonson's popularity began to fade with the death of his champion, King James I, in 1625. Ben Jonson died at 65 in 1637 in Westminster, London.

May 12th

*Imagination will often carry us
to worlds that never were.
But without it
we go nowhere.*

Carl Sagan
Astronomer, Cosmologist and Writer
(1934 - 1996)

Carl Sagan's family visited the 1939 New York World Fair when he was five years old and the experience triggered a life-long fascination in the unknown mysteries of the planets. His parents recognized their son's passion and encouraged him at every turn.

Sagan was an active member of the Ryerson Astronomical Society at the University of Chicago. In 1956, he received a Master of Science degree in Physics followed four years later with a PhD of Philosophy. Sagan served as a lecturer and researcher at Harvard University until the late 1960's. He was also an advisor with NASA during the Apollo and Mariner missions. Sagan's popularity peaked with the award-winning (Emmy and Peabody) PBS *Cosmos* series in 1980. The series reached over five hundred million people in 60 countries making it the most-watched PBS production. Sagan aggressively championed research for possible extraterrestrial life throughout his career.

The Pulitzer Prize author was married three times and had five children. Over a number of years, Sagan underwent three bone transplants dealing with myelodysplasia (MDS). Carl Sagan died of pneumonia at 62.

May 13th

***Not all those who wander
are lost.***

J.R.R. Tolkien
Writer and Poet
(1892 - 1973)

J.R.R.Tolkien (John Ronald Reuel), referred to as the "father of modern fantasy literature", was born in Bloemfontein in the Orange Free State (modern-day Free State Province) in South Africa. Tolkien's father, Arthur, a successful British bank manager, was transferred from London to Bloemfontein before J.R.R.'s birth.

While on a visit to England with his mother, Mabel, and his younger brother, Hilary, his father suddenly died of rheumatic fever. The shattered family moved in with the maternal grandparents. Young Tolkien became an eager student learning to read and write before the age of five. Mabel Tolkien succumb to a battle with diabetes in her mid-30's. The young Tolkien brothers were placed in the care of Father Morgan of the Birmingham Catholic Oratory. John graduated from Oxford's Exeter College with honors in English Literature in 1915. A year later, he married Edith Bratt (27), a fellow orphan he had met when he was 16. He then served as a Second Lieutenant on the front lines in France. John Ronald returned to his beloved Edith after WWI and devoted the next 35 years as an English literature university professor.

During his teaching years, Tolkien wrote several classic novels which had a tremendous impact on fantasy literature – *The Hobbit* (1937) and *The Lord of the Rings* (1954). J.R.R. Tolkien died in late 1973 and was buried with the lady he had loved for 65 years, Edith, who passed away less than two years earlier.

May 14th

You can't wait for inspiration.
You have to go after it with a club,

Jack London
Writer and Journalist
(1876 - 1916)

Jack London (John Griffith Chaney) was born to Flora Wellman, a music teacher in a poor district of San Francisco. The earthquake of 1906 devastated the city of San Francisco and official records were lost. Young Jack's biological father has never been legally identified. The belief is that a William Chaney, an astrologer Flora knew, was his natural father.

In 1876, Flora Wellman married a gentleman named John London. The new family settled in Oakland, California, where young London appears to have had a somewhat normal life. London attended the University of California in Berkley. He left the campus to join the search for gold in the Klondike. Life in the rugged Klondike proved to be dificult for many gold hunters. London developed scurvy which caused much damage to his body. By the turn of the century he decided to earn a living as a writer prompted in part by the increase in the number of magazines looking for adventure short stories. In 1903, one of his most famous stories, *The Call of the Wild*, was sold to the Saturday Evening Post for an impressive $750 and book rights for $2,000. The book skyrocketed to national and then international success and London was on his way to great wealth. *White Fang* (1906) also enjoyed international popularity.

London's good health was severely compromised during his Klondike Gold Rush days. On November 22, 1916, Jack London died of uremic poisoning in his ranch in Sonoma County, California. He was 40.

May 15th

***How old would you be
if you didn't know
how old you are?***

Satchel Paige
Baseball Player
(1906 - 1982)

Satchel Paige was born Leroy Robert Page in Mobile, Alabama. After the death of his father in the mid-1920's his mother, Lula Page, changed the family name by adding an "I". The nickname "Satchel" came from his childhood job carrying bags at the train station.

By his early teens, Satchel had a juvenile record for theft and was sent to reform school for six years until his eighteenth birthday. At 20, he joined the Chattanooga White Sox of the Negro Southern Baseball League for $250 per month. He lived on $50 and $200 was sent to his mother every month. Over the next two decades Satchel earned a reputation as the best pitcher in the all-black league. Jackie Robinson broke the black barrier in the major baseball leagues in 1947. In 1948, Satchel (42) became the oldest man to debut in the majors by joining the ranks of the Cleveland Indians. His first contract was for $40,000 for the final three months of the season. His final game as a major league pitcher was in September of 1965.

Satchel's baseball pitching career spanned an unbelievable forty years. He is considered by many baseball experts and players as having the hardest throw in baseball history. Leroy Satchel Paige, the first black pitcher in the American Baseball League, died of a heart attack weeks before his 76th birthday.

May 16th

Anyone can count the seeds in an apple, but only God can count the number of apples in a seed.

Robert H. Schuller
Spiritual Leader
(b. 1926)

Robert H. Schuller was born in the area of Alton, Iowa. The dedicated student earned a Master of Divinity degree from Western Theological Seminary at 24 years of age. He became an ordained minister in the Reformed Church.

In 1955, Schuller (29) launched the Garden Grove Community Church in Southern California in a drive-in theatre. Within six years a new church building complimented the existing space for 500 cars. The congregation continued to reach out to new followers eager for a "positive" faith. The beautiful glass structure designed by architect Philip Johnson and appropriately called the Crystal Cathedral was dedicated in 1980. When Schuller was 44 years old (1970), he launched a weekly broadcast called *Hour of Power*. Over a four decade period the broadcast has become the most watched church service in the world.

Robert H. Schuller and his wife, Arvella, have been married for more than six decades and have five grown children. The economic crisis did not spare the Crystal Cathedral. As the first decade of the 21st century drew to an end the church was facing a financial crisis.

May 17th

*We don't stop playing because we grow old.
We grow old because we stop playing.*

George Bernard Shaw
Playwright
(1856 - 1950)

George Bernard Shaw was born in Dublin, Ireland, in the mid-19th century to a grain merchant (George Carr Shaw) and a professional singer (Lucinda Elizabeth). Shaw had two older sisters. His mother left her husband taking her two daughters when young Shaw was 16. Lucinda joined her vocal coach in London. Young George remained in Dublin with his father. Shaw disliked the school system and the teachers and left to take a job as a clerk.

At 20, Shaw moved to his mother's London home where he dedicated himself to writing. Shaw's first financially successful writing venture was *The Devil's Disciple* in 1897. A year later he married Charlotte Payne Townshend and the marriage is reported never to have been consummated because the belief is that he was homosexual. The prolific writer was responsible an for incredible 65 plays in total, including *Caesar and Cleopatra* (1898), *Man and Superman* (1903) and *Major Barbara* (1905). Shaw perfected a writing style not popular in British drama at the time – strong, social issues dealt with the Shaw wit. One of his plays was exceptionally successful – *Pygmalion* (1912) which served as the basis for the popular stage production (1956) and motion picture (1964) titled *My Fair Lady*.

Shaw is the only writer to be awarded both a Nobel Prize in Literature and an Oscar for the 1933 screenplay for *Pygmalion*. Bernard Shaw died at 94.

May 18th

It is easier to build strong children than to repair broken men.

Frederick Douglass
Playwright and Poet
(1818 - 1895)

Frederick Douglass, born Frederick Augustus Washington Bailey, a slave in Maryland, became an eloquent leader of the abolitionist movement in the U.S. He was separated from his slave mother, Harriet Bailey, as an infant and never knew his father. Harriet died before his 7th birthday.

At twelve, Frederick was sent to Baltimore as a slave to the Auld household. Mrs. Auld secretly introduced young Frederick to the alphabet contrary to the current law forbidding blacks to read. When he was fifteen the defiant young Frederick was sent to a "slave breaker" where he was repeatedly whipped. At 19, he successfully escaped to New York City with the help of a free black lady named Anna Murray with whom he had fallen in love. They were married in 1838. Once in hiding they took the family name "Douglass". Frederick became an exceptional orator in great demand on the lecture circuit, including Europe. The British and Irish were so taken by the 28-year-old they raised the funds necessary to buy his freedom. He founded The North Star, a newspaper championing abolition of the slave trade. After the Civil War, Douglass was appointed Consul-General to Haiti.

Douglass has been named as one of the 100 Greatest African Americans in U.S. history. Frederick Douglass died of a heart attack in early 1895 in Washington, D.C.

May 19th

A pessimist sees the difficulty in every opportunity; an optimist sees the opportunity in every difficulty.

Sir Winston Churchill
Statesman
(1874 - 1965)

Sir Winston Churchill, one of greatest orators in British history, was born with a speech impediment similar to his father. Churchill was a descendant of the aristocratic Spencer family on his father's side. His mother, Jennie, was the daughter of a wealthy American business entrepreneur.

Young Winston was a rebellious child and a less than average student. Finally once enrolled at Harrow School at 14 as a live-in student he found a focus as a military cadet and began to flourish academically. A growing distance developed between the young man and his parents who seldom visited him. His father, Sir Randolph, an influential politician, died while Winston (21) was a Second Lieutenant with the Queen's Own Hussars. In order to enhance his meager military pay, Winston served as a war correspondent for various London newspapers reporting in his own style on military campaigns in Cuba and India. He made a name and added to his income.

In 1904, Churchill (34) was introduced to a young lady named Clementine Hozier. The couple had five children. Churchill entered politics and served his country twice as Prime Minister – 1940-45 and 1951-55. Sir Winston Churchill died nine days after suffering a fatal stroke at the age of 96.

May 20th

They who dream by day are cognizant of many things which escape those who dream only by night.

Edgar Allan Poe
Writer and Poet
(1809 - 1849)

Edgar Allan Poe, known as the master of the macabre, was born as Edgar Poe in Boston, Massachusetts. David Poe, his actor-father abandoned the family in 1810 and his mother, also an actress, died of pneumonia when Poe was still an infant. Young Edgar was taken in by John Allan, a successful Richmond, Virginia, merchant and his wife, Frances. The couple never formally adopted the young boy but did change his name to Edgar Allan Poe.

Young Poe led a somewhat undisciplined life during his youth. Edgar was enrolled at the University of Virginia. During his short university career Poe amassed gambling debts and left the campus becoming estranged from the Allans whose patience had been exhausted. In 1830, he was accepted as a cadet at West Point Military Academy but within a year forced a court martial in order to be dismissed. A wealthy Baltimore businessman found him an assistant editor position with the Southern Literary Messenger but he managed to get fired within weeks. He married his 13-year-old cousin at 26. His published poems began to draw attention and in 1845 his poem, *The Raven*, made him famous instantly but he received only $9 for the publication. After his wife's death at 25, Poe's drinking became a serious problem.

In 1849, Poe was found disoriented on a Baltimore street in clothes other than his own. His death remains a mystery.

May 21st

***The more I see
the less I know for sure.***

John Lennon
Musician and Song Writer
(1940 - 1980)

John Lennon - the name immediately brings to mind such disciplines as songwriter, singer and social activist. John was born in Liverpool, England, to Julia and Alfred Lennon.

John's merchant seaman father was away from the family for long stretches of time and finally vanished completely for over six months. Young five-year-old John was placed with his mother's sister, Mimi, where he lived most of his young life. At 22, a rebellious John married Cynthia Powell who was pregnant with his child. At that very same time in 1962, The Beatles burst onto the British music scene and Beatles manager, Brian Epstein, encouraged all to keep both the marriage and the pregnancy a secret. Their marriage didn't survive the decade. The Beatles magic combination of John Lennon, Paul McCartney, George Harrison and Ringo Star were featured on *The Ed Sullivan Show* in February, 1964, and 'Beatlemania' was born. The Lennon-McCartney writing team produced some of the most commercially successful and critically acclaimed pop songs in history. An excess of drugs and the sudden death of Epstein in 1966, signaled the end of The Beatles. By the late 1960's Lennon was collaborating with Yoko Ono whom he married in 1969. A year later, in 1970, The Beatles officially broke up.

Lennon's solo career produced a number of successful albums. The genius of John Lennon was prematurely and tragically silenced when he was murdered by a deranged stalker.

May 22nd

We wish to be happier than other people; and this is difficult, for we believe others to be happier than they are.

Montesquieu
Philosopher
(1689 – 1755)

Montesquieu was born, Charles-Louis de Secondat, in the southwest of France of noble ancestral lineage. Charles-Louis was raised and educated in the Catholic faith. When his maternal uncle died young Charles-Louis inherited a substantial amount of money plus the title Baron de Montesquieu.

Charles-Louis (26) married Jeanne de Lartigue the same year King Louis XIV (1638-1715) died. The transition to the child king (Louis XV at five years of age) had a great influence on Montesquieu and his writings. He made his literary mark with the release of *Lettres persanes* (*Persian Letters*) in 1721. Montesquieu's greatest contributions to the world was the 1748 publication of *L'esprit des lois* (*The Spirit of the Laws*). His social and political concepts were controversial and were eventually banned by the Catholic Church. Montesquieu's theories were favored by the leaders of the emerging America, notably James Madison, the father of the U.S. constitution. Montesquieu believed in a society where "no man should fear another" and promoted a three-tiered government model with an 'executive', a 'legislative' and a 'judicial'. He also encouraged a major rethinking of slavery.

Montesquieu became totally blind in his last years. In 1755, at the age of 66, Montesquieu died in Paris.

May 23rd

You can tell more about a person by what he says about others than you can by what others say about him.

Leo Aikman
Journalist
(1908 - 1978)

Leo Aikman was born in Dana, Indiana, at the beginning of the 20th century. The small town of Dana was a farming community with a population of approximately 600.

Aikman enrolled at DePauw University where he graduated with a Bachelor of Arts degree. He also earned a Masters degree in American History at the University of Michigan.

Leo Aikman began his career as a member of the National Parks Service in Washington, DC, and remained with the dedicated team until 1941. At 33, Aikman became a historian with the Kennesaw Mountain National Battlefield Parks in Marietta, Georgia. The park honors the 5,350 Civil War soldiers who gave their lives during the June, 1864, battle.

Aikman began writing a column in 1948 with the Atlanta Constitution. He spent a total of thirty years as a columnist with the Constitution.

Leo Aikman died at the age of 70.

May 24th

***May you live
all the days of your life.***

Jonathan Swift
Cleric and Writer
(1667 - 1745)

    Jonathan Swift was born in mid-17th century Ireland. The Dublin native's father was Irish and his mother was British. Young Swift was born several months after his father's sudden death. His distraught mother placed young Jonathan with his paternal uncle and returned to England.
    Swift received a B.A. degree from Dublin University at 19 and his pursuit of a Masters degree was interrupted by the 1868 Glorious Revolution of Ireland. He joined his mother in England where he was employed as personal assistant to Sir William Temple, a British diplomat, to help with his memoirs. Swift (20) became the tutor of Ester, the eight-year-old daughter of one of Temple's servants. Swift developed Menière's's disease which followed him throughout his life. In 1692, Swift earned his Masters degree from Oxford. Two years later he was ordained in the Church of Ireland. During this period he wrote and published two works which established his as a serious writer – *A Tale of a Tub* and *The Battle of the Books*. When he was 59, Swift published the book he is best remembered for – *Gulliver's Travels*.
    The belief is that Swift and Ester, whom he met when she was 8, were secretly married in 1913. Ester died at 50 when Swift was 61. In 1742, Swift (75) suffered a debilitating stroke which resulted in the loss of speech. He was declared of "unsound mind" and died in 1745. He was buried by Ester's side in the cathedral. Swift's will set up a fund to establish a psychiatric hospital which is still in operation.

May 25th

Children have never been very good at listening to their elders, but they have never failed to imitate them.

James Baldwin
Writer and Civil Rights Activist
(1924 - 1987)

James Baldwin survived his childhood years in Harlem to emerge as an important writer and an enthusiastic Civil Rights activist. His single mother had married a preacher named David Baldwin.

As a young man, Baldwin relocated to Paris in the hope of escaping the growing prejudice in the U.S. Life on Paris' left bank allowed Baldwin to further explore his own sexuality and develop his writing style. He desperately wished to be recognized as more than an American black writer. Baldwin accomplished his dream with a series of powerful novels – *Go Tell It on the Mountain* (1953), *Giovanni's Room* (1956), *Another Country* (1962) and *Tell Me How Long the Train's Been Gone* (1968). Baldwin captured the turbulent times of the 1960's in the United States.

Baldwin, the writer, was frequently the subject of criticism that his full-time presence in Europe kept him out of touch with the real America. But time and time again Baldwin answered the criticism with yet again another work emphasizing black life in the U.S.

Baldwin died of stomach cancer in Saint-Paul-de-Vence, France. He was buried outside of New York City.

May 26th

The chain of wedlock is so heavy that it takes two to carry it – and sometimes three.

Alexandre Dumas
Playwright and Poet
(1802 - 1870)

Alexandre Dumas, one of the most widely read French authors, was born in Villers-Cotterêts, France. Dumas' father, Thomas-Alexandre Dumas, a general in Napoleon's army and a descendant of African lineage, died when Dumas was four-years-old. Dumas's mother, Marie-Louise, the daughter of an innkeeper, was unable to give her son a proper education but her story-telling did give young Dumas a vivid imagination.

When Dumas was twenty he moved to Paris in the employment of the office of Louis Philippe, the Duke of Orléans. By the time he reached 27, Dumas had found financial stability with the release of popular plays, including *Henry III and His Court* (1829) and *Christine* (1830). In his mid-30's, Dumas created a literary writing factory employing other writers to feed the ever-growing appetite for serialized dramas in periodicals. Dumas' wealth was often depleted by his excessive lifestyle. Dumas made his lasting mark in world literature with three novels – *The Three Musketeers* (1844), *The Count of Monte Cristo* (1846) and *The Man in the Iron Mask* (1847). His novels have been translated in almost one hundred languages and were the basis of countless movies.

Alexandre Dumas died in 1870 and was buries in Villers-Cotterêts but in 2002 President Jacques Chirac had him interred in the Panthéon in Paris along side Victor Hugo and Émile Zola.

May 27th

The best way to predict your future is to create it.

Peter F. Drucker
Educator and Consultant
(1909 - 2005)

Peter F. Drucker (the 'F' for Ferdinand), was born in what is now part of Vienna, Austria. His father, Adolf, was a lawyer within the civil servant structure and his mother, Caroline, studied medicine. The Lutheran-Protestant home was always the scene of meetings with various intellectuals.

Young Drucker worked as a journalist while he attended the University of Frankfurt. At 22, he graduated with a PhD in international law. Within two years Drucker was forced to flee Germany because of his early writings. He traveled to London and then eventually settled in the U.S. where he devoted over six decades of his life as a university professor first in New York and then in California. While in London, Drucker (25) met and married a fellow university student named Doris Schmitz. During the early 1940's, Drucker served as consultant for some of the major multi-national companies such as IBM, General Motors and Coca-Cola. In his popular book, *Concept of the Corporation* (1946), he developed his theory of large companies having serious social responsibilities beyond their walls. Eventually he took his message to Canada and Japan where he drew large followings.

Over sixty years, Drucker wrote 39 books which were translated in more than thirty languages. Peter F. Drucker died a week before his 96th birthday with his last literary work published after his death.

May 28th

He who finds discontentment in one place is not likely to find happiness in another.

Aesop
Fabulist
(620 - 564 BC ?)

Aesop, undoubtedly the most famous fabulist in literary history, remains a mystery, centuries after the first reporting of his existence. History has recorded numerous versions of his life and his physical appearance and all are unsubstantiated. A rather sketchy biography can be pulled together from historical facts and legends.

Aristotle (384-322 BC) tells us that Aesop was born in approximately the year 620 BC along the coast of the Black Sea in a city called Mesenbria modern-day Nesembra. According to Aristotle's account, Aesop was a slave to the philosopher Xanthus and later gained his freedom. Aesop is also reported to be exceptionally ugly, almost monstrous. By the Classic Greek age, Aesop, fact or legend, had become part of the folklore and his tales of talking human-like animals widely quoted. None of Aesop's original writings survived the centuries.

At one point in history, Aesop is reported to be black of Ethiopian descent. The belief was substantiated by the fact that many of the fables were about creatures known to be from Africa – camels, elephants and apes. Aristotle wrote that Aesop was sent to the city of Delphi on a diplomatic mission where he was executed in 564 at approximately 56 years of age.

May 29th

I have noticed even people who claim everything is predestined, and that we can do nothing to change it, look before they cross the road.

Stephen Hawking
Physicist and Cosmologist
(b. 1942)

Stephen Hawking's parents moved from London to Oxford during his mother's pregnancy away from the dangers of Hitler's Luftwaffe bombing raids. Dr. Frank Hawking was a biologist at the National Institute for Medical Research in London. Young Hawking proved to be an average student with less-than-average study habits and a stronger interest in horse-back riding.

Hawking attended Oxford and later Cambridge to study astronomy and cosmology. Once on campus Hawking began to develop symptoms which would lead to a shocking diagnosis – ALS, commonly referred to in the U.S. as Lou Gehrig's disease. He stubbornly continued to work on his PhD with the help of his doctoral tutor. By the age of 32, Hawking's battle with ALS reached another stage leading to a tracheotomy and a complete loss of speech. Since then a voice synthesizer has allowed Hawking to communicate with the aid of messages inputted into a computer. Hawking's research in quantum gravity and theoretical cosmology has made him an academic celebrity. He was married twice and has three grown children.

Stephen Hawking, the recipient of the U.S. Presidential Medal of Freedom, continues his work as Director of Research at Cambridge.

May 30th

Our prime purpose in this life
is to help others.
And if you can't help them,
at least don't hurt them.

Dalai Lama
Spiritual Leader
(b. 1935)

Dalai Lama was chosen at the age of two by an official delegation of Tibetan monks to succeed the 13th Dalai Lama. The young Lhamo Döndrub became formally the 14th Dalai Lama and spiritual leader of Tibetan Buddhism on November 7, 1950, at the age of 15.

During the 1950's, the People's Republic of China was attempting to gain control of Tibet. In early 1959, the Tibetan movement clashed with Chinese troops. The young 24-year-old Dalai Lama was forced to flee to India with a large contingency of Tibetans. The Dalai Lama was quick to denounce the violent actions of the Chinese and create a Tibetan government in exile. The charismatic and eloquent young leader soon won the support of the United Nations and the free world.

Over the decades the exiled government established hundreds of monasteries and nunneries with the firm determination to protect the Tibetan culture and Tibetan Buddhism.

The Dalai Lama continues to this day his struggle to win world-wide support in his fight for human rights for the Tibetan people.

May 31st

You can make more friends in two months by becoming really interested in other people, than you can in two years by trying to get other people interested in you.

Bernard Meltzer
Broadcaster
(1916 - 1998)

Bernard Meltzer was born in Manhattan, New York. Meltzer earned a Civil Engineer degree from City College of New York and a Masters degree from the University of Pennsylvania.

During his early adult life Meltzer worked as a real estate contractor and property evaluator. Later he served as a professor of finance and economics at the University of Pennsylvania. In the early 1970's, Meltzer (57) launched a second career as a radio broadcaster on WOR-Am in New York City. His program, *What's Your Problem?*, became extremely popular reaching 600,000 listeners per hour. Meltzer was on the air for a total of 23 hours each week.

The soft-spoken folksy Meltzer shared advice on virtually any problem tossed his way by the eager phone-in audience. The topics on any given day would range from romance to investment, from plumbing to family crisis issues, and Meltzer's distinctive soothing voice would always offer comfort. During his late 60's, he was diagnosed with Parkinson's disease but continued on air until the mid-1990's. Bernard Meltzer died of pneumonia in a Manhattan nursing home at the age of 81.

> **"To cut through the red tape."**

The 21st century legal system is a product of thousands of years of evolution. The ancient Egyptian culture, going as far back as 3000 BC, had developed a code of laws to resolve civil issues and judge criminal acts. Laws and the judicial system evolved with civilization. The methods of conducting trials over the centuries took various dramatic forms. 'Trial by Ordeal' had the accused put to the test by being forced to undergo physical challenges with success translated as innocence. By the beginning of the 12th century such trial forms were banned.

Two main legal systems have established themselves in a great percentage of the world. In France, Napoleon Bonaparte introduced the Napoleonic Code in 1804 which borrowed many aspects of ancient Roman law. In the 21st century, the Napoleonic Code has formed the basis for legal systems in such countries as Italy, Spain, Mexico, the Nederland's and Poland.

The development of English Law traces its roots back to the signing of the Magna Carta in 1215. The charter, a by-product of the rebellion against King John of England, eventually led to the creation of English Law which is used in most English-speaking countries in the world, including the United States.

Law, in its essence, is a "rigid conformity to formal rules". The accepted practice throughout the centuries was to secure bundles of legal documents destined for storage with red tape. When the bundles were required, the court clerk had *"to cut through the red tape"*.

June 1st

Adversity has the effect of eliciting talents, which in prosperous circumstances would have lain dormant.

Horace
Philosopher
(65 BC – 8 BC)

Horace (Quintus Horatio Flaccus) was born the son of a free slave. His beloved father, a farmer in the village of Venusia, was determined his son have a proper education despite the high cost. His father transplanted himself to Rome to oversee Horatio's primary education. Later Horatio was sent to Athens to study Greek and philosophy. Father and son shared a special bond which surfaces in Horatio's later writings.

As a young man Horace served under Brutus in the Battle of Philippi in which Augustus emerged victorious. After his military service Horace became part of a literary circle which included Virgil (70-19 BC) and Maecenas, a close friend of Augustus. Maecenas became Horace's life-long friend and mentor. The poems in Horace's vast collection were penned in Greek meter. *Ars Poetic,* written in the year 18 BC when Horace was 47 years old, was studied by writers for centuries and influenced such poets as France's Pierre Corneille and England's William Shakespeare.

Horace, who was forever quick to attribute any of his success to his father, undoubtedly became the leading poet during the Augustine age. Horace died at 57.

June 2nd

The point of living, and of being an optimist, is to be foolish enough to believe the best is yet to come.

Peter Ustinov
Writer, Director and Actor
(1921 - 2004)

Peter Ustinov was born in London of Russian-German parents. Young Peter grew up in a household of intellectuals. His father was a successful journalist and his mother, Nadia, was a painter and ballet designer.

Ustinov developed a love for languages and accents which would serve him well in his performing career. At 18, he appeared on stage in *White Cargo* (1939) and discovered his deep passion for the arts. His sharp wit and ease with languages soon drew the attention of theatre, film and television producers in Britain and the United States. Ustinov won a number of major performing awards, including two Academy Awards. In 1990, he was knighted Sir Peter Alexander Ustinov.

During his later years Sir Ustinov turned his attention to the world stage. He worked relentlessly on behalf of UNICEF as a Goodwill Ambassador and fundraiser. His role as ambassador for the world organization was so appreciated that then Executive Director of UNICEF, Carol Bellamy, represented the United Nations Secretary-General at his funeral in 2004.

June 3rd

***If you want things to be different,
perhaps the answer is
to become different yourself.***

Norman Vincent Peale
Minister and Writer
(1898 - 1993)

Norman Vincent Peale, raised in a Methodist home, was born in Bowersville, Ohio. He attended Bellefontaine High School. He graduated from Ohio Wesleyan University and conducted his theological studies at Boston University. Peale was ordained a Methodist minister in 1922.

In 1932, Peale joined the Reform Church in America as pastor of Manhattan's Marble Collegiate Church. Under Peale's leadership the church membership grew tenfold. His preaching style and his writings made him one of the most popular preachers in the United States. Peale co-founded a psychiatric clinic with psychoanalyst Smiley Blanton. They also co-authored a number of religious-psychiatric self-help books. In the mid-1930's, Peale's radio program, *The Art of Living*, was launched and broadcast on radio and television for 54 years. *The Power of Positive Thinking* was published and immediately faced praise from his followers and criticism from the psychiatric community for its simplistic message. Peale was a political ally of Richard Nixon and a family friend officiating at Julie Nixon's wedding. He created an uproar when he stated that the election of a Catholic president like John F. Kennedy would lead to the loss of free speech. He was forced to retract the statement.

Norman Vincent Peale died of a stroke in 1993.

June 4th

Time stays long enough for anyone who will use it.

Leonard da Vinci
Master of Arts and Science
(1452 - 1519)

Leonardo da Vinci, considered to be one of the greatest painters in history, was actually blessed with a multitude of extraordinary talents. During his lifetime he acquired profound knowledge in science, architecture, mathematics and engineering. Da Vinci is often referred to as likely the most diversely talented person – a true Renaissance Man.

Da Vinci was born in Vinci in the area of Florence, Italy, the son of Piero da Vinci, a legal notary. Leonardo's mother is believed to have been a peasant woman named Catherina. During his youth Leonardo did not show the signs of a gifted child. At fourteen he was placed as an apprentice to an artist named Verrocchio where Leonardo acquired all the skills necessary. At 20, he began one of the most celebrated and productive artistic career in history. Over the span of five decades Leonardo da Vinci gave the world such exquisite pieces of art as *The Last Supper* and *Mona Lisa*. His inventive mind also foresaw such future technology as the helicopter, calculator and the use of solar power.

Da Vinci enjoyed a wide and diverse circle of friends, including mathematician Luca Pacioli. The final three years of his life were spent living within the Vatican during the time the masters, Michelangelo and Raphael, were working. Leonardo da Vinci died on May 2, 1519, at 67.

June 5th

***Don't cry because it's over,
smile because it happened!***

Dr. Seuss
Writer
(1904 - 1991)

Dr. Seuss (Theodor Seuss Geisel) published a total of 44 children's books which delighted millions upon millions of people – young and old alike. The Seuss books have been the basis of an impressive three motion pictures, a Broadway play, eleven television specials and four series.

Geisel was born in Springfield, Massachusetts, the son of German immigrant parents. His father, Theodor Robert, managed the family brewing company. Geisel's middle name originated from his mother's maiden name – Henrietta Seuss. Geisel's gift as an illustrator served him well throughout his life. He contributed to the Dartmouth College magazine on a regular basis. A drinking escapade involving ten undergraduates resulted in Geisel's loss of extracurricular activities. To circumvent the situation, Geisel began using the pen name Seuss. During WWII Geisel served as Commander of the U.S. Animation's Department where he produced war propaganda short films. After the war, Geisel's career as a writer-illustrator of children's books blossomed with critically-acclaimed works: *Horton Hears a Who!* (1954), *The Cat in the Hat* (1957), *How the Grinch Stole Christmas* (1957) and *Green Eggs and Ham* (1960). Millions of Dr. Seuss books have been purchased by parents and grandparents.

Theodor Seuss Geisel battled throat cancer for several years before dying at 87.

June 6th

To live we must conquer incessantly, we must have the courage to be happy.

Henri-Frédéric Amiel
Writer and Philosopher
(1821 - 1881)

Henri-Frédéric Amiel, a direct descendant of the Huguenots, was born in Geneva, Switzerland. He became an orphan early in his life when he suddenly lost both his parents. Amiel studied at universities in both Heidelberg and Berlin before returning to his native Geneva at the age of 28.

In 1849, Amiel was appointed (28) a professor at the Geneva Academy where he remained until his death in 1881. During his 32 years at the Academy, Amiel taught Aesthetics and Philosophy. Over the course of his lifetime, he wrote a diary which was published after his death, *Journal Intime* (*Private Journal*) quickly gained a reputation throughout Europe and was translated into English by Mary A. Ward. Amiel also wrote several books of poems.

Leo Tolstoy (1828-1910) and the French writer, Blaise Pascal (1632-1662) were influenced by Amiel's passionate and painful search for God. Henri-Frédéric Amiel died at the age of 60 in his native Geneva.

June 7th

Truth titillates the imagination far less than fiction.

Marquis De Sade
Philosopher and Poet
(1740 - 1814)

Marquis de Sade (Donatien Alphonse François de Sade) was born in Paris to the Comte Jean-Baptiste de Sade and Marie-Eléonore de Maille. The young de Sade was schooled by an uncle before he attended the Jesuit Lycée. He reached the rank of Colonel during the Seven Year War.

When the Marquis was 23 he agreed to an arranged marriage with Renée-Pelagie de Montreuil which produced three children. The adult de Sade began to frequent prostitutes on a regular basis as well as become involved in sexual relationships with male and female members of his household staff. The incidents escalated in frequency and seriousness, including the reported kidnapping and abuse of a woman and later involved in the poisoning of prostitutes. Over the period of his 51 adult years, the Marquis de Sade spent 32 years in prison or in an asylum. He was imprisoned for ten years in the Bastille and transferred to an asylum just two weeks before the historic storming of the Bastille on July 14, 1789.

De Sade authored a collection of novels, plays and short stories, many of them while imprisoned, depicting strange sexual fantasies. History has had conflicting opinions of de Sade but without doubt he is remembered as fascinating. Marquis de Sade died at 74.

June 8th

*The obscure we see eventually,
the completely apparent
takes longer.*

Edward R. Murrow
Journalist
(1908 - 1965)

Edward R. Murrow (Egbert Roscoe Murrow), born in Polecat Creek, North Carolina, was the youngest of three brothers of Quaker parents, Roscoe and Ethel Murrow. The Murrows lived in a log farm house without the benefit of plumbing or electricity. The struggling family moved to Blanchard, Washington, in 1914 where they cleared land near the Canadian border.

Despite great poverty young Egbert managed to enroll at Washington State University graduating in 1930. During his stay on campus he changed his first name to Edward. By 1935, Murrow (27) started a lifetime job with the CBS. At that stage in the network's history, CBS Radio had two individuals in the news department – Murrow and Robert Trout. The outbreak of WWII gave birth to broadcast journalism and Murrow was at the forefront of the world-changing events from London rooftops. He became a celebrity as a result of his brave and articulate coverage. Murrow made the transition to television in the early 1950's and invented television news as we know it today. In the mid-1950's, the CBS News team, headed by Murrow's *See It Now* primetime program, took on the battle with Senator Joseph McCarthy's official investigation into Communist activities eventually leading to the Senator's downfall. Murrow, considered the father of broadcast journalism, lost his battle with lung cancer and died at 57.

June 9th

*Some cause happiness
wherever they go;
others, whenever they go.*

Oscar Wilde
Writer, Playwright and Poet
(1854 - 1900)

Oscar Wilde was raised during the mid-19th century in an upper class home of intellectuals. Young Oscar was introduced to poetry and a love of writing at an early age by his poet-mother. Lady Jane Wilde doted on her three children – William ('Willie'), Oscar and Isola.

Sir William Wilde, Oscar's surgeon-father, had three out-of-wedlock children before his marriage to Lady Jane. The three children were never part of Sir William's family even though he provided financial assistance for their well-being and education.

Oscar enjoyed the benefits of the finer schools of the day – Trinity College in Dublin, and Magdalen College, Oxford. Wilde, born and raised a Protestant, studied Catholicism and seriously considered converting following an audience with Pope Pius IX in Rome.

At the height of his success and while his famous play, *The Importance of Being Earnest*, was still on stage in London, Wilde was convicted of gross indecency with other men and imprisoned for two years. After his release he settled in France never to return to England. He converted to Catholicism on his death bed.

June 10th

If my mind can conceive it,
and my heart can believe it,
I know I can achieve it.

Jesse Jackson
Clergyman and Activist
(b. 1941)

Jesse Jackson was born Jesse Louis Jackson in Greenville, South Carolina. His mother, Helen Burns, a sixteen-year-old, was involved with a professional boxer named Noah Louis Robinson. Helen (18) married Charles Henry Jackson who legally adopted young Jesse.

Jackson dropped out of Chicago Theological Seminary in 1960 to have a stronger presence in the growing civil rights movement. At 27, Jackson was ordained without the benefit of a theological degree and joined the Martin Luther King, Jr, team for the historical 1965 Selma to Montgomery march. On April 4, 1968, Jackson stood in the motel parking lot when the shot rang out striking Dr. King, changing the course of the movement. Jackson struggled with the new leadership and eventually formed his own civil rights group. His successful high-profile international activism during the 1980's led him to place his name as a candidate for the presidential nomination for the Democratic party in 1984 and again in 1988. After the two unsuccessful attempts he became Senator for the District of Columbia between 1991 and 1997.

During a post-election rally the camera caught a teary-eyed Jackson in the crowd as he listened and cheered on President-elect Barack Obama.

June 11th

Life affords no higher pleasure than that of surmounting difficulties.

Samuel Johnson
Writer and Lexicographer
(1709 - 1784)

Samuel Johnson, born a sickly child, grew up to be considered one of the most distinguished men of letters in the English language. His mother, Sarah Ford, was over 40 years of age when Samuel was born in Lichfield, England. Samuel's father, Michael, was a struggling bookseller.

Young Johnson was a bright, inquisitive child and forever curious to explore the numerous books in his father's bookstore. Despite his father's financial misfortunes, Johnson received an education equal to his blossoming intelligence. By the time Johnson reached six he began to show signs of health issues. He developed unusual physical behavior in the form of odd uncontrollable gestures and tics. The condition followed him throughout his life and made it difficult to be placed in a public form of employment. Modern medicine identifies his condition as Tourette syndrome. Johnson left Oxford without a degree because of finances and likely due to his physical condition.

Johnson is best remembered for his contribution to the English language during the 18th century. After toiling for nine consecutive years, he produced the *Dictionary of the English Language* (1755). The "Johnson Dictionary", as it was called, ruled the language for 150 years until the publication of the Oxford Dictionary in 1928. In his mid-70's, the large man survived a serious stroke. Within 18 months Samuel Johnson slipped into a coma and died at 75.

June 12th

Lovers don't finally meet somewhere.
They're in each other all along.

Rumi
Philosopher, Poet and Theologian
(1207 - 1273)

Rumi (Jala ad-Din Muhammad Rumi) was born in the Balkh Province of modern-day Afghanistan. During the period 1215-1220 when the Mongols invaded much of central Asia, Rumi's father transplanted his family.

During his early travels Rumi met a mystic poet named Attar. The 18-year-old was greatly influenced by the writings of the famous poet. In his early 30's Rumi became an Islamic Jurist. Rumi and his followers traveled throughout the Middle East sharing Rumi's philosophy. He encouraged the use of music, dance and poetry to practice personal faith.

Rumi's spiritual philosophy was firmly based on unconditional love, tolerance and charity. His belief that all religions lead to God has made him and his teachings widely accepted.

Rumi died at 66. His philosophy and writings had a great influence on Persian literature.

June 13th

***A rolling stone
can gather no moss.***

Publilius Syrus
Writer and Poet
(1st Century BC - ?)

Publilius Syrus's personal history is sketchy but his influence during the 1st century is unchallenged. The precise dates of his birth and death have been lost through the centuries. What is known is that Publilius was born a slave brought to Rome and auctioned off in the city marketplace. He was likely from the ancient town of Antioch founded by one of Alexander the Great's generals and near the modern city of Antakya, Turkey.

Over time his Roman master became impressed with Publilius' natural intelligence, granted him his freedom and offered an education. Eventually Publilius matured as a writer and performer of his own plays throughout Italy. Julius Caesar became aware of his popularity and invited him to perform at the Roman Games in 46 BC. Publilius' writings always delivered a moral and in time his works were studied in schoolrooms through the Empire. His writings were not preserved through the ages with a mere small collection under the title *Sentiniae* (*Sentences*).

Since other writers contributed to Publilius' work it is difficult to determine with certainty what was authored by the former slave. One of the famous quotes found in the collection was – *"The judge is condemned when the guilty is acquitted."*

June 14th

***Man should forget his anger
before he lies down to sleep.***

Thomas de Quincey
Author and Intellectual
(1785 - 1859)

Thomas de Quincey was born in Manchester, England, the son of a successful London merchant and an intelligent and dominant mother. Young Thomas was frail as a child and developed as a solitary and withdrawn young man. His father died when Thomas was 11 and the family moved to Bath.

Thomas began to excel in junior school but he was transferred to a school with a lesser academic reputation because his mother feared his intelligence would go to his head. By 15, the bright young Thomas was enrolled at Oxford and much was expected of him. He dealt with periods of depression and eventually abandoned his studies. In 1802, Thomas (17) wandered through England and Wales with limited funds. He returned to Oxford but turned to opium as an escape. He left university without receiving his degree. In 1816, de Quincey (31) married and he and his wife, Margaret, had eight children during their 21-year marriage until her death in 1837. At the age of 36, de Quincey wrote *Confessions of an English Opium-Eater* which was released in serial form in a London magazine. *Confessions* established his reputation as a serious writer and he earned a living contributing to various periodicals.

De Quincey struggled with two issues most of his adult life – debts and opium. He suffered from intestinal problems and at the age of 74, Thomas de Quincey died in Edinburgh.

June 15th

***Forgiveness is
the most tender part of love.***

Johnny Sheffield
Actor
(1931 - 2010)

Johnny Sheffield was born John Matthew Sheffield Cassan in Pasadena, California. Johnny's father, Reginald, was an actor and his mother, Louise, a Vassar graduate with a great passion for literature.

At the age of seven, young Johnny became a child actor in a successful Broadway play called *On Borrowed Time*. Within a year the young actor was starring opposite Johnny Weissmuller and Maureen O'Sullivan in MGM's *Tarzan Finds a Son* in 1939. Young Johnny was 8 years old. The movie proved to be very popular and the production company made a total of eight Tarzan films with Sheffield. The last Tarzan movie Sheffield starred in was released in 1947 when he was 16. Sheffield starred in the lead role of 12 other jungle movies as *Bomba, the Jungle Boy* (1949-1955). In addition to the popular jungle films, Sheffield was cast in six other non-jungle movies, including the classic *Knute Rockne, All American* (1940) starring Pat O'Brien. Following a failed television pilot, Sheffield, then 24, enrolled at the UCLA and earned a business degree.

John and Patricia Sheffield were married in 1959 had three children. At 79, John Sheffield died of a heart attack hours after a fall from a ladder at his California home.

June 16th

Writing is the only profession where no one considers you ridiculous if you earn no money.

Jules Renard
Writer
(1864 - 1910)

Jules Renard (Pierre-Jules Renard), the product of an unhappy childhood, grew up to be a member of France's prestigious Académie Goncourt by the age of 43. The man of letters was responsible for twenty-one novels, seven plays and an impressive journal written during his all too short life.

Renard was born in Châlons-du-Maine, France, the last of four children of François and Anna-Rose. Young Renard passed on higher education in favor of serving in the French military. Following his service years, Renard (24) married Marie Morneau and settled in Paris. He immediately began to contribute to newspapers and periodicals. During his early years Renard befriended two fellow writers who would enjoy their own illustrious careers – playwright Alfred Capus (1858-1922) and actor Lucien Guitry (1860-1925). Renard's most famous novel, the autobiographical *Poil de carotte* (*Carrot Top*) about the childhood of a redheaded boy, was written in 1884 when he was 30. Between the age of 23 and until his death, Renard wrote a journal which would influence future writers like Britain's Somerset Maugham.

Renard struggled with arteriosclerosis throughout his last years. Jules Renard died of the condition at the age of 46.

June 17th

The highest reward for a person's toil is not what they get for it, but what they become by it.

John Ruskin
Art Critic
(1819 - 1900)

John Ruskin was a British art critic whose essays exercised a great deal of influence during the Edwardian and Victorian periods. Ruskin's more than 250 literary works covered a range of topics from art to science to environment and left lasting marks.

Ruskin was born and raised in London the only son of a successful wine merchant and his wife. He was home-schooled during his early years and eventually enrolled at Christ Church, Oxford. Despite a long period of serious illness the university granted him a degree. Ruskin was still in his teen years when he began to contribute essays to weekly art periodicals. In 1843, Ruskin, then only 24, authored one of his major critical essays called *Modern Painters* creating controversy and eventually alienated many of the artists of the day. Gradually the growing Impressionism movement began to minimize Ruskin's influence as an art critic.

Ruskin was married for a short six years and, by his own admission, the marriage was never consummated. His biographers have long disputed his sexuality. John Ruskin died January 20, 1900. A month later The Ruskin Literary and Debating Society was established in Toronto, Canada.

June 18th

There is no comparison between that which is lost by not succeeding and that which is lost by not trying.

Francis Bacon
Philosopher, Politician and Writer
(1561 - 1626)

Francis Bacon set three goals for himself at an early age. Young Bacon decided his life's work would consist of serving his country, uncovering truths and serving his church.

Bacon earned the respect and support of first, Queen Elizabeth I and then King James I. In 1603, King James knighted Bacon. Sir Francis Bacon rose to the influential role of Lord Chancellor but struggled through several financial obstacles. By 1621, Sir Bacon's political career ended in disgrace with the king stepping in at the last moment to save him from the Tower of London. Sir Francis Bacon was an important part of the Scientific Revolution. His scientific philosophy led the way to a new method of scientific research based on a systematic approach to experimental theories. Sir Bacon's method, often referred to as the Baconian Method, established him as the "father of empiricism".

In early 1626, Sir Bacon was conducting experiments to develop a process to preserve meat products over a period of time. During the evening of April 9, 1626, he was collecting large amounts of snow to further his experiments. Within days he became very ill and died of pneumonia. Sir Francis Bacon was 65.

June 19th

What the teacher is, is more important than what he teaches.

Karl Menninger
Psychiatrist
(1893 - 1990)

Karl Menninger was born in Topeka, Kansas, in the closing years of the 19th century the oldest of three sons of Dr. Charles Menninger, general practitioner, and his wife, Florence. His parents encouraged their children to fulfill their dreams and ambitions. Karl struggled with the career choices in his path but decided to share his father's passion for knowledge and medicine.

After attending the University of Wisconsin, Menninger enrolled at Harvard Medical School and studied psychiatry under an inspiring teacher named Dr. Southard. Following his internship at Boston Psychopathic Hospital, he returned to Topeka to open the Menninger Clinic with his father introducing the noble concept of addressing the medical and psychiatric needs of the community. Within a few years the father and son team proudly built the Menninger Sanitarium. The Menninger's second son, William, also a psychiatrist, joined the family business. In 1930, Karl Menninger authored *The Human Mind* and gained an instant international reputation. The Menninger family also established a centre to treat mentally challenged children called The Southard School in honor of Dr. Karl's Harvard teacher.

In 1981, President Jimmy Carter awarded Dr. Karl the Presidential Medal of Freedom. Dr. Karl Menninger died in Topeka, Kansas, at the age of 96.

June 20th

*I am only one, but I am one.
I cannot do everything,
but I can do something.
And I will not let what I cannot do
interfere with what I can do.*

Edward Everett Hale
Clergyman and Writer
(1822 - 1909)

Edward Everett Hale was born in Boston Massachusetts, the gifted child of Nathan Hale, owner-founder and editor of the Boston Daily Advertiser. The Hales were distant cousins of Helen Keller. Edward's father was actually the nephew of Nathan Hale who was executed for espionage by the British during the Revolutionary War.

At 13, Edward enrolled at Harvard and graduated in 1839 one of the university's youngest graduates. He was ordained a minister in 1846 and between the years 1846 and 1899, Hale served as pastor of various churches in Massachusetts. Hale and his wife, Emily Baldwin Perkins, were parents to eight sons and one daughter.

Hale became a prolific writer with a strong commitment to the abolition of slavery, a champion of education and a defender of the working class. He was the writer or editor of over 60 books on a wide range of topics. Hale also established himself as an exceptional writer of the short story form, especially with the release of *The Man Without a Country* (1863) and *The Skelton in the Closet*.

Edward Everett Hale died in 1909 at the age of 87.

June 21st

A fanatic is one who sticks to his guns whether they're loaded or not.

Franklin P. Jones
Journalist and Writer
(1908 -1980)

Franklin P. Jones was born in Saratoga, New York, at the beginning of the 20th century. The State of Pennsylvania became his life-long home when he left New York to attend Haverford College, one of the leading arts colleges in the U.S. He graduated from Haverford with a Bachelor of Science degree in 1933.

Jones' first full-time job was as a crime reporter for the Philadelphia Record in 1934. He remained with the newspaper for twelve years eventually leaving as a member of the editorial board when the Record closed its doors in 1946. The following year Jones launched a second career when he joined Gray and Rogers Advertising Agency out of Philadelphia. He was the firm's head of the 40-member public relations department. In 1954, he became a partner and retired at 52 to devote his full attention to writing. Jones penned an endless treasure of material, including quotable quotes such as "The only thing about having nothing to do is you can't stop and rest."

Franklin P. Jones lost his battle with cancer in December of 1980 after what could be called a good life.

June 22nd

Tears shed for self are tears of weakness, but tears shed for others are a sign of strength.

Billy Graham
Spiritual Leader
(b. 1918)

Billy Graham (William Franklin Graham) was born and raised on a dairy farm in Charlotte, North Carolina. His parents, William Franklin and Morrow Coffey Graham, were members of the Associate Reform Presbyterian.

At 16, young Graham attended a revival gathering in Charlotte under the guidance of evangelist Mordecai Ham which led to his conversion. Graham studied theology at the Florida Bible Institute. In 1943, Graham (25) earned a degree in anthropology from Illinois' Wheaton College. While at Wheaton he met the 'love of his life' and in August of that year he and Ruth Bell married. At this moment the Grahams are blessed with five adult children, nineteen grandchildren and 28 great-grandchildren. Graham became pastor at Village Church in Illinois where he got his first experience with radio evangelism. Between 1948 and 1952, the young Graham served as President of Northwestern College in St. Paul, Minnesota. During the late 1940's, Graham attracted national attention with his revival meetings often held in over-sized circus tents. Graham has preached to hundreds of millions in nearly two hundred countries and reached an equal number by way of radio and television. Billy Graham was named by Gallup as the seventh most admired person in the 20th century, was awarded the Presidential Medal of Freedom. Graham, who has been battling Parkinson's disease since the mid-1990's, lost his beloved wife, Ruth, in 2007.

June 23rd

Man's mind is so formed that it is far more susceptible to falsehood than to truth.

Desiderius Erasmus
Scholar and Priest
(1466 – 1536)

Desiderius Erasmus was ordained into the priesthood at 26 years of age (1492) after his theological studies at an Augustine monastery. Soon after being ordained Erasmus was appointed secretary to the Bishop of Cambrai where his intellectual abilities flourished.

Following his travels throughout Europe, Erasmus began challenging the Catholic Church and its leaders to reform. His first book, *Handbook of the Militant Christian*, was published in 1503. Three years later Erasmus took the challenge to the public by anonymously publishing *Julius Exclusus*, chastising Pope Julius II for waging war and amassing a huge fortune. Erasmus continued his confrontations with the church before and after being formally released from his religious vows in 1517.

Erasmus' confrontational style failed to trigger the Christian reform he promoted in his writings. Gradually he distanced himself from the church and its leaders. Erasmus was judged harshly in the century following his death.

Desiderius Erasmus died at 70.

June 24th

Nothing happens unless first a dream.

Carl Sandburg
Poet, Historian and Folkorist
(1878 - 1967)

Carl Sandburg, born in Galesburg, Illinois, to a poor Swedish couple, gave up on school at the age of 13 to deliver milk products in a milk wagon in his hometown. Over his youth, Sandburg, who was affectionately called "Charlie" by family and friends, held a collection of jobs, including bricklayer and farm hand. After a short stay at Lombard College he turned his attention to journalism with the Chicago Daily News.

At 20, Sandburg volunteered to serve with the 6th Illinois Infantry at the outbreak of the Spanish-American War. Following a second short stint at Lombard College, he moved to Milwaukee, Wisconsin, where he married Lillian Steichen and raised three daughters. The Sandburgs returned to Illinois where he devoted all his time to writing under the name Charles Sandburg. The 1920's were the beginning of a prolific period of time when he produced the memorable Sandburg writings, including the *Rootabago* series (1930's), *Potato Face* (1931) and the three-part Abraham Lincoln biography – *The Prairie Years* (1926), *Grows Up* (1928) and *The War Years* (1930). In 1945, he wrote the historical novel *Remembrance Rock*.

Sandburg was awarded three Pulitzer Prizes for his poetry (*The Complete Poems* and *Corn Huskers*) and *Abraham Lincoln: The War Years*. The writer who best captured 20th century America also won a Grammy in 1959. Carl "Charlie" Sandburg died at his North Carolina home in his 89th year.

June 25th

I think one's feelings waste themselves in words; they ought all to be distilled into actions which bring results.

Florence Nightingale
Nurse and Writer
(1820 - 1910)

Florence Nightingale, or "The Lady with the Lamp", as history remembers her, was born into an upper-class British family in Florence, Italy, and named in honor of her birth city. Her father, William Edward Shore, inherited the Nightingale coat of arms from his maternal uncle.

At the age of 17, Florence changed the course of her life after she felt the call of God. Against the wishes of her family and friends she turned her back on the benefits of the life of a wealthy young lady and pursued nursing. With the aid of an influential politician-friend named Sidney Herbert, Florence headed to the front lines at the outbreak of the Crimean War (1853-56) with a staff of 38 nurses, including her aunt. The dedicated Nightingale would make final rounds to check on the wounded with a lamp in her hand. In recognition for her work a fund raising drive in Britain created the Nightingale Foundation to train young nurses. The Nightingale Training School was established in 1860. She took an active role in the school by writing the curriculum.

In the late 1870's, Nightingale trained and mentored North America's first fully trained nurse, Linda Richards, who is recognized as one of the great nursing pioneers. Florence Nightingale, who suffered from brucellosis since her mid-30's, died in her sleep at the age of 90.

June 26th

***Try to reason about love
and you lose your reason.***

Anton Chekhov
Physician and Playwright
(1860 - 1904)

Anton Chekhov, who considered himself a physician first and a writer second, became one of the finest short story craftsmen in literary history. Throughout his life, and a prolific writing career, Chekhov practiced medicine.

Chekhov was born in the port city of Taganrog, Russia, the third of six children of a grocery merchant named Pavel. The Chekhov family would gather around their mother, Yevgeniya, who was a fabulous story teller. When Chekhov was 16, his father was forced into bankruptcy and the family moved to Moscow to face poverty. Young Anton remained in Taganrog to complete his schooling. Three years later he joined his family and was admitted to medical school at Moscow University. In order to cover his own expenses and help his family, Chekhov turned to writing and quickly attracted the attention of major publishers. He was able to move his family into a proper home as he graduated from medical school. As his writing career took flight he began to develop health issues. His play, *Ivanov*, was a success and established him as a serious playwright. At 37, Chekhov survived a hemorrhage of the lungs.

Chekhov's relatively short writing career produced a number of classic plays and short stories (*The Lady with the Dog*) which influenced writers such as James Joyce and George Bernard Shaw. Anton Chekhov succumbed to tuberculosis in 1904 at 44.

June 27th

The value of marriage is not that adults produce children, but that children produce adults.

Peter de Vries
Writer
(1910 - 1993)

Peter de Vries, a Chicago, Illinois, native was educated in a religious system (Dutch Christian Reformed Church). He attended and graduated from Calvin College in 1931.

After his school years, de Vries spent his twenties working at a variety jobs such as vending machine operator, salesman and radio actor before finding his calling as editor of Poetry magazine. In 1944, writer James Thurber recommended de Vries for a position with the widely read The New Yorker magazine. De Vries spent the next 13 years with the magazine. The prolific writer wrote twenty-three novels between 1940 (*But Who Wakes the Bugler?*) and 1986 (*Peckham's Marbles*). Four of de Vries novels served as the basis of Hollywood movies – *The Tunnel of Love* (1958), *Reuben, Reuben* (1970), *How Do I love You* (1970 - based on his novel *Let Me Count the Ways?*) and *Pete 'n' Tillie* (1972 - based on *Witch's Milk*).

In 1983, de Vries was elected to the American Academy of Arts and Letters. Peter de Vries died at 83 in Norwalk, Connecticut.

June 28th

It is a statistical fact that the wicked work harder to reach hell than the righteous do to enter heaven.

Josh Billings
Humorist and Lecturer
(1815 – 1885)

Josh Billings, was born Henry Wheeler Shaw in Lanesborough, Massachusetts, into an illustrious American political family. Billings' father (Henry Shaw), grandfather (Samuel Shaw) and an uncle (John Savage) all served in the U.S. Congress during the first half of the 19th century.

Following high school in his hometown, Billings enrolled at Hamilton College. An innocent prank resulted in his expulsion during his sophomore year. During the dead of night he had removed the clapper from the school's tower bell. He turned his attention to earning a living and over the next decade toiled as an auctioneer, a farmer and in the coal mines. Billings and his wife, Zipha, moved to Poughkeepsie, New York, where he worked as a journalist. Under the pen name Josh Billings, he wrote a collection of folksy books, including *Farmers' Allminax* (1870), *Everybody's Friend* (1874) and *Trump Kards* (1887).

Literary scholars rank Josh Billings second to Mark Twain (Samuel Clemens) as a humorist. Josh Billings died in Monterey, California, at 67.

June 29th

A single rose can be my garden,
a single friend, my world.

Leo Buscaglia
Playwright and Poet
(1924 - 1998)

Leo Buscaglia, was born Felice Leonardo Buscaglia in Los Angeles, California, the youngest of four children of Italian immigrants. He was raised Roman Catholic and later studied Buddhism.

Following graduation from Theodore Roosevelt High School in Los Angeles, Buscaglia joined the U.S. Navy during the early years of WWII. After the war ended he enrolled at the University of Southern California. In 1963, Buscaglia earned a PhD and joined the teaching faculty and remained with the university until he retired. The suicide of one of his students in the late 1960's had a great impact on him and changed his teaching attitude. With the university's blessing he launched a new non-credit course called *Love 1A* where there were no grades and no failing. A PBS executive arranged to have one of Buscaglia's "Love" lectures videotaped and aired during a pledge drive. The viewer response was such that Buscaglia became a PBS regular. The television exposure led to lectures and books. At one point, Buscaglia had five books on the New York Times Best Sellers list. His books have sold nearly twenty million copies in seventeen languages.

Leo Buscaglia died of a sudden heart attack at his Nevada home at 74.

June 30th

There's only one corner of the universe you can be certain of improving, and that's your own self.

Aldous Huxley
Writer
(1894 - 1963)

Aldous Huxley was born in Surrey, England, as part of the famous British Huxley family. Aldous' father, Leonard, was a noted educator-writer and his grandfather, Thomas Henry, was a reputable zoologist. Both Aldous' brothers, Julian and Andrew, became highly-respected biologists. In addition, Aldous' mother, Julia, was an educator who founded Prior's Field School in Surrey.

When Huxley was 17, he developed a condition called Keratitis Punctata, an inflammation of the eye's cornea, which left him partially blind for a number of years. He managed to graduate from Oxford with a degree in English literature. After university Huxley remained at Oxford as a French professor where one of his students was named Eric Blair, later known by his writer name, George Orwell, who found literary fame with his novel called *Nineteen Eighty-Four* (1949). Huxley published his first novel in 1921 (*Crome Yellow*) and was responsible for an outpouring of essays and short stories but his best remembered for his novel *Brave New World* (1932).

Huxley was also attracted to parapsychology and mysticism and experimented with psychedelic drugs, especially LSD. Aldous Huxley was diagnosed with laryngeal cancer at the age of 66 and died in on November 22, 1963, the day President Kennedy was assassinated.

> **"Once in a blue moon."**

Most calendar years have twelve full moons displaying their splendor in each of the twelve months. The lunar phase, known as a full moon, happens when the moon and the sun are directly on the opposite sides of the earth. Tradition suggests that a full moon encourages temporary odd behavior but psychologists have never been able to substantiate such folklore.

The definition of a month can vary from culture to culture but the lunar month is measured from one full moon's cycle to the next full moon's cycle. The length of the moon's cycle is exactly 29.53059 days totaling 354.37 days per year. The solar year contains approximately eleven extra days. The accumulation of those extra days results in an extra, or 13th, moon every two or three years.

The term "blue moon" to identify the extra moon dates back to the mid-16th century. Since the church made reference to the individual moons by given names in order to identify certain ecclesiastic events; the extra moon caused a problem. The label "blue moon" allowed the church to maintain its schedule.

The rarity of a blue moon gave birth to a new phrase which meant "a rare event". The phrase was – *"Once in a blue moon"*.

July 1st

You are not only responsible
for what you say,
but also for what you do not say.

Martin Luther
Clergyman and Scholar
(1483 - 1546)

Martin Luther was born in Eisleben, Germany, to Margarethe and Hans Luder (later Luther). Young Martin was baptized as a Roman Catholic. Martin's father prepared him for a career in law and was schooled accordingly in his youth. At nineteen, he enrolled at the University of Erfurt where he was awarded a Master's degree in 1505. After a year of law Martin transferred to theology and was ordained in 1507.

In 1512, Luther received a PhD in Theology at the University of Wittenberg and spent his entire life as a professor at the university. By 1517, he wrote *The Ninety Five Theses* as a scholarly dispute with the Church's practice of "selling indulgences". Luther maintained that forgiveness was a blessing to be received only from God and the sale of indulgences only offered false assurances to the faithful. Within a year *The Ninety Five Theses* document was circulated throughout Europe setting the stage for a public confrontation with Rome. Pope Leo X dispatched a number of papal envoys only to have Luther take a stronger stand. The defiance led to Luther being excommunicated in 1521 and the beginning of the Protestant Reform.

Luther suffered from Ménière's disease and angina. A stroke resulted in a loss of speech. On February 18, 1546, Martin Luther died at 62.

July 2nd

An atheist is a man who has no visible means of support.

John Buchan
Writer and Diplomat
(1875 - 1940)

John Buchan, 1st Baron of Tweedsmuir and the 15th Governor General of Canada, was born in Perth, Scotland, to John Buchan, a minister, and his wife, Helene Jane. Young Buchan studied the classics at the University of Glasgow and law at Oxford.

After graduation, Buchan pursued a career in diplomacy becoming an assistant to the High Commissioner to South Africa. In 1907, he was admitted to the Bar and married Susan Charlotte Grosvenor later that same year. Eventually the Buchan family consisted of four children. In 1910, Buchan (35) launched a career in politics and published his first adventure novel – *Prester John*. Buchan served Britain both as a member of the House of Lords and as Director of Information during WWII. At the outbreak of the war, Buchan released his most popular novel, the spy-thriller, *The Thirty-Nine Steps*, which served as the basis for Alfred Hitchcock's 1935 *The 39 Steps* movie.

John Buchan was appointed as Canada's representative of King George V in the role of Governor General of Canada in 1935. The new Governor General visited every part of the country in his numerous travels, including the Arctic regions. Buchan oversaw, on behalf of Canada, the historic transition after the abdication of Edward VIII in the late 1930's.

Governor General John Buchan died five days after a stroke while still in office.

July 3rd

Anything that is of value in life only multiplies when it is given.

Deepak Chopra
Physician and Motivational Speaker
(b. 1946)

Deepak Chopra grew up in New Delhi, India, with dreams of one day becoming a famous actor. In time, he followed in his father's footsteps and entered medicine. Dr. Krishan Chopra was a successful cardiologist in India.

Young Chopra completed his primary schooling at St. Columba's School and graduated from the All India Institute of Medical Sciences in 1968 with a specialty in endocrinology. After years teaching at Boston University School of Medicine and serving as Chief of Staff at the New England Memorial Hospital, Chopra became fascinated with the Transcendental Meditation technique. In 1985, he left the hospital and joined the Maharishi Mahesh Yogi to study Ayurveda more commonly referred to as alternative medicine.

In 1987, Chopra published the first of more than 55 wellness books which have been translated into three dozen languages and reached sales of over twenty million copies. His message has been received with both praise and skepticism because of its simplistic approach to medicine. Since the 1980's, Chopra has faced criticism from the medical community as well as from within his own circles. Nonetheless Chopra has a huge and devoted following.

Chopra heads up the Chopra Centre for Well Being founded in 1996 in La Jolla, California. He also hosts a weekly radio program on Sirius and writes a column for the San Francisco Chronicle.

July 4th

How much more grievous are the consequences of anger than the causes of it.

Marcus Aurelius
Statesman and Philosopher
(121 - 180)

Marcus Aurelius, remembered by history as the Philosopher-King, was born Marcus Aurelius Augustus into a prominent and somewhat wealthy Roman family. Marcus lost both parents in his young years and was raised in the care of his paternal grandfather.

Emperor Hadrian was impressed with the character of young Marcus and nominated him for the exclusive College of the Salii to study religion and philosophy. When Emperor Hadrian died in 138, Antoninus assumed the throne as Antoninus Pius and, according to the late Emperor's wishes, adopted young Marcus, then 17, and Lucius Commodus, the son of the Emperor's close friend to succeed him upon his death. Marcus continued his education and developed his skills as an orator with the help of his Latin instructor, Fronto. In 145, a marriage, pre-arranged by Emperor Antoninus Pius, united Marcus (24) and Faustina. Over their long married life they had fourteen children.

In 161, Emperor Antoninus Pius died and the Roman Senate appointed Marcus Emperor but Marcus insisted he and his adopted brother, Lucius, share the office according to Emperor Hadrian's wishes. Over a two-decade period, Marcus governed either alone or co-shared the role of Emperor. Marcus Aurelius, considered one of the most important Stoic philosophers, died at 59.

July 5th

True eloquence consists of saying all that should be said, and that only.

François de la Rochefoucauld
Author
(1613 - 1680)

François de la Rochefoucauld, who received no formal education during his childhood, grew up to establish the essay as an accepted form of literature. By the age of ten, young François was serving in the French Army. In 1629, La Rochefoucauld (16) fought in the siege of Cassel. During his military career he was wounded several times, including a serious head wound at 33.

La Rochefoucauld was born in Paris the eldest son of an illustrious French family. His father, the 5th Duc de La Rochefoucauld, served as a minister in the court of Louis XIII until his death in 1650. At 15, François La Rochefoucauld married Andrée de Vivonne and the couple raised eight children during their 41-year marriage. Andrée died in 1670. La Rochefoucauld aggressively opposed Cardinal Richelieu and at one point was imprisoned in the Bastille and then exiled (1632-1642) by the Cardinal. Following his exile, La Rochefoucauld turned his energies to a very productive writing period which gave the world two powerful works – *Mémoires* (1664) and *Maximes* (1665).

In his final year, La Rochefoucauld became an invalid. On March 17, 1680, François de la Rochefoucauld passed away in Paris.

July 6th

There is nothing with which every man is so afraid as getting to know how enormously much he is capable of doing and becoming.

Soren Kierkegaard
Philosopher and Theologian
(1813 - 1855)

Soren Kierkegaard, often labeled the "father of Existentialism", was born in Copenhagen, Denmark, one of seven children into a reasonably wealthy and influential Danish family. His father, Michael Pedersen, was a well-read gentleman who had a passion for philosophy. Young Soren's less-educated mother, Ane Sorensdatter, had been a house maid in the Kierkegaard household. Michael Kierkegaard developed a great guilt about impregnating Ane and passed the predisposition to guilt to his son.

Kierkegaard spent his entire school life in Copenhagen, first at the Borgerdyd Gymnasium and then pursuing theological studies at the University of Copenhagen. He carried his father's passion for philosophy into his adulthood and was greatly influenced by the writings of Socrates. Kierkergaard believed that individuals should learn to use their own resources to stretch themselves beyond the images society designs for people. During his later years, he conducted an on-going attack on the Danish Church despite the fact his older brother, Peter, was Bishop of Aalborg. Scholars believe Kierkegaard lost control and created a sensation in Denmark.

Soren Kierkegaard collapsed on one of his favorite walks through Copenhagen and died a month later.

July 7th

We joined our hands, and with our hands, our hearts.

William Shakespeare
Playwright and Poet
(1564 -1616)

William Shakespeare, recognized by scholars as the greatest writer in the English language, is responsible for a large volume of literary work, including 38 plays plus an endless number of sonnets and poems. Shakespeare's literary genius has influenced writers over the centuries.

William was born and raised in Stratford-upon-Avon, in the central district of England, the third of eight children of John and Mary Shakespeare. Young William was likely schooled at King New School a short distance from the Shakespeare home. The scholars believe Shakespeare's artistic life began in the mid-1580's and by 1594 was an actor-playwright member of the company known as Lord Chamberlain's Men (later the King's Men). By the end of the 16th century, Shakespeare had become a wealthy writer with his plays featured at the Globe theatre. The precise order Shakespeare wrote his plays has forever been a point of discussion. His plays include such classics as *The Merchant of Venice*, *Romeo and Julie*, *Hamlet*, *King Lear* and *Macbeth*.

Shakespeare retired to Stratford-upon-Avon with Anne Hathaway, his wife of over thirty years. William Shakespeare died at 52.

July 8th

But far more numerous was the herd of such who think too little and talk too much.

John Dryden
Playwright and Poet
(1631 - 1700)

John Dryden, the eldest of fourteen children, was born in the rectory of the All Saints Church in Aldwincle, England. His maternal grandfather was the pastor of the All Saints congregation. John's parents were Erasmus Dryden and Mary Pickering.

At 13, young Dryden was sent to Westminster School, recently established by Queen Elizabeth I, where he studied the classics and the art of rhetoric. His education at Westminster had a great influence on his later writings. Dryden earned a Bachelor of Arts degree from Trinity College, Oxford. A few months after his graduation his father died and Dryden moved to London with a small inheritance to launch his writing career. At 29, Dryden published his first successful poem, *Heroique Stanzas*, and established himself as the most respected poet of his time. Dryden reluctantly devoted time to writing plays for the theatre revival in England but soon returned to poetry. After the overthrow of King James, Dryden fell out of favor and lost his position as Poet Laureate. One of his most notable achievements was as a translator – *The Works of Virgil* (1697).

Dryden is recognized as the most dominant writer of the Restoration which is often referred to by scholars as the Age of Dryden. John Dryden died in London at 69.

July 9th

To live in hearts we leave behind is not to die.

Thomas Campbell
Poet
(1777 - 1844)

Thomas Campbell, the Scottish-born poet who settled in London in his twenties, was instrumental in the founding of the University of London. Campbell was born in Glasgow, the youngest son of Alexander, a trading firm executive who lost much of his own fortune during the American Revolution.

Young Thomas's higher education years were all spent in Glasgow, first at Glasgow High School and then the University of Glasgow. Campbell's gift for writing poetry was recognized early in life. When he was 20, Campbell transplanted himself to Edinburgh where he began his writing career alongside Sir Walter Scott. He was able to cover his expenses with the help of income from private tutoring. His first years produced *The Wounded Hussar* (1797) and *Epistle to Three Ladies*. In 1803, Campbell (26) and Matilda Sinclair, his second cousin, married and made London home. His means of financial support was derived from his role as foreign news translator with the London Star newspaper. In 1819, one of his greatest literary contributions, *Specimens of the British Poets*, was published to much acclaim. Within two years he was appointed to the prestigious role of editor of the New Monthly Magazine.

Matilda Campbell died at an early age in 1828. Later Campbell's health became an issue and he withdrew from public life. Thomas Campbell died in France at the age of 66.

July 10th

A mother is not a person to lean on but a person to make leaning unnecessary.

Dorothy Canfield Fisher
Author, Educator and Activist
(1879 - 1958)

Dorothy Canfield Fisher, was born Dorothy Frances Canfield in Lawrence, Kansas, but spent most of her adult life in Vermont. Her father, James Hulme Canfield, was an academic who was president of Ohio State University. Flavia Camp, her mother, was an artist and writer in her own right.

Dorothy took her Bachelor of Arts degree from Ohio State University and earned a PhD in romance languages at Columbia University in 1904. In 1907, Canfield (28) married John Redwood Fisher and they had a son and a daughter. The couple spent time in Rome where Dorothy became acquainted with Maria Montessori. Later Canfield Fisher introduced the Montessori Method in the U.S. She was extremely impressed by the system and wrote *A Montessori Mother* (1912). Canfield Fisher became the education system's greatest champion. At the outbreak of WWI, Canfield Fisher followed her husband to France as he served his military obligation. She volunteered her service to helping soldiers blinded in action and French refugee children. Canfield Fisher wrote a number of novels, including *The Bent Twig* (1915) and *Her Son's Wife* (1926), but is best remembered for her children's book called *Understood Betsy* (1916). During the 1940's, Eleanor Roosevelt named Canfield Fisher one of the ten most influential women in the U.S.

Dorothy Canfield Fisher died in Vermont at 79.

July 11th

The reading of all good books is like a conversation with the finest of men of past centuries.

René Descartes
Writer and Philosopher
(1596 - 1650)

René Descartes, claimed as the "father of modern philosophy" by many, was born in La Haye, France, to Jeanne and Joachim Descartes. His mother died when young René was an infant. Descartes' father became a politician.

Descartes followed his father's wishes and earned a degree in law from the University of Poitiers. After graduating in 1616, he traveled through Europe for a number of years gaining life experiences, including being present at the Battle of White Mountain near Prague in 1620. At the age of 32, Descartes moved to the Dutch Republic and lived in approximately a dozen Dutch cities until his death. Descartes had acquired a wealth of knowledge in mathematics and philosophy. After nearly 400 years, Descartes' *Meditations on First Philosophy* (1641) is still considered a valuable text book at universities worldwide. He also developed a method which allowed geometric shapes to be quantified in algebraic equations. The theory, called the Cartesian Coordinate System, bridges the two disciplines of algebra and geometry.

Descartes' work ("*Je pense donc je suis.*" or "*I think, therefore I am*") still has an impact on the 21st century in both philosophy and mathematics. René Descartes died of what is believed to be pneumonia at the early age of 53 while in Stockholm tutoring Queen Christina of Sweden.

July 12th

It is better to be approximately right than precisely wrong.

Warren Buffett
Entrepreneur and Philanthropist
(b. 1930)

Warren Buffett, one of the top five richest men in the world, does not have a cell phone, a computer in his office and drives his own car. He also lives in the same Omaha home he bought in 1958.

Buffett was born in Omaha, Nebraska, to Howard and Leila Buffett. His father served four terms in the United States Congress resulting in the Buffett family moving to Washington, D.C., where young Buffett completed his high school. At the age of nineteen, Buffett graduated from the University of Nebraska with a degree in Business Administration followed by a Master's in Economics from Columbia Business School in 1951. A year later, he married Susan Thompson and they eventually had three children. Buffett started his business career in his father's investment firm and by 1970 headed his own company called Berkshire Hathaway Inc. Over the years the investment holding company acquired stock in a collection of successful enterprises such as Coca-Cola, Capital Cities/ABC, the Washington Post, General Electric and others.

After the death of his estranged wife in 2004, Buffett married his long-time friend, Astrid Menks. With a commitment to leave his children just enough to take care of them, Buffett has pledged to give away 99% of his fortune, valued near 50.0 billion in 2010, through his foundation.

July 13th

The wise man is not the man who gives the right answers; he is the one who asks the right questions.

Claude Levi-Strauss
Anthropologist
(1908 - 2009)

Claude Levi-Strauss, considered to be one of the most influential social anthropologists of modern time, began his academic life as an average student. He later studied law at the Sorbonne. In time he gave up law in favor of philosophy and later anthropology.

Levi-Strauss was born in Brussels while his father, a painter, was on assignment. He grew up and was educated in Paris. After his graduation from the Sorbonne in 1931, he spent a few years teaching high school but left teaching to join a French cultural group in Brazil. While in the country Levi-Strauss visited the rain forest to study the social structures of the Brazilian Bororo and the Nambikwara tribes. His four years in Brazil shifted his focus to social anthropology. The importance of his PhD thesis, *The Elementary Structures of Kinship*, was instantly recognized worldwide. In 1955, Levi-Strauss (47) wrote a semi-autobiographical book (*Tristes Tropiques*) which once again drew world attention. He struck another chord within the anthropological community with the 1962 release of *La Pensée Sauvage* (*The Savage Mind*).

In 2008, Claude Levi-Strauss became the first living member of the Académie Française to celebrate his 100th birthday.

July 14th

If you don't like something, change it.
If you can't change it,
change your attitude.

Maya Angelou
Writer and Poet
(b. 1928)

Maya Angelou found the inner strength to survive a challenging early life to become a major name in modern literature. Over the decades she has carried many mantels, including that of poet, activist, dancer, playwright, producer, actor (*Roots*) and professor.

During the 1950's Maya became active in the growing civil rights movement. She served as Northern Coordinator for Dr. Martin Luther King Jr. Later Maya joined Malcolm X to help him create the Organization of African American Unity. Malcolm X was assassinated shortly after the movement's launch. Dr. King was assassinated on her 40th birthday. Since the death of her friend, Maya has sent flowers to his widow, Coretta Scott King every single year until Mrs. King's death in 2006.

Maya has continued to be an influential force in America's black community. On January 20, 1993, Maya was invited to read her poem, *On the Pulse of Morning*, at the inauguration of President Bill Clinton. She is a popular invited speaker on the lecture circuit.

July 15th

There are no strangers here;
only friends you haven't yet met.

William Butler Yeats
Playwright and Poet
(1865 - 1939)

William Butler Yeats, one of the most important literary figures to emerge out of the 20th century, suffered from poor school grades and a difficulty with languages as a child. In high school he suddenly took an interest in poetry and by 20 had published his first poems. He quickly became a member of a circle of budding poets and thrived on the regular exchange of ideas.

Yeats was born in County Dublin, Ireland, to John Yeats, a painter, and Susan Mary, who came from a wealthy business family. The Yeats family was very artistic with Yeats' brother, Jack, a successful painter, and his two sisters leading members of the arts movement in Dublin. Yeats became a prolific and successful poet and playwright. His poetic output was impressive in form and style – *Poems* (1895), *The Secret Rose* (1897) and *The Wind Among the Reeds* (1899). Yeats was instrumental in the founding of the Abbey Theatre in Dublin. His play, *Cathleen Ni Houlihan*, opened the theatre in 1904.

Yeats (51) married late in life to Georgie Hyde-Lees and they had two children. He was the first Irish writer to be awarded the Nobel Prize in Literature in 1923 soon after Ireland was granted independence. He served two terms in the Irish Senate (1922 and 1925).

William Butler Yeats died in a hotel in Paris at 74.

July 16th

I have often regretted my speech, never my silence.

Xenocrates
Philosopher and Mathematician
(396 - 314 BC)

Xenocrates was a disciple of Plato and took over the leadership of the Platonic Academy when his master died in 347 BC. He further developed Plato's philosophy by adding the element of mathematics.

Xenocrates was likely born in either 396 or 395 BC in Chalcedon, Greece, an ancient maritime town in what is now a district of Istanbul named Kadikoy. He moved to Athens to pursue his education. Xenocrates joined Plato and his followers in spreading the philosophy of the master teacher. The Platonic Academy was established by Plato in 387 BC when Xenocrates was a child of nine. Aristotle studied at the Academy for twenty years from 367 BC until Plato's death.

In his role as the head of the Platonic Academy, Xenocrates produced an impressively large volume of writings and developed every aspect of the Academy's curriculum. In addition, he devoted more time to his two passions – metaphysics and ethics. Xenocrates followed Plato's thinking but added clarity to his master's philosophic work.

Xenocrates reportedly died from a fall at the advanced age of 82.

July 17th

Life is the flower for which love is the honey.

Victor Hugo
Writer and Political Activist
(1802 - 1885)

Victor Hugo, was born in the early years of the 19th century, grew up witnessing some of France's greatest political and social struggles. Napoleon proclaimed himself Emperor when Hugo was two months old. The events shaped Victor Hugo as a person and influenced his prolific literary output.

Hugo first captured the attention and imagination of the people of France from the poetry he wrote in his early 20's, including *Les Orientales* and *Les Feuilles d'automnes*. In 1829, Hugo (27) released his first publically-acclaimed novel – *Le dernier jour d'un condamné* (*The Last Days of a Condemned Man*). Two years later Hugo published a novel which would establish him as the "people's writer" – *Notre-Dame de Paris* (*The Hunchback of Notre-Dame*). The work of fiction had a remarkable social impact on the Paris of the day. Over a period of 17 years, Hugo structured and wrote the novel which would dramatically depict, in over 1200 pages, the misery and injustice of 19th century France. *Les Misérables* (1862) was released to an anxious reading public in serial form with the first part titled *Fantine*.

Victor Hugo, the writer and the political activist, publically labeled Napoleon III a traitor. Hugo was exiled in the mid-1800's. He and his family lived on the Island of Guernsey for decades and where he wrote *Les Misérables*. Hugo died at 83. His funeral procession in Paris drew over a million people.

July 18th

Love: A temporary insanity curable by marriage.

Ambrose Bierce
Journalist and Short-story Writer
(1842 – 1913)

Ambrose Bierce was born in Horse Cave Creek, Ohio, the tenth of thirteen children of farmers, Marcus and Laura, who shared their passion for literature. Young Ambrose developed a keen interest in his parents' passion.

At the outbreak of the Civil War Ambrose enlisted in the Union Army and was hailed a hero for the rescue of a fallen comrade behind enemy lines. First Lieutenant Bierce fought at the famous Battle of Shiloh (1862) at the age of twenty. The Battle of Shiloh was one of the bloodiest battles of the Civil War resulting in 3,477 dead and almost eleven thousand wounded soldiers. Two years later Bierce received a serious head wound at the Battle of Kennesaw Mountain in 1864. After the end of the Civil War Bierce and Molly Day married in 1871 and raised three children in the San Francisco area. He turned his full attention to writing for various newspapers and magazines, including William Randolph Hearst's San Francisco Examiner. Bierce was a highly respected writer with a unique writing style. He is recognized as one of the best short story writers of the 19th century. His stories included *An Occurrence at Owl Creek Bridge* and *The Boarded Window*. Bierce's most often quoted work was the satirical *The Devil's Disciple* (1906).

Bierce's death was clouded in mystery. In 1913, he reportedly joined Pancho Villa's rebels as an observer and disappeared without a trace. He was 71.

July 19th

*Good teaching is more
a giving of the right questions
than a giving of the right answers.*

Josef Albers
Educator and Artist
(1888 - 1976)

Josef Albers, a gifted teacher and artist, was born in Bottrop, Germany. In his lifetime, Albers created the foundation for what scholars consider the most influential and innovative programs in the field of art education.

Young Albers developed a fascination for art and form as a child. His parents encouraged his studies in Berlin and Munich. In 1920, Albers enrolled as a 32-year-old mature student at the prestigious Weimar Bauhaus and studied art under Johannes Itten. Albers impressed the staff and was invited to remain as a teacher. By 1925, he had earned a position as a full-time professor. The year 1933 marked Adolph Hitler's rise to power and the closure of Weimar Bauhaus. Albers and his wife, Anni, a former art student, moved to the United State's east coast. Albers spent 17 years sharing his passion for art at Black Mountain College in North Carolina before being invited to head the design department at Yale where he remained until he retired at 70.

In 1963, he released *Interaction of Color* presenting his theory about color in art. Albers' teaching and art represents the all-important blending of Europe's traditional style with the new approach in America. His contributions were officially recognized when he was made a member of the American Academy of Arts and Sciences in 1973. Josef Albers died at 88.

July 20th

A real friend is one who walks in when the rest of the world walks out.

Walter Winchell
Journalist and Broadcaster
(1897 - 1972)

Walter Winchell was born Walter Winschel (one 'l') in New York City at the end of the 19th century. His unique writing style and voice delivery made him one of the most recognized people over three decades in the U.S. At his peak, Winchell's daily syndicated column was read by over 50 million people in 2,000 newspapers worldwide. During that same period another 20 million listeners tuned in to his Sunday evening radio broadcast.

Winchell was attracted to vaudeville as a teenager. He would write notes about his fellow cast members and leave them on the backstage bulletin board for everyone's amusement. He took his unique style to the Vaudeville News and eventually at 32 he was writing a daily column for the New York Daily Mirror. During the late 1940's his unusual radio program displaced *The Fred Allen Show* and *The Jack Benny Show* in the ratings.

When the communist scare gripped the U.S., especially the entertainment community, Winchell made the mistake of championing Senator Joseph McCarthy's witch hunt. Winchell's mesmerizing hold on the American public ended. A new audience rediscovered the distinct Winchell (62) delivery as the narrator of ABC's *The Untouchables*.

Walter Winchell died of prostate cancer at 74.

July 21st

It is in the character of very few men to honor without envy a friend who has prospered.

Aeschylus
Playwright and Soldier
(524 BC - 456 BC)

Aeschylus was successful at both his callings in life – soldier and writer. He proved to be brave in the one and inventive in the other. And he left his mark in both disciplines.

Aeschylus's young life was not well documented and much of the details were lost over the centuries. Scholars believe Aeschylus was born in 525 or 524 BC in the small town of Eleusis near the Aegean Sea north of Athens in the region of Attica. He was born into a wealthy and influential family with ancestral ties to Greek nobility. Aeschylus would have been educated in the classics. Records do show that he wrote his first play in his mid-20's. At the age of 35, Aeschylus and his brother, Cynegeirus, participated in the Battle of Marathon against the Persians where Cynegeirus was killed in action. Eighteen years later (472 BC) a play, *The Persians*, written by Aeschylus won the first prize at the competition in the city of Dionysia. The playwright had a great influence on the development of the Greek theatre both in content and style.

Aeschylus was blessed with two sons, Euphorion and Euaon, who became renowned poets. A favorite Aeschylus quotation is inscribed on Robert F. Kennedy's gravesite. Aeschylus died in 456 BC while visiting Sicily.

July 22nd

The difference between school and life? In school, you're taught a lesson and then given a test. In life, you're given a test that teaches you a lesson.

Tom Bodett
Writer and Voice Actor
(b. 1955)

    Tom Bodett was born in Champaign, Illinois. In his early thirties, Bodett contributed to National Public Radio's *All Things Considered* program while he was in Alaska as a contractor building homes. He received a call which introduced him to another aspect of the entertainment business. He was invited to be the spokesman for a major U.S. motel chain. A quarter of a century later, Bodett was still associated with the commercial campaign.

    In 1986, Bodett wrote *As Far As You Can Go Without a Passport*. Three years later he hosted his own program on the National Public Radio network. *The Loose Leaf Book Company* featured book reviews, author interviews and, at times, dramatizations of book excerpts. During that same period (2000), Bodett wrote his first children's book – *Williwow!* Bodett has also been part of the voice over cast of various animations.

    Tom Bodett lives in Dummerston, Vermont, where Rudyard Kipling lived during the 1890's and wrote *The Jungle Book*. Bodett continues to be an active part of the National Public Radio family.

July 23rd

Fault always lies in the same place: with him weak enough to lay blame.

Stephen King
Writer
(b. 1947)

Stephen King has become one of the most popular writers in the horror-fantasy genre. During his writing career, King has published over fifty novels, five non-fiction books and a collection of short stories.

King was born in Portland, Maine, to Nellie Ruth and Donald King. His father, a merchant seaman, abandoned the family when Stephen was two, leaving his mother with the responsibility of raising two boys on her own. The family moved from state to state seeking financial stability before finally settling in Durham, Maine, when Stephen was eleven. Nell supported her family as a caregiver for the mentally challenged. King graduated from the University of Maine with a degree in English in 1970. He sold his first story as a professional writer, *The Glass Floor*, in 1967. King discovered another audience for his exceptionally well-crafted stories with the release of his first movie, *Carrie,* in 1976. A string of successful films based on his work followed, including *The Shining* (1980), *Stand By Me* (1986), *Misery* (1990), *Shawshank Redemption* (1994) and *The Green Mile* (1999).

In 1999, King was struck by a van while walking near his home. The accident resulted in a collapsed lung and a leg so fractured that amputation was discussed. King and his wife, Tabitha, also an author, continue to make Maine their home.

July 24th

Fame is a vapor, popularity an accident, riches take wing, and only character endures.

Horace Greeley
Editor and Politician
(1811 - 1872)

Horace Greeley, at the age of 30, launched the New York Tribune which set new standards in U.S. journalism and served as the most influential newspaper between the 1840's and the early 1870's. Greeley was the sole and dedicated editor of the newspaper until his death.

Greeley was born at the beginning of the 19th century in Amherst, New Hampshire, to Zaccheus and Mary Greeley, poor struggling farmers. Greeley (20) set out to make his mark in New York City. By his mid-twenties he had launched two weekly periodicals – the *New Yorker* and the political *Log Cabin*. In short time, his weeklies reached a circulation of 90,000. At 30, he merged both entities into the *New York Tribune* (1841) which later became the *New York Herald Tribune*. The newspaper, built on high journalistic standards, became the strongest voice in the U.S. By early 1860's, the newspaper had the envious subscription of over 300,000. Greeley's well-crafted editorials took an aggressive stand against slavery and promoted other liberal reforms. Greely, the champion of the working man, served in the U.S. Congress in the late 1840's. One of his editorials encouraged settlers with his famous *"Go West, Young Man!"* rally. Greeley ran a campaign against Ulysses S. Grant for the presidency in 1872 and suffered a huge defeat. Greeley died before the final election count in late November, 1872.

July 25th

You can easily judge the character of a man by how he treats those who can do nothing for him.

Johann Wolfgang von Goethe
Playwright and Poet
(1749 - 1832)

Johann Wolfgang von Goethe, considered one of the greatest writers of modern German literature, was born in Frankfurt, Germany. Goethe's work in morphology and homology were further developed by noted naturalists of the 19th century such as Charles Darwin.

Goethe studied law in Leipzig and was eventually admitted to the Bar in Frankfurt in 1771. At 25, Goethe wrote a novel, *The Sorrows of Young Werther*, which instantly rewarded him with a worldwide reputation. *Sorrows*, based in great part on his own life experiences, earned more attention than it did financial success since copyright and royalty laws were yet to be enforced. *Sorrows* did offer him a place in the court of the Duke of Saxe-Weimar which led to a personal friendship with the Duke. The world embraced *Sorrows* with such passion that the 1774 novel is frequently referred to as the first "best seller" in history. Goethe's lengthy erotic poem, *Faust*, created another sensation and later served as the basis for operatic interpretations.

Goethe had a great impact on the 19th century both with his literature and his important study of color – *The Theory of Colors* (1810). Johann Wolfgang von Goethe died in Weimar, Germany, at 82.

July 26th

Wisdom is knowing what to do next; virtue is doing it.

David Starr Jordan
Ichthyologist and Peace Activist
(1851 - 1931)

David Starr Jordan was the most important ichthyologist of the late 19th century and first part of the 20th century. Jordan devoted his life to the study of fish life and, in association with the Smithsonian Institute, conducted countless studies of fishery throughout the U.S. Jordan's influence on the branch of zoology is felt to this day.

Jordan was born in Gainesville, New York, and studied at both Cornell and Butler universities before graduating from Indiana University School of Medicine. In 1875, Jordan began a series of valuable field trips in Indiana and Wisconsin and later on the American and Canadian west coast. At the age of 34, Jordan became the youngest president of a major educational institution in the U.S. as he took over the leadership of Indiana University. Later he led Stanford University for twenty-five years until his retirement, first as president and then as chancellor.

Jordan was also well known as a peace activist taking a strong position against war in general. He also opposed the U.S.'s involvement in WWI. David Starr Jordan died at the age of 80.

July 27th

We have thirty-five million laws trying to enforce Ten Commandments!

Earl Wilson
Journalist
(1907 - 1987)

Earl Wilson, born Harvey Earl Wilson in Rockford, Ohio, became one of the leading newspaper columnists in the U.S. His newspaper column ran six days each week for a total of forty-one years in the New York Post.

Wilson graduated from Heidelberg College and earned a degree in journalism from Ohio State University in 1931. He worked at the Washington Post before moving to New York City. In 1935, he joined the staff of the New York Post where he met and married Rosemary, a secretary at the newspaper. By 1942, Wilson (35) launched a daily column called *It Happened Last Night* (later *Last Night with Earl Wilson*) covering New York City's Broadway scene. Wilson, who was nicknamed Midnight Earl, would set out every late afternoon to uncover material for his column accompanied by his devoted wife. The two were inseparable. Wilson would always refer to Rosemary in the column as "B.W." for Beautiful Wife. In 1971, Wilson wrote a behind-the-scene book called *The Show Business Nobody Knows*. He also authored two other books which proved very controversial – *Show Business Laid Bare* (1974) and *Frank Sinatra – an Unauthorized Biography* (1976) in which he revealed details of John F. Kennedy's extramarital affairs.

Wilson struggled with Parkinson's disease and retired after four-plus decades. Earl Wilson died at 77, a year following the death of his beloved "B.W."

July 28th

***It is only with the heart
that one can see clearly,
for the most essential things
are invisible to the eye.***

Antoine de Saint-Exupéry
Writer and Aviator
(1900 - 1944)

Antoine de Saint-Exupéry lived a rich and full life as an aviator and writer and devoted a great part of his life to both passions. He was a pioneer in the early days of international postal flight. He captured his experiences in the prize-winning novel, *Night Flight* (*Vol de Nuit*). In 1935, Saint-Exupéry and his navigator narrowly survived a crash in the Sahara desert while racing against time to break the existing flying record between Paris and Saigon. The experience served as the basis for *The Little Prince*.

At the outbreak of WWII, and during the time he wrote *The Little Prince*, Saint-Exupéry lived in North America – New York City and Quebec City. At the age of 43 he returned to Europe and flew reconnaissance missions behind enemy lines to collect intelligence on German troops. On the evening of July 31st, 1944, he flew his P-38 Lightning on a mission out of Corsica, North Africa, and never returned. A few days later the body of a French pilot was found off the Island of Frioul near Marseille but never properly identified.

In 1998, 54 years later, a fisherman found a piece of an aviator's flight suit south of Marseille. Attached to the fabric was a silver identification bracelet with Saint-Exupéry's name as well as his wife's name.

July 29th

The best portion of a good man's life is the little, nameless, unremembered acts of kindness and love.

William Wordsworth
Poet
(1770 -1850)

William Wordsworth, along with contemporary, Samuel Taylor Coleridge, developed and further defined the Romantic Age in England, encouraging poetry to be the "real language of men". The two co-authored *Lyrical Ballads* in 1778 based on folk tradition and included Wordsworth's *Tintern Abbey* and Coleridge's classic *The Rime of the Ancient Mariner*.

Wordsworth was born the second of five children of John and Ann Wordsworth in Cockermouth, England, in the beautiful north lake district. John Wordsworth, a lawyer, was absent most of young William's childhood but did introduce his son to the poetry of Shakespeare and Milton. When his mother died in his eighth year, William was sent to a school in Lancashire and he didn't see his siblings for ten years. He was eventually reunited with his only sister, Dorothy, and they became inseparable. When Wordsworth was 21, he spent time in France during the Revolution and fell in love with Annette Vallan who would give birth to their daughter, Caroline. The war between England and France kept them apart for ten years but by then he was engaged to marry childhood friend, Mary Hutchinson and raised five children.

Wordsworth never lost touch with Annette and his daughter, taking care of them financially even in his will. William Wordsworth died of pleurisy at 80.

July 30th

Silence is argument carried out by other means.

Che Guevara
Physician and Revolutionist
(1928 - 1967)

Che Guevara was a key figure of the Cuban Revolution during the 1950's. The stylized image captured by photographer, Alberto Korda, has come to symbolize 'rebellion' within popular culture.

Guevara's early years offered little indication of the place he would hold in Latino history. He was born Ernesto Guevara, the eldest of five children, in Rosario, Argentina. Guevara's father, Ernesto Guevara Lynch, was of Irish descent and his mother, Celia, was Spanish. The Guevara home enjoyed an extensive library where young Ernesto discovered the poetry of John Keats and the philosophy of Jean-Paul Sartre. Guevara interrupted his medical studies at the University of Buenos Aires to take a nine-month motorcycle trip through South America which would change his life. A month after graduation in 1953, Dr. Guevara set out on his quest determined to see a "borderless united Hispanic America". In 1955, Guevara met the Castro brothers, Fidel and Raul, and he dedicated himself to their cause. Within a year the three were involved in guerilla warfare ending in 1959 with the overthrow of the Batista regime.

After the Cuban Revolution, Guevara carried his military revolution philosophy to the Congo and then to Bolivia. In 1967, an informant led the Bolivian military to Guevara's mountain rebel camp. On October 9th, 1967, Guevara was executed by orders of the Bolivian President. Che Guevara is remembered by some as a hero and by others as a terrorist.

July 31st

***It is not how old you are,
but how you are old.***

Marie Dressler
Actress
(1868 - 1934)

Marie Dressler, born Leila Marie Koerber, discovered at an early age she had a talent to entertain her family. The talent would lead her to win an Oscar for her performance opposite Wallace Berry in *Min and Bill* (1931).

Dressler was born in Cobourg, Ontario, Canada, to Austrian Alexander Koerber and Anna Henderson. At fourteen, her parents allowed her to fulfill her dreams by taking a chorus girl role in an opera company production. Within a decade she made her debut on Broadway. By the 1890's, Dressler had established herself as a major vaudeville performer. In her mid-30's, she met a young fellow Canadian looking for a job in show business. The young man was Mack Sennett who would later offer Dressler (42) her first film role for his own Keystone Studios where such actors as W.C. Fields, Gloria Swanson and Bing Crosby got their start. Sennett teamed her up with another Keystone actor named Charlie Chaplin. Over her career, Dressler appeared in more than 40 films, including *The Patsy* (1928), *One Romantic Night* (1930) and *Tugboat Annie* (1933). Dressler's autobiography, *The Life Story of an Ugly Duckling*, reflected her insecurities of her appearance.

In early 1934, Dressler was diagnosed with terminal cancer but the information was kept from her by a very sympathetic friend, MGM boss Louis B. Mayer. Marie Dressler died on July 23, 1934, in Santa Barbara, California. She was 65.

"The Upper Crust."

During the centuries prior to 1500, the average person, if they were fortunate, would have the benefit of two meals in a day. The main meal, dinner, was served at mid-day while the evening meal, supper, was lighter. The lower classes of Europe were forced to rely on only those food goods they could cultivate from their own harvests. A poor harvest placed horrific hardships on a family. The poor ate barley, rye and oat-based meals with home-grown vegetables rounding off most diets. The potato was introduced later in the 16th century.

The average hard-working lower class male survived on approximately 2,000 calories per day while a male member of nobility consumed as much as 5,000 calories. Tradition reports that a typical monk suffered from obesity because they consumed as much as 6,000 calories per day but spent little time in any physical activity. Most lower-class kitchens had a large kettle in the fire pit. A meal consisted of reheating whatever might have sat in the pot from a previous meal.

Bread was a popular food since it was prepared from product grown in the family field. A raw collection of dough was placed directly on the hot bricks in an oven resulting in the bottom section of the loaf more cooked than the top. The baked loaf was shared according to status within the family unit – the bottom for the individual members of the family while the top section, or *"the upper crust"*, was saved for the master of the house.

August 1st

Do not fear to be eccentric in opinion, for every opinion now accepted was once eccentric.

Bertrand Russell
Philosopher and Social Critic
(1872 - 1970)

Bertrand Russell is considered one of the leading logicians of the 20th century. The impressive output of his writings has had great influence on various disciplines throughout the world. Russell grew up in a home where radical thought was promoted. Both his parents died during his childhood.

Russell frequently challenged the status quo. During WWI he was a leading voice in a small circle of intellectuals who championed pacifism. In his mid-forties (1916), he lost his position as a Cambridge lecturer because of his strong anti-war stance. He served six months in prison. Russell's voice continued to be heard as he defiantly took public positions against Hitler and Stalin during the pre-WWII years. Russell was also very vocal about the U.S.'s role in the Vietnam conflict. He took an equally strong and public stand in favor of nuclear disarmament during his late years.

Russell remained active well into his nineties writing his three-volume autobiography (1967-1969). Bertrand Russell died of influenza at 97 in Wales.

August 2nd

*I don't know the key to success,
but the key to failure is
trying to please everyone.*

Bill Cosby
Actor and Educator
(b. 1937)

Bill Cosby was born William Henry Cosby Junior in Philadelphia, Pennsylvania, the first of four sons. His devoted mother, Anna, was a maid and his father, William Henry Senior, was a seaman who served in WWII.

William quickly fell into the role of "class clown" during his early school years in Philadelphia. By grade 10, William had failed and left school to take on odd jobs eventually joining the U.S. Navy. While in the Navy, he was assigned to a veterans' hospital to care for casualties of the Korean War. The life-changing experience made him appreciate the value of physical therapy and led him to complete his education. During the 1960's, Cosby became a Grammy Award-winning stand-up comedian. In 1965, producer Sheldon Leonard cast 28-year-old Cosby with actor Robert Culp in the television spy series, *I Spy* (1965-1968). Cosby, forever the educator, made use of his two successful series (*Fat Albert* - 1972-1979 and *The Cosby Show* - 1984-1992), to encourage higher education. Cosby's PhD dissertation was based on the *Fat Albert* series' impact on the elementary school curriculum.

Cosby authored a dozen books beginning with the 1986 release of *Fatherhood*. Bill Cosby has won four Emmy's, countless Grammy's and in 2003 was honored with the prestigious Bob Hope Humanitarian Award.

August 3rd

The discovery of what is true and the practice of that which is good are the two most important aims of philosophy.

Voltaire
Writer, Playwright and Philosopher
(1694 - 1778)

Voltaire was one of the great free thinkers of his century. He took every opportunity to challenge the status quo of his time.

He proved to be a prolific writer and created works in almost every literary form, including some two thousands writings. His literary work touched on many disciplines – books, plays, poetry and essays. Researchers have collected over 20,000 personal letters.

Voltaire exercised a great deal of influence on the development of the method of recording history. He broke away from the traditional form of writing historical books. Voltaire's *The Age of Louis XIV* (1752) introduced a writing style that changed the form of historiography.

Voltaire literary works often ridiculed the French institutions of the day and the Catholic Church. He never retracted his public criticism of the Church and was denied a Christian burial. His friends managed to secretly bury his body in the abbey in Champagne, France. On July 11, 1791, his remains were returned to Paris in a funeral procession involving over a million people.

August 4th

*I find television very educational.
Every time somebody turns on the set,
I go into the other room
and read a book.*

Groucho Marx
Entertainer
(1890 - 1977)

Groucho Marx, born Julius Henry Marx over a butcher shop in New York City, became one of the iconic American comedy performers. Young Julius and his siblings grew on the Upper East Side. Minnie Marx became a devoted stage mother encouraging her sons to pursue a career in show business.

The Marx siblings (Julius, Milton, Arthur plus a friend named Lou) started their career as the singing Four Nightingales. Eventually the brothers realized they were getting more laughs from their improvised humor on stage and evolved into The Marx Brothers, minus Lou. The act conquered Vaudeville and Broadway before Hollywood came calling. The Marx Brothers (now called Groucho, Chico and Harpo) won the hearts of film audiences with their very distinctive stage persona in 13 movies. Groucho starred in an additional thirteen Hollywood-produced movies. In 1947, Groucho (57) became the unique host of the long-running *You Bet Your Life* series. The series ran for 14 seasons on all three networks of the time – CBS, ABC and NBC.

Marx's comedic uniqueness exercised great influence on a generation of performers, including Johnny Carson, Woody Allen and Bill Cosby. Groucho Marx died of pneumonia at the age of 86.

August 5th

A journey is best measured in friends, rather than miles.

Tim Cahill
Writer
(b. 1944)

Tim Cahill was born in Nashville, Tennessee, and raised in Waukesha, Wisconsin. He was originally drawn to a career in law before, luckily for the reading public, he turned his attention to professional writing.

Cahill attended the University of Wisconsin on a swimming scholarship. While on campus Cahill established long-lasting friendships with guitarist-songwriter Steve Miller and singer-songwriter, Boz Scaggs. Cahill was fortunate to find a mentor in professor William Wiegand who encouraged him to pursue writing. Cahill earned a Master's degree in Creative Writing from San Francisco State University. Over the decades he became a high-profile writer traveling to over 100 countries often placing himself in difficult and dangerous situations.

Cahill is the founding editor of *Outside Magazine*. He has recounted his travel experiences in some ten books, including his under 24-hour record-setting drive from the southern tip of Argentina to the most northern part of Alaska – *Road Fever* (1991).

In 2008, Cahill's wife, Linnea, was killed in a tragic traffic accident. Tim Cahill lives in Livingston, Montana.

August 6th

Failing is not falling down,
failing is not getting up.

Daniel Enright
Television Producer
(1917 - 1992)

Daniel Enright became one of the major U.S. network game shows producers with partner Jack Barry in the 1950's. During the early days of television network shows were often owned and controlled by major sponsors.

The late fifties were witness to a scandal involving some of the more successful network shows. Barry & Enright Productions' *Twenty-One*, sponsored by Geritol, became the focus of an aggressive Congressional Committee investigation. The committee discovered that some of the prime time quiz shows were "scripted" for the sake of drama and ratings. One of the most high-profile contestants was a university professor named Charles Van Doren who delivered an emotional public confession admitting he had been supplied answers. The confession forced him to resign his duties as co-host on NBC's *Today Show* and to relinquish his teaching position at Columbia University. The committee concluded that no illegal activity had taken place but immediately recommended a change in the laws governing game shows.

Both Jack Barry and Dan Enright were banished from network television for a full two decades. The 1994 Robert Redford-directed movie, *Quiz Show*, captured the details of the quiz scandal.

August 7th

If your ship doesn't come in, swim out to it.

Jonathan Winters
Comedian and Actor
(b. 1925)

Jonathan Winters (Jonathan Harshman Winters III), born in Bell brook, Ohio, grew up to become one of the most gifted comedians and highly respected performers. His mother, Alice, was a Ohio radio personality and his father, Jonathan Harshman Winters II, was a descendant of the founder of the Winters National Bank, now part of the JPMorgan Chase company.

After his parent's separation, young Jonathan lived with his maternal grandmother. In 1942, Jonathan (17) joined the U.S. Marine Corps and spent the next three years in the Pacific. Following his Marine Corps service, he studied art at the Dayton Art Institute. In 1948, Winters married a fellow- student named Eileen and launched a career in radio as Johnny Winters. Radio allowed him to further develop his natural talents of creativity and comedic timing. By the early 1960's, Winters was a regular in the New York City nightclubs and on *The Tonight Show* first with Jack Paar and later with Johnny Carson.

Winters has appeared in over 50 movies (*It's a Mad, Mad, Mad, Mad World*) and such television shows as *Mork and Mindy*. The winner of the Mark Twain Prize for American Humor lives in Santa Barbara, California. His beloved wife of 60 years, Eileen, died of breast cancer in 2009.

August 8th

*I am always doing that
which I cannot do,
in order that I may learn
how to do it.*

Pablo Picasso
Painter and Sculpture
(1881 - 1973)

Pablo Picasso was born in Malaga, Spain, the first child of Don Jose Ruizy Blasco and Maria Picasso Lopez. The family was middle class with Don Jose serving as a professor of art. Young Pablo demonstrated a great interest in drawing during his early years.

When Pablo was 13, two life-changing events took place – his younger sister, Coruna (7), died of diphtheria and the family moved to Barcelona. Young Picasso was allowed to enroll at the Barcelona School of Fine Arts despite his age. In short time, Picasso's skills surpassed his father's talents as well as those of his professors. The family sent the budding artist to the Royal Academy in Madrid.

Picasso spent most of his adult life in France. His painting style matured by the turn of the 20th century when Picasso and Georges Braque launched the avant-garde art movement known as Cubism. Picasso's *Les Demoiselles d'Avignon* (1907) is considered the birth of Cubism.

Picasso married twice in his life and was involved in numerous relationships producing four children. Pablo Picasso died in France at the age of 91.

August 9th

*Reflect upon your present blessings,
of which every man has plenty;
not upon your past misfortunes,
of which all men have some.*

Charles Dickens
Writer
(1812 - 1870)

Charles Dickens's early childhood in 19th century London contributed to the making of undoubtedly the most popular writer of the Victorian era. Young Dickens was himself a product and survivor of the rather harsh social conditions of London's working class.

At an early age, while his father was in debtor's prison, young Dickens was forced to toil in a shoe polish factory housed in a damp, rat-infested warehouse. One of the other young workers by the name of Bob Fagin befriended Dickens. Dickens's photographic memory offered him a wealth of rich, fascinating characters and storylines. In later years Dickens used the prison setting in a serialized novel called *Little Dorrit* (1855-1857) and one of the memorable characters in *Oliver Twist* (1839) became Fagin. The experiences of an unhappy childhood served as the basis of another classic novel – *David Copperfield* (1850). One of the literary gems in Dickens' inventory, *A Christmas Carol* (1843) was reportedly written in a short number of weeks in order to cover the expenses related to the birth of a fifth child.

Charles Dickens died in 1870 at the age of 58.

August 10th

Obstacles are those frightful things you see when you take your eyes off your goal.

Henry Ford
Industrialist
(1863 - 1947)

Henry Ford was born just outside Detroit, Michigan, to an Irish-born Englishman (William Ford) and a Michigan native (Mary). Henry, the oldest of seven children, outlived every member of the Ford family. Three years after his mother's death in 1876, Henry (14) abandoned school to work as a machinist.

In 1888, Ford (25) married Clara Bryant and in their 62-year marriage had one child named Edsel. In his mid-20's, Ford became an engineer with the recently-formed Edison Illumination Company. Within ten years he launched the short-lived Detroit Automobile Company. Two years later he founded the Henry Ford Company with the financial backing of Harold Willis. A year later, Ford left the enterprise as a result of a difference of operating strategy. The company continued without Ford under the name Cadillac Automobile Company. By 1903, he and partner, Alexander Malcomson, (along with brothers John and Horace Dodge) formed the Ford Motor Company with $28,000 capital.

For more than a century the Ford Motor Company has survived harsh competition, a depression and two world wars. William Clay "Bill" Ford, the great-grandson of Henry Ford, is guiding the family business into the 21st century as Executive Chairman.

August 11th

The way I see it,
if you want the rainbow,
you gotta put up with the rain.

Dolly Parton
Singer and Songwriter
(b. 1946)

Dolly Parton, 'The Queen of Country Music', was born in Sevierville, Tennessee, the fourth of twelve children of Robert and Avie Parton. The 14-member Parton family lived in a one-room cabin. Poverty was a way of life.

By the age of nine, young Dolly's singing career was launched with appearances on local radio and television. Immediately after high school, Dolly moved to Nashville and within a year signed on as a pop singer with Monument Records. At 20, she married Carl Thomas Dean, the owner of an asphalt company. Forty-five years later the couple continues to keep their childless married life private. Parton's Nashville career got a boost as a member of the Porter Wagoner musical family. Her solo career blossomed during the 1970's with the release of her own songs, including *Coat of Many Colors*, *Jolene* and *I Will Always Love You*. Parton has proven to be an astute business person with such successful ventures as the Dollywood Amusement Park and Sandollar Productions, producer of such popular movies as *Father of the Bride* (1991), *Father of the Bride, Part II* (1995) and *Sabrina* (1995) starring Harrison Ford and Julia Ormond.

The winner of eight Grammys and the Lifetime Achievement Award continues to devote her energy to philanthropy.

August 12th

What counts can't always be counted; what can be counted doesn't always count.

Albert Einstein
Physicist
(1879 - 1955)

Albert Einstein overcame an early speech problem to become one of the leading physicists in the world. The "father of modern physics" is credited with creating a revolution in the world of physics with the discovery of the theory of general relativity.

Albert's parents enrolled young Einstein in a Catholic school during his first years. The bright and inquisitive young Einstein was eventually sent to the Luitpold Gymnasium for more advanced studies. In 1900, Einstein earned a teaching diploma from the Zurich Polytechnic where he met and married a fellow student named Mileva Naric. The couple was separated for the last five of their fifteen year marriage which ended in divorce in 1919. Einstein and his second wife, Elsa Lowenthal, were married for 17 years before she lost her battle to heart disease in 1936. The Einsteins were on a lecture tour in California in 1933 when Adolf Hitler gained political control of Germany. They never returned to Germany choosing to settle in Princeton, New Jersey, where Albert was attached to Princeton University.

Prior to the beginning of WWII, Albert Einstein and Bertrand Russell authored and signed the Russell-Einstein Manifesto underlining the dangers of nuclear weapons. In his lifetime Einstein was responsible for more than 300 scientific papers. Albert Einstein worked until his death at 76.

August 13th

Do not walk behind me,
I may not lead.
Do not walk in front of me,
I may not follow.
Walk beside me and be my friend.

Albert Camus
Writer
(1913 - 1960)

Albert Camus survived the extreme poverty of his early childhood in Algiers. He eventually earned the equivalent of an M.A. thesis at the University of Algiers. Camus, an avid soccer player as a talented goalkeeper for the university team, was diagnosed with tuberculosis at the age of 17. He was forced to end his athletic career and to become a part-time student.

During his early post-graduate years, Camus became an active member of the French Communist Party. He saw the movement as a means to combat the inequities which existed in Algeria between the native Algerians and the "Pieds-Noirs" (Black-feet). The Pieds-Noirs represented the European colonists who had settled in Algeria. Camus' own parents were Pieds-Noirs. He was eventually denounced by the Communist Party. Camus rejected all political labels.

The journalist-turned-philosopher was a strong advocate against capital punishment. In 1957, Camus became the first African-born writer to be awarded the prestigious Nobel Prize for Literature.

August 14th

*I long to accomplish
a great and noble task,
but it is my duty to accomplish
small tasks as if they were
great and noble.*

Helen Keller
Author, Lecturer and Activist
(1880 - 1968)

Helen Keller lost her sight and hearing at the age of 19 months from likely scarlet fever or meningitis. A young partially blind instructor named Anne Sullivan broke through the barrier and eventually taught Helen to communicate by touch and feel. The uplifting personal story was captured in the award-winning 1962 movie *The Miracle Worker* (Patty Duke and Anne Bancroft).

Mark Twain (Samuel Clemens) became Keller's champion early in her life and introduced the Keller family to his friend, wealthy industrialist, Henry Rogers. Rogers eagerly covered all the expenses for Helen's education. Keller defied all the odds and overcame her physical limitations to become the first blind-deaf person to earn a university degree. During her lifetime she authored 12 books and countless articles. Keller and her companion, Anne Sullivan, traveled the world on a number of lecture tours. In 1903, Keller (22) wrote a popular autobiography entitled, *The Story of My Life*. The Helen Keller International organization was established in 1915 to encourage research. Keller's devoted instructor and lifelong companion, Anne Sullivan, died in 1966. During the early 1960's Keller then (81) suffered a number of strokes. She spent the final years in her Connecticut home.

August 15th

*Start by doing the necessary,
then the possible,
and suddenly you are doing
the impossible.*

Saint Francis of Assisi
Spiritual Leader
(1181 - 1226)

Saint Francis of Assisi (Giovanni Francesco di Bernardone) gave up the worldly life of a wealthy young man to rise and become one of the most venerated saints in the Roman Catholic Church.

Young Francesco answered the call following a spiritual awakening in his mid-twenties. Francesco left all his worldly possessions to live the simple life of a preacher roaming the Italian countryside. He chose not to be ordained a Catholic priest and his growing community of devoted followers was quickly known as the 'lesser brothers'.

The Franciscan Order was officially recognized by Rome in 1210. Francesco was 29 years of age. The Franciscan Order quickly spread to all parts of the known world. Francesco made such a personal impression that the Franciscan Order was recognized as the "custodians of the Holy Land' on behalf of Christianity.

Francesco developed great affection for God's creatures, calling them his "brothers and sisters". In 1226, at the early age of 45, Francesco succumbed to his frail health. Folklore has it that a dying Francesco found the strength to thank his donkey for carrying him all of its life and the donkey wept.

August 16th

A man's sense of self is defined through his ability to achieve results. A woman's sense of self is defined through her feelings and the quality of her relationships.

John Gray
Writer
(b. 1951)

John Gray has become one of the most successful and wealthiest relationship authors worldwide. He has released twelve books on human relationships which have been distributed in 45 languages with sales reaching over fifty million copies.

Gray was born in Houston, Texas, the fifth of seven children of a Texas oilman and a co-owner of a spiritual bookstore. Young John abandoned his university studies to join the Maharishi Yogi where he spent nine years as a celibate monk. He returned to his studies and eventually earned a PhD in 1982.

In 1992, Gray published a book which catapulted him to fame and fortune. *Men are from Mars, Women are from Venus* explored the basic differences between the two sexes on emotional levels, communicating skills and personal needs and values. The book shot to the top of the best sellers' list.

John Gray remains a popular speaker on the lecture circuit. Gray and his wife, Bonnie, live in Northern California.

August 17th

The nice thing about being a celebrity is that if you bore people they think it's their fault.

Henry Kissinger
Playwright and Poet
(b. 1923)

Henry Kissinger (Heinz Alfred Kissinger) was born in Furth, Germany. His father was a schoolteacher and his mother a devoted housewife. The Jewish Kissinger family fled from Germany in 1938 when Hitler took control of the country's future. They landed in New York City.

Young Henry worked his way through college with the help of a job in a shaving brush factory. WWII interrupted his studies in 1943 when he enlisted in the U.S. Army. Kissinger received the Bronze Star for his service, including the late 1944-early 1945 Battle of the Bulge.

Kissinger earned a PhD at Harvard in 1974 and joined the teaching faculty. He served as advisor to Governor Nelson Rockefeller in the 1960's. Kissinger played a very high profile role as Secretary of State under Richard Nixon and later Gerald Ford. He was awarded the Nobel Peace Prize for orchestrating the end of the Vietnam conflict.

Henry Kissinger and his wife, Nancy, live in Kent, Connecticut. Son David is head of Conaco Productions, Conan O'Brien's production company.

August 18th

*Love is an irresistible desire
to be irresistibly desired.*

Mark Twain
Writer
(1835 - 1910)

Mark Twain (Samuel Clemens) was born within days of Haley's Comet's close encounter with Earth. The Clemens family of seven children (Samuel being the sixth) suffered tragic losses. Three of the children did not live beyond childhood and a fourth (brother, Henry) was killed in a riverboat explosion before his 20th birthday. Samuel's father, a district judge, died of pneumonia when Samuel was 11.

In his early 30's, Samuel, under the pen name Mark Twain, was sent on an assignment abroad by a newspaper to write a series of 'travel letters' later published (1869) as *The Innocents Abroad*. The trip proved life-changing as a result of a chance meeting with his future brother-in-law. Twain married the love of his life, Olivia, in 1870. His family of three daughters (a son died at 19 months) became the entire focus of his life. The family traveled with Twain on his many lecture tours. He often claimed his family was "a nation upon itself".

Mark Twain proved to be very successful and earned a great deal of money – an unusual accomplishment for writers of the day in their living years. The Twains settled in Hartford, Connecticut, where they built a beautiful home, now a museum honoring the writer.

Twain died in 1910, six years following the death of his beloved Olivia.

August 19th

*As you grow older you will discover
you have two hands,
one for helping yourself,
the other for helping others.*

Audrey Hepburn
Actress and Humanitarian
(1929 - 1993)

Audrey Hepburn was born Audrey Kathleen Ruston in Brussels, Belgium. Her father, Joseph, added the hyphenated Hepburn to the family name mistakenly believing he was a descendant of James Hepburn (1536-1578), the third husband of Mary, Queen of Scots.

The Hepburn-Ruston family faced great hardships leading up to and during WWII. Young Audrey's health was compromised due to malnutrition. Her war-time struggles and the memories of children in danger would have a great influence on her adult life. During the post-war late 40's, Hepburn launched her career in the chorus lines on the London stage. In 1951, she was cast in the lead role of the stage production of *Gigi*. Hepburn's impressive film career included such memorable movies as *Roman Holiday* with Gregory Peck (1953), *Sabrina* (1954 – Humphrey Bogart and William Holden) *My Fair Lady* in 1964. The beautiful lady won a total of seven Best Actress awards and received another 17 nomination and is considered the third greatest female screen legend.

Hepburn's own childhood experiences led her to the life of a dedicated humanitarian as Goodwill Ambassador for UNICEF. Audrey Hepburn lost a short battle with cancer and died in her Switzerland home at the age of 64.

August 20th

Forgive your enemies,
but never forget their names.

John F. Kennedy
Statesman
(1917 - 1963)

John F. Kennedy, the second son of entrepreneur, Joseph Kennedy, and socialite, Rose Fitzgerald, did not, as a young person, show any signs of the important role he would play later in life. John was frequently rebellious as a young man and often sickly as a child, including being pulled out of school for a full year because of a leukemia scare.

For a great part of his youth, John lived in the shadow of older brother, Joseph Junior. The young Joe, football hero and war hero, was being groomed for the highest of political office in the U.S. John traveled extensively throughout Europe and the Soviet Union to formulate his university thesis – later published as a book entitled *Why England Slept*. Thirty-year-old John served as commander of the famed PT-109 until it was rammed by a Japanese destroyer. The tragic war death of Joe, Jr (1944) thrust John into his brother's role. Following the war John served in the U.S. Congress for 6 years and 8 years in the Senate before being elected President in 1960. His presidency was faced with great challenges – conflict with Nikita Khrushchev (1960), Bay of Pigs (1961) and the Cuban Missile Crisis (1962).

John Fitzgerald Kennedy, or JFK as he was affectionately known, was assassinated in 1963.

August 21st

Dying is a very dull, dreary affair.
And my advice to you
is to have nothing to do with it.

W. Somerset Maugham
Playwright and Writer
(1874 - 1965)

Somerset Maugham published his very first work at the age of sixteen - a biography of Italian opera composer Giacomo Meyerbeer. The rather small and frail Maugham became a literary giant in his lifetime.

By 23, Somerset Maugham had written his first critically acclaimed novel while still a medical student. The 1897 publishing of *Lisa of Lambeth* proved to be extremely popular with both the critics and the reading public. A full decade after his first work, Maugham began to write a string of successful novels, plays and short stories, including *Lady Frederick* (1907) and *The Magician* (1908). Maugham's medical training and his homosexuality proved to be of great value in his writings. A rather quiet and withdrawn gentleman, Maugham's male partners were frequently his best researchers.

Maugham had numerous relationships with both men and women. In 1917, he married a divorcee (Syrie Wellcome) and fathered a daughter. By the time WWI started, Maugham, then 40, had become a famous and wealthy writer. He served with the British Red Cross as an ambulance driver. During this period he wrote two of his masterpieces – *Of Human Bondage* (1915) and *The Moon and Sixpence* (1916). In 1927, Maugham and his wife divorced. He resumed his relationship with Frederick Haxton until Haxton's death in 1944.

August 22nd

Angels can fly because they take themselves lightly.

G. K. Chesterton
Writer and Journalist
(1874 - 1936)

G.K. Chesterton made use of his clever wit and his own style of humor to become one of the most widely read writers throughout the 20th century. A great deal of his prolific output remains in print to this day.

G. K. Chesterton's writings covered numerous areas and disciplines, including poetry, fiction, philosophy, literary and art criticism, playwriting and biographical works. In addition, Chesterton was a journalist. In his youth, the avid reader was greatly influenced by Charles Dickens, Robert Browning and St. Thomas Aquinas. In turn, Chesterton would have tremendous influence on the writings of later writers, such as Ernest Hemingway, Agatha Christie and the creator of the *Harry Potter* series, J. K. Rowling.

Chesterton's quick wit became his trademark in his writings as well as his day-to-day social life. During WWI, a British lady queried why this healthy man was not "out at the front" to which the near 300 pound Chesterton replied – "Madam, if you go around to the side, you will see that I am!"

The writer whom his friend, George Bernard Shaw, once called "a colossal genius" died at 61. Chesterton had converted to Catholicism some dozen years before his death. His estate reflected how successful this early 19th century writer had been – over 2.0 million in today's U.S. currency.

August 23rd

Many of life's failures are people who did not realize how close they were to success when they gave up.

Thomas Edison
Scientist
(1847 - 1931)

Thomas Edison's father, Samuel Ogden Edison, escaped from Canada because of his involvement in the unsuccessful Mackenzie Rebellion in 1837. Young Edison was home-schooled by his devoted mother.

In his teens, Edison saved the life of a three-year-old and the boy's father, a train station agent, rewarded Edison by giving him a job as a telegraph operator. The two events sent Edison on an historical path which would impact the world. Within a few years (1869), Edison applied for and was granted his first patent – the electric vote recorder. He proved to be one of the most prolific inventors with over one thousand patents.

Edison's financial success is directly related to two facts – the creation of the first industrial laboratory and various mass-production factories. His business acumen eventually led to establishing a number of successful companies some of which remain in operation to this day, including General Electric.

Edison's personal philosophy of non-violence led him to avoid developing weapons to kill man or beast. Some scholars refer to Edison as one of the most influential figures in modern history. Edison died at 84 and was buried at his Glenmont estate in New Jersey.

August 24th

***We are as much alive
as we keep the earth alive.***

Chief Dan George
Band Chief, Poet and Actor
(1899 - 1981)

Chief Dan George was born Geswanmouth Slahoot in North Vancouver, British Columbia. At the age of 5, the young boy was taken from his family and placed in the government Indian Residential School System. The government-driven program which was introduced in 1840 was created as a means to force assimilation of aboriginal peoples into the general population. The use of their language and the practice of their faith were forbidden. At that point young Geswanmouth' name was changed to Dan George.

George's post-war years were spent in various jobs, including construction and longshoreman. He also served in the important role of Band Chief of the Tsleil Waututh Nation. At the advanced age of 60, George had the opportunity to launch another career as an actor in the CBC's *Caribou Country* television series. In 1970, George (71) was nominated for a Best Supporting Actor Oscar for his memorable role as Old Skins Lodge in *Little Big Man* starring Dustin Hoffman and Faye Dunaway. George co-starred in a string of other Hollywood films, including Clint Eastwood's 1978 *The Outlaw Josey Wales*.

George was made an Officer of the Order of Canada in 1971. Chief Dan George died in 1981 at the age of 83. In 2008, Canada Post honored the Chief with a postage stamp.

August 25th

Wise men talk because they have something to say. Fools talk because they want to say something.

Plato
Philosopher
(427 BC - 347 BC)

Plato, the founder of one of the first schools for higher learning in the Western culture, is responsible for much of the foundation for a range of subjects such as philosophy, mathematics and logic. Plato's philosophy is detailed in his writings – thirty-six dialogues and thirteen letters.

Plato's own personal pride for his family comes through in his philosophy. The glorification of the family is an underlining theme of one of his dialogues – *Charmides*. Plato frequently dealt with one of the cornerstones of the family, the father-son relationship. In other dialogues, such as *Republic* and *Phaedo*, Plato promotes the belief in the immortality of the soul and of the after-life. His philosophy demonstrates in *Laws* and *Statesman* what the ideal government should consist of by comparing it to the human body – 'appetite' – the 'workers', 'spirit' – the 'guardians' and 'reason' – the 'rulers'.

Scholars have debated over the centuries the order in which Plato's dialogues and letters were actually written but no one argues the importance his writings have had on the development of Western philosophy.

August 26th

In the hopes of reaching the moon men fail to see the flowers that blossom at their feet.

Albert Schweitzer
Philosopher, Physician and Missionary
(1875 - 1965)

Albert Schweitzer, the son of a Lutheran pastor, grew up surrounded with both theology and music. His father exercised a great influence on young Albert, including introducing his son to a great love of organ music.

At 30, Albert Schweitzer dedicated his life to medical missionary work. Schweitzer returned to university as a student and earned a Doctorate in Medicine in order to qualify for the medical missionary program. A year after his marriage to Helene Bresslau, the couple headed to Africa at their own expense to establish a hospital. Over time Schweitzer dealt with various life-threatening maladies which threatened the African communities, including malaria, heart disease and leprosy. The German-born Schweitzers, and Mrs. Schweitzer being of Jewish descent, were interned by the French military during WWI. The hospital in Lambarene, Africa, continued to expand throughout the decades.

The Albert Schweitzer Fellowship, established in 1940, has helped thousands of young people from various walks of life to pursue public service. The selfless Schweitzer spirit inspired many individuals over the decades, including actor Hugh O'Brian who launched his own Youth Leadership Foundation.

August 27th

*In a country well governed,
poverty is something to be ashamed of.
In a country badly governed,
wealth is something to be ashamed of.*

Confucius
Philosopher
(551 - 479 BC)

Confucius, born Kong Qiu, was an influential scholar, teacher and philosopher of Chinese history. His teachings were instrumental in the early development of Chinese thinking and social behavior.

Confucius' philosophy is captured in five classics he is believed to have either written himself or edited, including *Analects of Confucius*. His writings underline the importance of morality, both personal and governmental, justice and social relationships. Confucius placed great emphasis on knowledge and the ability to think for one's self.

During the 16th century Italian Jesuit, Matteo Ricci, began to translate and study the works of Confucius. The translation of "Confucius" established it as the most commonly used name in the Western world.

Confucius' philosophy was carried forward after his death by his many disciples. Since no undisputable proof exists of the authorship of the writings, modern scholars remain cautious what can be attributed directly to the one the Chinese respectfully call the Greatest Master.

August 28th

No one could make a greater mistake than he who did nothing because he could do only a little.

Edmund Burke
Statesman and Philosopher
(1729 - 1797)

Edmund Burke spent the greater part of his first two decades in his native Dublin, Ireland, before transplanting himself to London. As a student at Trinity College, Burke excelled at debate and established the Edmund Burke Debating Club, a talent which would serve him well in his future political life. The club, later called the College Historical Club, is still in existence to this day making it the oldest undergraduate organization in the world.

After years as a successful writer Burke was drawn into politics. In 1765, at 36, he joined Britain's House of Commons as a member of the Whig Party. During the early years of his political career he was accused of having strong Catholic ties and of having been educated at a Jesuit school at a time in Britain when Catholics could not hold public office. Burke defended himself always maintaining he was loyal to the Anglican Church as his father had been. Over a 30-plus year career in British politics, Burke distinguished himself as an exceptional statesman and orator. He was best known for taking strong, and at times, unpopular positions. Burke eloquently supported the cause of the American Revolution to the point where his home had to be protected by military guards. He also took firm stands against capital punishment and the anti-Catholic laws. Burke has been often labeled by scholars as the "philosophical founder of modern conservatism". Edmund Burke died at 68.

August 29th

***You must be willing to do the things today
others don't do in order to have
the things tomorrow others won't have.***

Les Brown
Motivational Speaker
(b. 1945)

Les Brown was born in Liberty City, an under-privileged area of Miami, Florida. At the age of six weeks, Les and his twin brother, Wes, were adopted by a single woman named Mamie Brown. The family lived in great poverty. Les had great difficulty focusing and concentrating at school and was branded a "slow learner". The label was not accurate but damaged his self-esteem for years.

Despite having a minimum formal education, Brown was driven to educate himself with reading and life experiences. During the late 60's, he became a high-profile morning radio DJ in Columbus, Ohio. Brown also served three terms as a Ohio Sate legislator. He authored a successful self-help book entitled *Live Your Dreams* which propelled him into a career as a motivational speaker. His clients include Chrysler, 3M and Xerox.

In 1995, Brown married super star Gladys Knight. The couple eventually divorced. Brown continues to be in great demand as a guest speaker and motivational coach.

August 30th

Treat a man as if he were
what he ought to be
and you help him become
what he is capable of being.

Johann Wolfgang von Goethe
Writer
(1749 - 1832)

Johann Wolfgang von Goethe was born into a German Lutheran family which enjoyed a high social profile in Frankfurt. His parents were determined to offer all their children the best education possible. His father surrounded the children with fine literature and made private tutors available. Young Goethe became fascinated with the writings of the great masters at an early age.

Goethe earned a degree in law but his passion for literature and his interest in natural science drew him in another direction. The extra-ordinary success of his first novel, *The Sorrows of Young Werther*, catapulted him into the public eye and earned him the life-long favor of the Duke of Saxe-Weimar and a place in the court. At 33, Goethe was granted the noble "von" recognition by his friend, the Duke. Many of Goethe's literary work were based on personal experiences, including his numerous romantic relationships. During his early 40's, Goethe began a relationship with the strong-willed Christiane Vulpius and settled in Weimar. After 18 years together and several children, the couple married in the Duke of Saxe-Weimar's court chapel.

Goethe's literary output established him as one of the key writers in German literature and in the Romanticism movement. Johann Wolfgang von Goethe died in his 82nd year.

August 31st

When you come to the end of your rope, tie a knot and hang on.

Franklin D. Roosevelt
Statesman
(1882 - 1945)

Franklin D. Roosevelt was the 35th President of the United States. He became a major figure leading up to and during the Second World War. Roosevelt was the only president to serve for twelve consecutive years. He was the fifth cousin of President Theodore Roosevelt (1901-1909).

Roosevelt was born in Hudson Valley, New York, the only child of Sara Ann Delano and James Roosevelt who was 51 at the time of Franklin's birth. Both the Roosevelt and Delano families were well-established and wealthy families. Roosevelt was a 'C' student at Harvard but his charismatic personality made him a favorite all through his political life. He served as Governor of New York State between 1929 and 1932.

In 1932, the Democratic Party nominated Roosevelt to run against incumbent Herbert Hoover. Roosevelt's optimistic outlook despite the persistent economic gloom propelled him into the White House. Roosevelt was diagnosed with polio which eventually led to paralysis.

Roosevelt married Eleanor Roosevelt, a distant cousin, in 1905. The couple had six children but the marriage was never considered a success. Franklin Delano Roosevelt died in 1945 at 63 with his life-long friend, Lucy Mercer by his side.

"Don't throw the baby out with the bath water!"

Lifestyles prior to the 16th century in Europe were harsh throughout the known world of the time, especially for the lower classes. Work, for the masses, generally meant toiling for long endless hours in dusty fields or in unhealthy environments within the city walls. Peasants often were infested with lice and fleas and remained dirty for days and weeks. Personal hygiene, including dental hygiene, ranked extremely low to the task of simply surviving from day to day.

The art of cleanliness varied from culture to culture but, in general, a simple bath was considered a luxury for the common folks. The importance of cleanliness was not practiced although the washing of hands and face was more common. Running water systems did not exist and the value of hot water bathing remained unknown for some time. The occasional bath would be enjoyed in cool water and usually without the benefit of soap or shampoo-like substances. Water, drinking or cleaning, was a precious commodity rationed in every household.

Individual homes, other than the castles of the nobility, did not have interior bath tubs. Baths consisted of a big wooden tub filled with cold water. The man of the house had the privilege of the nice clean water, then all the other sons and men, then the women and finally the children. And last of all - the babies! By then, the water was so dirty you could actually lose someone in it.

Hence the saying - "*Don't throw the baby out with the bath water!*"

September 1st

***We make a living by what we get,
but we make a life by what we give.***

Sir Winston Churchill
Statesman
(1874 - 1965)

Sir Winston Churchill, born Winston Leonard Spencer-Churchill, chose to use the name Churchill as his politician-father had done. Winston devoted his life to his country and became one of the most respected politicians in modern times. He also served as an officer in the British Army in various military campaigns.

Churchill entered political life at the age of 32 as a Member of Parliament for the Oldham district of London and remained in the House of Commons for the next 58 years. During the 1930's, Churchill was a lone voice in England warning of the danger emerging in a changing Germany. At the beginning of WWII, Churchill was named First Lord of the Admiralty and a member of the all-important War Cabinet. The resignation of Prime Minister Neville Chamberlain in May of 1940 led to Churchill being named his replacement. His skills as an orator and his defiance of the Hitler military machine inspired the British people to follow his leadership. He remained in office under King George VI until Hitler was defeated. Churchill was called to serve as Prime Minister a second time in the early 1950's (1951-1955).

Churchill is the only British Prime Minister to be awarded the Nobel Prize in Literature. Winston Churchill died at 90 and the state funeral in 1965 drew the largest group of world leaders ever assembled.

September 2nd

Management is doing things right:
Leadership is doing the right things.

Peter F. Drucker
Educator and Consultant
(1909 - 2005)

Peter Ferdinand Drucker grew up in a household of intellectuals in Vienna, Austria, to become one of the world's most influential and widely read business consultants. He single-handedly revolutionized big corporation thinking about the workplace and the customer.

Drucker, educated in Austria and Germany, left Germany with his young bride as Adolf Hitler rose to power in 1933. Drucker eventually found sanctuary in the United States during his mid-twenties where he became a citizen in 1943. Drucker's early fascination with the behavior of people led him to focus on the workplace. He created a consulting firm in the 1940's which proved to be in great demand throughout the world, especially in Japan. Drucker's management philosophy encouraged a community environment where respect for the worker be practiced. He repeatedly preached that a corporation's greatest asset was the people. He warned senior management not to allow profit to be the company's sole goal. Drucker also predicted many of the business directions of the 20th century – decentralization and privatization.

The last thirty years of Drucker's life were spent at the Claremont Graduate University as Professor of Social Science and Management. His last lecture was in 2002 at the age of 92. Peter Drucker died a week shy of his 96th birthday.

September 3rd

*The one thing we can never
get enough of is love.
And the one thing
we can never give enough of is love.*

Henry Miller
Writer and Painter
(1891 - 1980)

Henry Miller was born Henry Valentine Miller in Manhattan, New York, to Louise Marie and Heinrich, a tailor. The German Catholic family moved to Brooklyn when Henry was a child. His higher level education was limited to one semester at the City College of New York. In 1917, at the age of 26, Miller married Beatrice Wickens. Miller would marry five times in his life plus a long-term relationship in Paris with French writer Anaïs Nin.

In 1930, Miller, while still married to his second wife, transplanted himself to Paris on his own. During his early years in Paris he worked at the Chicago Tribune's European office as a proofreader. Miller's first critically acclaimed novel, *The Tropic of Cancer* (1934) was banned in North America because of the explicit language and sexual descriptions. A number of his most memorable works, including *Black Spring* (1936) and *The Tropic of Capricorn* (1939), triggered numerous obscenity trials when the books were eventually published in the U.S.

Miller, who was also painter of over 2,000 watercolors, is considered one of the key figures leading to the sexual revolution of the 1960's. Henry Miller died of circulatory complications at his California home. He was 88.

September 4th

Better to have loved and lost than never to have loved at all.

Alfred Lord Tennyson
Poet
(1809 - 1892)

Alfred Lord Tennyson, the fourth of twelve children born to the rector of Somersby, was born into a middle-class family which had royal ancestral ties. Young Alfred attended Trinity College in Cambridge where he was awarded the prestigious Chancelor's Gold Medal at 20. In 1827, Alfred (18) and his older brother, Charles, published a collection of poems – *Poems by Two Brothers*.

Tennyson's first solo publication in 1830 at the age of 21, *Poems Chiefly Lyrical* included one of his most famous poems – *Claribel and Mariana*. In his early 40's, Tennyson married his childhood friend, Emily Sellwood. The eldest of their two sons, Hallam, eventually became the Governor-General of Australia. Tennyson is considered to be one of the finest craftsmen of Victorian English. Several of his poems remain important works in English literature, including *Ulysses* (1833) and his masterpiece, *The Charge of the Light Brigade* (1855), written to honor the British cavalrymen during the Crimean War. In 1850, Tennyson was appointed Poet Laureat by Queen Victoria and dutifully served in his official role until his death.

Tennyson reluctantly accepted the title of Lord at the age of 74. Alfred Lord Tennyson quietly died at 83.

September 5th

*Forgiveness is the answer
to the child's dream
of a miracle by which
what is broken is made whole again
what is soiled is made clean again.*

Dag Hammarskjold
Writer and Diplomat
(1905 - 1961)

Dag Hammarskjold was born in Jönköping, Sweden, the youngest of four sons of Agnes and Hjalmar Hammarskjold, the former Prime Minister of Sweden (1914-1917). The Hammarskjold children excelled in school and young Dag earned a Bachelor of Laws, a Master's degree in Political Economy at the Uppsala University and a PhD from Stockholm University.

Hammarskjold worked his way up to the chairmanship of the Sveriges Riksbank (1941-1948) before serving in a number of political positions. In 1951, Hammarskjold was appointed Vice Chairman of the Swedish delegation to the United Nations. Within two years he was elected by an overwhelming 57-3 vote as UN Secretary-General. During his eight-year term, Hammarskjold presided over a number of historical events, including the 1956 Suez Crisis and the Congo conflict of the early 1960's. In mid-September of 1961, Hammarskjold was flying to negotiate a cease-fire when his DC-6 plane crashed. Three inquiries failed to identify the cause of the crash leading to much speculation that he was assassinated. Dag Hammarskjold is the only UN Secretary-General to be awarded a posthumous Nobel Peace Prize.

Dag Hammarskjold was 56.

September 6th

You can conquer almost any fear if you will only make up your mind to do so. For remember, fear doesn't exist anywhere except in the mind.

Dale Carnegie
Writer and Lecturer
(1888 - 1955)

Dale Carnegie, born Dale Breckinridge Carnagey to a poor Missouri farmer, grew up to exercise the greatest impact on personal self-improvement, salesmanship, public speaking and the world of corporate business during the first half of the 20th century. Young Dale managed to juggle his daily chores on the farm and his education at the Missouri State Teacher's College.

Following graduation, Carnegie launched the beginning of a successful career in sales which earned him national recognition. In 1911, with $500 in savings, he pursued his dream of becoming a lecturer. Within a short period and a slight change to his name, he had launched the Dale Carnegie Course, introduced the Dale Carnegie Training Program for businessmen and had written several self-help books. By 1914, he was earning $500 each week which translates to $10,000 per week in today's currency.

The poor country boy wrote one of the most influential books, *How to Win Friends and Influence People* (1936), which had sold over 5 million copies by the time of his death. Dale Carnegie died at 66 from Hodgkin's disease.

September 7th

***Opportunities multiply
as they are seized.***

Sun Tzu
Military Leader
(544 BC - 496 BC)

Sun Tzu, the Chinese military genius, was reportedly born in 544 BC although the precise dates of his birth or death were never recorded. Scholars believe Sun Tzu served as a general during the reign of King Helü of WU who was reportedly born in 514 BC. What is clear is that Sun Tzu had a great influence on Asian history and culture.

Over the past centuries historians have debated many aspects of Sun Tzu, including his existence as a real historical figure. Modern scholars have accepted his existence and recognize his importance in Asian history as a military general and strategist. Sun Tzu is considered the likely author of *The Art of War*, one of the most widely read books on military strategy and philosophy. *The Art of War* covered a wide rage of subjects beyond war philosophy, including the value of diplomacy.

Sun Tzu and his writings have influenced many military and political leaders over the centuries, including Napoleon Bonaparte in his march across Europe. General Colin Powell studied *The Art of War* in preparation for the Persian Gulf War in the 1990's.

Tradition suggests that Sun Tzu died in his late 40's.

September 8th

*It's fine to celebrate success
but it is more important
to heed the lessons of failure.*

Bill Gates
Entrepreneur and Philanthropist
(b. 1955)

    Bill Gates, ranked among the top richest men in the world over a number of years in the early part of the 21st century, was born William Henry Gates III in Seattle, Washington. His father, Williams H. Gates II, was a successful Seattle-based lawyer and his mother, Mary, served on the Board of Directors of the First Interstate Bank.

    Gates' parents encouraged a law career which led Bill to enroll at Harvard in 1973. Within a few years, Gates (21) and a high school friend named Paul Allen registered Microsoft. By 1980, the fledgling company became a major software program supplier to IBM. Microsoft began developing and licensing operating software to the growing industry hardware vendors. The company then created and launched Microsoft Windows in mid-1985 when Gates and Allen were barely 30. The Microsoft success made Gates a billionaire before he turned 32 (1987). He has repeatedly placed among the list of wealthiest men in the world since the early 1990's.

    The Bill and Melinda Gates Foundation has been Gates' focus since relinquishing day-to-day involvement in mid-2008. The Gates have committed to giving the large percentage of their estimated 60-plus billion to charity in their lifetime.

September 9th

Behind every great fortune there is a crime.

Honoré de Balzac
Writer
(1799 - 1850)

Honoré de Balzac was born in Tours, France. His father, Bernard-François Balssa, one of eleven children, grew up in an extremely poor area in the south of France. Balssa, determined to elevate himself into France's nobility, changed his family name and added, without permission, the "de" prefix. To further secure his position, Balssa (51) married the 18-year-daughter of a wealthy merchant and they had four children.

Young Honoré and his siblings were sent away as infants to spend almost five years with a wet-nurse. At eight, Honoré began a seven-year stay at a grammar school. He struggled with loneliness and a dislike of his surroundings to the point of a suicide attempt in his teens. The absence of family bond is visible in many of his literary works. During his 20's and early 30's, Balzac unsuccessfully attempted to launch several business ventures all the while mass producing nine novels which were frequently banned. In 1832, Balzac (33) developed the concept of writing about all aspects of French society under one umbrella title – *La Comédie Humaine* (*The Human Comedy*). Countless novels were penned under *La Comédie Française,* including *Eugénie Grandet,* His literary output influenced many writers, including Charles Dickens, Edgar Allan Poe and William Faulkner.

In his mid-30's, Balzac began a 15-year correspondence relationship with the married Ewelina Hanska. Sadly, Balzac (51) died five months after marrying Ewelina. Victor Hugo delivered a touching eulogy at the funeral service.

September 10th

Happiness doesn't come from doing what we like to do but from liking what we have to do.

Wilferd A. Peterson
Writer
(1900 - 1995)

Wilferd A. Peterson was born Wilferd Arlan Peterson in Whitehall, Michigan at the turn of the 20th century. He served as Vice-President and creative director for a Grand Rapids, Michigan, advertising company for several decades. Peterson always claimed that his greatest inspiration came from his devoted wife of 58 years, Ruth, who died in her early 80's in 1979.

Peterson established himself as a well-respected writer by contributing inspirational essays for the popular magazine supplement called This Week which reached a readership of well over 13 million. His loyal readers led to his first book in 1949 – *The Art of Getting Along*. For over a quarter century, Peterson wrote a popular column for the Science of Mind nationally distributed magazine. His inspirational essays were frequently quoted and used by the Hallmark Greeting Card Company. His poem, *The Art of Marriage*, is considered the most recited words in marriage ceremonies, including Joanne Woodward and Paul Newman's wedding.

Wilferd A. Peterson lived a very productive life and died at the age of 95.

September 11th

It is folly for a man to pray to the gods for that which he has the power to obtain for himself.

Epicurus
Philosopher
(341 BC - 270 BC)

Epicurus established a philosophy centuries ago which has influenced thinkers throughout the ages into the 21st century. The school of Epicureanism based its philosophy on the principle that the main goal in life was to achieve happiness through peace and with the aid of life friendships.

Epicurus was born in the Athenian settlement on the Greek island of Samos where his parents had moved to as a young couple. Epicurus studied Plato's philosophy under Pamhilus. At the age of 35, Epicurus founded a school in Athens, opened to women and slaves, called The Garden because his small group of followers would meet on a regular basis in the beautiful garden. Most of the known 300 literary works of Epicurus have been lost and his philosophy survived because of his followers. Epicurus had a direct influence on the approach to science insisting that only complete observation and deduction could lead to pure scientific discoveries.

Epicurus suffered through numerous battles with kidney stones and eventually died a painful death at the age of 72.

September 12th

The most difficult secret for a man to keep is his own opinion of himself.

Marcel Pagnol
Writer and Film Maker
(1895 - 1974)

Marcel Pagnol was born at the end of the 19th century in Aubagne near Marseille, France. His father, Joseph, was a school teacher and young Marcel learned to read at an early age. Augustine, his frail mother, died at the age of 39 when Marcel was in his teen years.

Pagnol studied English literature at the University of Aix-en-Provence prior to WW I. He served in the French infantry for a short period but was eventually discharged because of his own frail health. Pagnol married at 21 and became an English teacher in the south of France for a decade. In his early 30's, he devoted all his time to writing, first as a playwright and then as a successful novelist. In 1931, after viewing his first talking motion picture, he decided to pursue a life as a filmmaker. Over the years, he produced a number of his own literary works as films.

In 1946, Pagnol (51), by then an established writer and filmmaker, was elected to the prestigious Académie française. He was the first filmmaker to be granted the honor. Marcel Pagnol died in 1974 in Paris. He was 79.

September 13th

A consensus means that everyone agrees to say collectively what no one believes individually.

Abba Eban
Politician and Diplomat
(1915 - 2002)

Abba Eban was born Aubrey Soloman Meir Eban in Cape Town, South Africa. The Eban family moved to Great Britain when Aubrey was a youngster. Eban studied the classics at Cambridge. He was very active in the Zionist Youth Movement.

During WWII, Eban served as an intelligence officer with the British Army eventually reaching the rank of a major. In 1947, he became attached to the United Nation's Special Committee on Palestine. During this period, Eban changed his first name to Abba, the Hebrew word for "father" because he had a vision he would be recognized as the father of Israel. Eban served his country well in numerous diplomatic roles, including Ambassador to the United States and Ambassador to the U.N. When he ended his dozen years of association with the U.N., Eban devoted three decades of his life as an active politician in Israel in various key roles in the Israeli parliament.

Eban devoted the last dozen years of his life writing and lecturing. Abba Eban died in his 87th year and was buried near Tel Aviv.

September 14th

Life is the art of drawing without an eraser.

John W. Gardner
Politician
(1912 - 2002)

John W. Gardner was born in Los Angeles at the beginning of the second decade of the 20th century. During WWII Gardner served in the United Sates Marine Corps attaining the rank of Captain by the end of the war.

In his late thirties, Gardner was appointed as president of the Carnegie Foundation and was active in the promotion of the advancement of teaching techniques. Gardner also created the John Gardner Fellowship at Stanford University. President Lyndon Johnson called upon Gardner's expertise to serve as Secretary of Health, Education and Welfare. Under Gardner's leadership the department launched Medicare and created programs to make education more readily available to young people of poor backgrounds. Gardner eventually resigned his government position under Johnson because of his strong anti-Vietnam War stance.

Gardner was awarded the Presidential Medal of Freedom in 1964. John W. Gardner died in California at the age of 89.

September 15th

Trying to squash a rumor is like trying to unring a bell.

Shana Alexander
Journalist
(1925 - 2005)

Shana Alexander, Shana Ager, was born in New York City into a family of intellectuals and artist. Her father, Milton Ager, was a composer of such popular tunes as *Happy Days are Here Again* and her mother, Cecelia, was a newspaper columnist. Young Shana graduated from Vassar College at 20 years of age with a major in anthropology and launched a career in journalism as a copy clerk. She married and divorced twice in her lifetime.

At 26, Alexander joined Life Magazine as a junior researcher earning the sum of $65 per week. She rose quickly through the editorial roles and began to write a regular column, *The Feminine Eye*, during the early 1960's. Her columns often attracted national attention. One magazine column became the 1965 Sidney Poitier and Anne Bancroft drama film entitled *The Slender Thread*. Alexander's career was marked with a number of "firsts" – the first woman staff writer and columnist for Life and the first female editor for McCall's. Her weekly *60 Minutes* debate segments with James Fitzpatrick were satirized by *Saturday Night Live*'s Jane Curtin and Dan Aykroyd.

Shana Alexander succumbed to her battle with cancer in 2005 at the age of 79.

September 16th

*Some days you're a bug,
some days you're a windshield.*

Price Cobb
Race Car Driver
(b. 1954)

Price Cobb has been actively involved on the American car racing scene for several decades.

On June 16th and 17th of 1990, the legendary Cobb (36) joined forces with British driver Martin Brundle (31) and Danish John Nielsen (34) to compete in the 58th Le Mans 24-hour Race in France. The 24-Hour Le Mans Race began in 1923. The day-long race is often referred to as the Grand Prix of Endurance. The racing teams must balance the endurance of their highly-tuned racing vehicles with the skills and endurance of the three individual drivers. The three drivers alternate behind the wheel on the track.

Nissan, Porsche and Jaguar have competed against each other for the prestigious trophy for decades. Porsche has won the race a total of 16 times.

The 1990 24-hour Le Mans Race was won by the Cobb-Brundle-Nielsen team for Jaguar.

The veteran Cobb also owned an Indy Racing League team during the late 1990's. Price Cobb currently resides in Madison, Wisconsin.

September 17th

*When you cease to dream,
you cease to live.*

Malcolm Forbes
Publisher
(1919 - 1990)

Malcolm Forbes, born into a famous American publishing family, enjoyed the lavish lifestyle of a multi-millionaire. Young Malcolm was born in Brooklyn, New York, and attended Princeton University. His father, B. C. Forbes, was the founding publisher of Forbes Magazine.

Following graduation, Forbes served in the United States Army Corps during WWII earning the rank of Staff Sergeant with the infantry. He received the Bronze Star and the Purple Heart. Between 1951 and 1958, Forbes devoted most of his thirties to public service as the Republican Senator for the State of New Jersey. At the age of 38, he left politics and became the guiding force behind Forbes Magazine when his father died. The death of his brother, Bruce Charles, in 1964, left him with full control of the magazine. Forbes became well known in social circles for his lavish lifestyle. He celebrated his 70th birthday by chartering a 747 and flying some 800 guests to Tangier, Morocco, including Elizabeth Taylor, Henry Kissinger and Barbara Walters.

In February, 1990, some six months after his 70th memorable birthday party, Malcolm Forbes died of a heart attack in his New Jersey home.

September 18th

*A journey is a person in itself,
no two are alike.*

John Steinbeck
Writer
(1902 - 1968)

John Steinbeck, considered one of the most important writers of the 20th century, spent many summers of his youth working with migrant workers on ranches in California. The life-changing experiences would prove to be the basis of several of his literary classics.

Steinbeck, originally of German-Irish ancestry, was born in Salinas, California, and received his passion for literature from his teacher-mother, Olive. He spent five years at Stanford University but left before earning a degree. By the age of 27 (1929), Steinbeck wrote his first novel – *Cup of Gold*. A number of books followed before his critically-acclaimed classics were published – *Of Mice and Men* (1937) and *The Grapes of Wrath* (1939). Over a very productive writing career, Steinbeck produced a total of 16 novels, six non-fiction books and five collections of short stories. His works were the basis of countless Hollywood-produced movies starring such greats as Henry Fonda, James Dean (*East of Eden*), Burgess Meredith, Lon Chaney Jr. Gary Sinise and John Malkovich.

Steinbeck was awarded the Pulitzer Prize for Fiction (1940) and the Nobel Prize for Literature in 1962. John Steinbeck died in New York City at 66 of heart failure.

September 19th

No other form of transportation in the rest of my life has ever come up to the bliss of my pram.

Osbert Lancaster
Cartoonist and Writer
(1908 - 1986)

Osbert Lancaster was born in London, England, in an upper-middle class working family. He was destined for a career in law but his drawing skills and his unique humor changed the direction of his life. He decided to study art at the Slade School of Art in London.

Lancaster began his career as a cartoonist at the Architectural Review and, at the age of 28 (1936), published the first of many satirical books called *Progress at Pelvis Bay*. In 1939, 31-year-old Lancaster launched a four-decade career as cartoonist for the Daily Express. During his life he drew over ten thousand humorous cartoons to the pleasure of a wide audience. Lancaster was knighted in 1975 by Queen Elizabeth joining a select group of three cartoonists to have been recognized by the honor.

Osbert Lancaster died at 77 of natural causes in his beloved Chelsea with his second wife, journalist Anne Scott James, by his side.

September 20th

Real difficulties can be overcome; it is only the imaginary ones that are unconquerable.

Theodore N. Vail
Industrialist
(1845 - 1920)

Theodore N. Vail became one of the most powerful and influential industrialists in the establishment of the telephone as a vital means of communications. He served as president of the American Telephone and Telegraph Company for 16 years in the young entity's history. He proved to be invaluable in the company's rapid growth.

Vail was born in the town of Malvern in mid-19th century Ohio. During his twenties he pursued his first love – medicine. But his second passion, the fascination with telegraphy, a new technology developed by his cousin, Alfred Vail, drew him away from medicine. Vail launched his career with the United States Telegraph Company which later changed its corporate name to Western Union. By the age of 31, Vail (1876) was appointed General Superintendent of the Union Pacific Mail service. Within two years he was at the helm of the American Bell Telephone Company created by Alexander Graham Bell's uncle.

Theodore Newton Vail died at the age of 74.

September 21st

My best friend is the one who brings the best out in me.

Henry Ford
Industrialist
(1863 - 1947)

Henry Ford, born and raised in the Detroit area of Michigan, likely has had the single greatest impact on the economic and social aspects of the city and the state. Ford left the employment of the Edison Illumination Company to begin one of the most impressive and successful careers of any American industrialist.

In 1908, the Ford Motor Company introduced the Model T (with the steering wheel on the left) for $825 or over $20,000 in today's currency. The company pioneered two other innovations – the production assembly line and the independent dealership franchise concept. By 1914, almost half of a million cars were produced for a price tag of $360 (approximately $7,000 today). Ford Motors answered the call of the country during the two world conflicts by transforming factories into weapon plants. Henry Ford suffered a number of strokes in 1919 and turned over control of the company to his only child, 26-year-old Edsel. After 23 years at the helm, Edsel succumbed to cancer at 49. Edsel's son, Henry Ford II, assumed the leadership of the family business and is considered to have rescued the company during the difficult post war years.

Henry Ford died of a cerebral hemorrhage at the age of 83.

September 22nd

There is nothing in a caterpillar that tells you it's going to be a butterfly.

Buckminster Fuller
Architect and Inventor
(1895 - 1983)

Buckminster Fuller became a guru of the architectural community during the 20th century. Bucky, to his close friends, revolutionized architectural design by repeatedly challenging the status quo. Fuller gained fame for his geodesic domes which have remained a part of modern day architecture.

Fuller was born Richard Buckminster Fuller in Milton, Massachusetts at the end of the 19th century. In his youth, Fuller was fascinated by design and frequently built his own tools to achieve the end result of a design. Fuller's intellect eventually led him to Harvard University where he was expelled on two different occasions. At 22, Fuller married Anne Hewlett and went into business with his father-in-law. The company failed a few years later leaving Fuller bankrupt and without employment. Fuller gained international recognition during the 1950's after he was awarded the patents for the geodesic dome. He formed Geodesics, Inc. which served as the licensee for the dome. Fuller lectured around the world and was elected a Fellow of the American Academy of Arts and Science in 1968 and was awarded the Presidential Medal of Freedom by President Reagan in 1983.

Buckminster Fuller died of a heart attack a few days before his 88th birthday while visiting his beloved wife of 66 years in the cancer ward. Anne Fuller died hours later.

September 23rd

Always remember that you are absolutely unique. Just like everyone else.

Margaret Mead
Anthropologist
(1901 - 1978)

Margaret Mead became one of the most influential and respected anthropologists of the 20th century. The at-times controversial academic made skilful use of the mass media to advance her research.

Mead was born in Philadelphia, Pennsylvania, during late 1901 but grew up in Doylestown in an intellectual family. Her mother was a sociologist and her father an economics professor. Mead earned a Master's degree (1924) and a PhD (1929) at Columbia University. In her early twenties, Mead travelled to the South Pacific to study attitudes towards sex. In 1928, her findings were published in *Coming of Age in Samoa* and were greeted with the predicted shock and criticism.

Mead taught anthropology at both Columbia University (1954-78) and Fordham University. The trice-married Mead was made a member of the Academy of arts and Science (1948) and awarded the Presidential Medal of Freedom by President Carter in 1979. Margaret Mead died of pancreatic cancer a month before her 77th birthday.

September 24th

People who say it cannot be done should not interrupt those who are doing it.

George Bernard Shaw
Playwright
(1856 - 1950)

George Bernard Shaw, the Irish-born son of a lower-middle class couple, transported himself to London, England, at the age of twenty and became one of the most important writers of the English language. At an early stage in his career he turned his attention from the profitable task of a literary critic. Over a period of six decades, Shaw gave the world sixty-three plays plus an impressive output of novels, essays and private correspondence – more than a quarter million letters.

Shaw's plays began to be performed at the end of the 19th century and continue to be produced more than a hundred years later. His writings championed the plight of the working class. Shaw joined the pro-socialism movement called the Fabian Society and delivered emotional speeches for the rights of men and women.

Shaw's influence as a writer is felt to this day in all parts of the world. The Shaw Festival in a charming Canadian town called Niagara-on-the-lake in the province of Ontario debuted with two plays and grew to a celebration of Shaw with some 800 performances each summer.

George Bernard Shaw enjoyed a relatively healthy life and died at 94.

September 25th

The doors of wisdom are never shut
Benjamin Franklin
Politician and Scientist
(1706 - 1790)

Benjamin Franklin earned the unofficial title of "The First American" because of his unrelenting struggle for independence from Great Britain. After a lifetime of championing an independent statehood, Franklin (70) became one of the most influential Founding Fathers of America.

Franklin was born the tenth son in a working class family in Boston, Massachusetts, at the turn of the 18th century. His father, Josiah, a candle maker and his mother, Abiah, fled the religious oppressions of England's King Charles I. Benjamin's father planned for his son to enter the clergy but the family ran out of funds. Young Benjamin had the benefit of only a few years of schooling before being forced into the workforce at 12. By 22, he had launched the influential newspaper, The Pennsylvania Gazette. Franklin held various political offices during his life, including 1st U.S Postmaster General (1775), Ambassador to France (1778) and Ambassador to Sweden (1782) and Governor of Pennsylvania between 1785 and 1788. Franklin also gained international renown as the inventor of the lighting rod, the Franklin stove, the bifocals and the odometer.

Benjamin Franklin died at 84.

September 26th

Generosity is giving more than you can. Pride is taking less than you need.

Khalil Gibran
Poet and Artist
(1883 - 1931)

Khalil Gibran, often spelt as "Kahlil", emigrated from his native Lebanon to little Lebanon in Boston's south district with his mother and his three siblings at the age of 12. Gibran's gambling-addicted father had been imprisoned for embezzlement by Lebanese authorities. With little formal education prior to arriving in North America, Gibran grew up to become the world's third best-selling poet next to Shakespeare and Lao-Tzu.

Gibran was born in poverty in Bsharri, part of the Ottoman Syria, which is modern-day Lebanon. Gibran's first literary endeavors were written in Arabic. In 1918, Gibran (35) wrote his first critical success in the form of a collection of poems published under the title – *The Madman*. The majority of his writing from 1918 on was in English. Gibran's primary theme was Christianity and centered on spiritual love with influences from numerous theologians. In 1923, Gibran (40) published his best known work which was 26 poetic essays in *The Prophet*. The collection found renewed popularity in the 1960's with the New Age movement and has never been out of print since the 1920's.

Khalil Gibran died of tuberculosis a few months following his 48th birthday.

September 27th

The pen that writes your life story must be held in your own hand.

Irene C. Kassorla
Psychologist
(b. 1943)

Irene C. Kassorla established herself as an internationally renowned psychologist with a respected specialty in education.

Kassorla earned a Master's degree from the University of California Los Angeles's Department of Educational Psychology in 1965. She was awarded a PhD from the University of London's Institute of Psychology three years later. Kassorla captured the attention of the international media with her extensive research with schizophrenia. The research led to countless lecture tours and television and radio interviews. She has authored three international best selling books, including the popular marriage guide – *Putting it All Together*.

Dr. Kassorla resides in Los Angeles with her husband and two daughters.

September 28th

*If I had to live my life over again
I'd make the same mistakes,
only sooner.*

Tallulah Bankhead
Actress
(1902 - 1968)

Tallulah Bankhead, one of the most remarkable actresses of the screen and stage, was born in a political family in Huntsville, Alabama. She was a devout Democrat and two of her relatives served in Alabama's state senate and her father was the Speaker of the House of Representatives.

Tallulah, named after her paternal grandmother, proved to be a overly-active child and was sent to a Catholic convent by her non-Catholic parents. At 15, Bankhead won a beauty contest which led to her pursuing an acting career in New York City. Within the year she made her acting debut and promptly established herself as a serious stage actress in London. Bankhead returned to the U.S. to star in such films as George Cukor's *Tarnished Lady* (1931) and *Devil and the Deep* (1932) with Gary Cooper, Charles Laughton and Cary Grant. She continued to woo audiences with her stage, film and television appearances well into the 1960's.

Bankhead took pride in her well-earned naughty reputation. Over the decades she was linked romantically with both male and female celebrities. Tallulah Bankhead died in New York City of double pneumonia at the age of 66.

September 29th

***In any contest between
power and patience,
bet on patience.***

W.B. Prescott
Union Leader
(1862 - 1916)

W.B. Prescott was born in Toronto, Canada, in the mid-19th century. Prescott earned an international reputation as a progressive union leader and a tireless advocate of fair practices in the workplace throughout North America.

The International Typographical Union was formed in 1852 to protect members of the growing industry. The printing industry had become an important part of North America's economy and the backbone of the ever-expanding newspaper business. In 1897, under the mature leadership of a young 35-year-old Prescott, the union championed ground-breaking working conditions, including a 48-hour week work week and a standard wage scale. The union later paved the way to the internationally accepted 40-hour week which spread to other unions and industries.

W.B. Prescott died in his home of apoplexy likely resulting from a cerebral haemorrhage at the age of 54.

September 30th

***My life has been filled
with terrible misfortunes;
most of which never happened.***

Montaigne
Writer and Politician
(1533 - 1592)

Montaigne's (Michel Eyquem de Montaigne) family established an extremely successful herring business under the leadership of young Michel's great-grandfather, Lord Ramon Felipe Eyquem. Michel's father, Pierre Eyquem, Lord de Montaigne, became mayor of Bordeaux. The young Michel was sent to live with a peasant family where he spent the first three years of his life away from his family. His first language was dictated by his father to be Latin at all times.

At the age of 24, Montaigne launched a career in law and became a counsellor of the court in Bordeaux. The loss of a dear friend, the poet Etienne de la Boétie, encouraged Montaigne to dedicate his life to writing his masterpiece – *Essais*. Montaigne was pressured into a marriage he did not favour. The reluctant couple had six daughters but only the second child reached adulthood. Montaigne shared his life between public service as a notable statesman and his writing. Montaigne became one of the most influential writers of the French Renaissance.

Having enjoyed excellent health most of his life, Michel de Montaigne died at 59 from complications of tonsillitis.

"It's raining cats and dogs."

The class structure in medieval times dictated style, size and comfort of the family home. The noble of Europe lived in castles or, at least, castle-like dwellings. There are numerous examples of these original castles throughout Europe since they were constructed out of stone. The walled-in castles were usually surrounded by villages built on taxable land owned by the resident of the castle.

Outside the castle walls life was dramatically different. A typical medieval cottage consisted of two smallish rooms – a kitchen including a large hearth primarily for preparing meals and a second room which served as sleeping quarters for all the occupants. The average cottage had no chimney or windows resulting in rather dark and smoky interiors. Whatever the shape or size of a cottage most roofs were made of thatch – layers of dried straw or heather allowing the rain water to flow off the roof.

Animals, domestic or farm, were forbidden from sharing the interior space of the family cottage. On cool evenings animals were left to their own devices to seek out warmth from wherever they could find it. The animals soon found the great amount of heat seeping through the thatched roof and would spend the cold, damp nights sleeping on the roof. When rained poured down on the village, the roof tops became slippery and sometimes the animals would slide off the roof.

Hence the saying - "*It's raining cats and dogs.*"

October 1st

Money is a singular thing.
It ranks with love
as man's greatest source of joy
and with death
as his greatest anxiety.

John Kenneth Galbraith
Economist and Politician
(1908 - 2006)

John Kenneth Galbraith was born in a small farming community in Ontario, Canada, called Iona Station. Young Galbraith's early years were spent in a one-room school and in nearby Dutton High School. His father, Archibald, was a working farmer and his mother, Sarah, became a political activist. Both his parents were strong advocates of the Canadian United Farmers movement in the 1920's.

The 6'8" Galbraith earned a Bachelor of Science in Agricultural Economics in 1931 in Canada and a PhD in the same discipline from the University of California three years later. During the late 1930's he became a U.S. citizen. Over the decades he taught economics at Harvard and Princeton. The prolific writer of four dozen books and countless articles evolved into the most influential economist of the 20th century. Galbraith served in various capacities under four presidents – Franklin Roosevelt, Harry S. Truman, John F. Kennedy and Lyndon Johnson.

Galbraith was awarded the Order of Canada in 1997 and President Clinton presented him with the Presidential Medal of Freedom in 2000. John Kenneth Galbraith died at the age of 97.

October 2nd

Life is not a matter of holding good cards, but sometimes, playing a poor hand well.

Jack London
Writer and Journalist
(1876 - 1916)

Jack London lived a short but exceptionally productive life to become one of the world's first financially successful fiction writers. London was born in San Francisco in a home which was later destroyed in the great fires following the earthquake which leveled much of the city in 1906.

Young London was, for the most part, self-educated. By the age of 10, he had devoured a novel written in 1875 by Ovida (the pseudonym of English novelist Maria Louise Ramé). The 1875 Ovida novel, *Signa*, greatly influenced London's later writing style. Following a short first marriage (Elizabeth Madden), London met and married his life's soul mate, Charmian Kittredge. The two were seldom, if ever, apart. They traveled the world together and shared their beloved ranch in Sonoma, California. London was fascinated with the written word, both as an avid reader and as a writer. The author of such classics as *Call of the Wild* (1903), *The Sea Wolf* (1904) and *White Fang* (1906), owned a personal library consisting of well over 15,000 titles.

Jack London quietly died at his ranch in Sonoma, California at the early age of 40.

October 3rd

***If you wish to travel far and fast,
travel light.
Take off all of your envies,
jealousies, unforgiveness,
selfishness and fear.***

Cesare Pavese
Writer and Poet
(1908 - 1950)

Cesare Pavese managed to make his mark in Italian literature of the 20th century despite a short life. Pavese is considered by scholars to be one of the major Italian novelists in the first half of the century.

Pavese was born in San Stefano in the northern part of Italy. Most of his schooling took place in the city of Turin. During the early years of his education, Pavese was drawn to English literature and actually based his thesis on the works of American poet Walt Whitman. His other obsession proved to be more dramatic. The young atheist became an active member of the growing fascist movement in Italy of the 1930's. He spent several months in prison and was eventually exiled to the south of Italy.

Disillusioned by politics and a failed romantic relationship, Cesare Pavese committed suicide by duplicating the death scene in one of his own novellas. He was only 41.

October 4th

The winds of grace are always blowing, but it is you who must raise your sails.

Rabindranath Tagore
Poet
(1861 - 1941)

Rabindranath Tagore was born the youngest of thirteen children in a wealthy and influential family in impoverished Calcutta, in an area now called West Bengal. His paternal grandfather was considered a prince by European royalty. Tagore's father was responsible for the flourishing of the philosophies of Raja Ram Mohan Roy, an educational and religious reformer from India.

Rabi, as he was affectionately called, grew up in a family of intellectual and creative people but his care was mostly in the hands of the family servants. His education was the responsibility of his older brother, Hemendranath. Tagore was exposed at an early age to Indian and Western art and literature. By 16, Tagore was responsible for some impressive writing originally believed by all to be the long-lost works of a great writer. During his long creative life he authored and translated a large volume of writings. In 1913, Tagore (54) was honored with the Nobel Prize in Literature.

Rabi's international reputation introduced him to a variety of people – from Albert Einstein to Robert Frost, from William Butler Yeats to Mussolini. Rabindranauth Tagore died at 80 in the Tagore ancestral home.

October 5th

I saw the angel in the marble and carved until I set him free.
Michelangelo
Sculptor, Painter and Architect
(1475 - 1564)

Michelangelo (Michelangelo di Lodovico Buonarroti Simoni) was born in Caprese near modern-day Tuscany. Michelangelo's Buonarroti ancestors established themselves as successful bankers in Florence over a number of generations. At the age of six, Michelangelo's father set his young son on a course which would change the face of art worldwide. Young Michelangelo apprenticed as a stonecutter. Later his father added to his son's education by placing the 13-year-old with a master painter.

In 1496, Michelangelo (21) settled in Rome. Within a year the young sculptor was commissioned to produce one of his most famous works – *The Pieta*. Over the following six-plus decades, the man often referred to as "the" Renaissance man, gave the world the long-lasting gifts of his genius – *The Statue of David* (1504), the over 300 biblical figures on the ceiling of the *Sistine Chapel* (1508-1512) and *The Last Judgment* (1534-1541).

Michelangelo lived a simple life often withdrawing himself from all social contact. Michelangelo, considered by modern scholars to be the greatest artist in history, died before the completion of his great design – St. Peter's Basilica in Rome. He was 88.

October 6th

Sanity is a madness put to good uses.
George Santayana
Writer and Philosopher
(1863 - 1952)

George Santayana, born Jorge Agustin Nicolas Ruiz de Santayana y Borras, grew up in the Spanish town of Avila. Young Jorge was the only child of his widowed mother's second marriage. The family eventually settled in Boston, Massachusetts, but Jorge's father returned to Spain with no father-son contact until he entered Harvard.

By his mid-twenties, Santayana had returned to the Harvard campus as a professor of philosophy listing an impressive number of students, including Walter Lippman, T. S. Eliot, Gertrude Stein and Robert Frost. As Santayana reached his 50's after some thirty years teaching, he decided to devote all his time to writing. During his writing period he wrote on a variety of topics. Santayana's 1905 five-volume, *The Life of Reason*, influenced a generation and his 1935 novel, *Last Puritan*, gave him financial independence.

The life-long bachelor-agnostic, who described himself as an aesthetic Catholic, spent the last years of his life as a resident-patient of the convent of the Blue Nuns of Mary in Rome. George Santayana died at 88.

October 7th

Bachelors know more about women than married men; if they didn't they'd be married too.

> H. L. Mencken
> Journalist
> (1880 - 1956)

H. L. Mencken (Henry Louis) was born in Baltimore to a cigar factory owner (August Mencken Sr.) and lived most of his years in the same house. The avid reader was so influenced at nine by Mark Twain's *The Adventures of Huckleberry Finn* that he dreamt of becoming a writer.

In 1899, Mencken fulfilled his boyhood dream and launched a lifelong writing career which would span seven decades. At 19, he joined the reporting staff of the Baltimore Morning Herald. Six years later, Mencken began writing editorials and a nationally syndicated column for the Baltimore Sun which would be his home for 43 years. Mencken also established himself as a serious novelist and short story writer. His circle of literary friends included F. Scott Fitzgerald, Sinclair Lewis and Alistair Cooke. Mencken was greatly influenced by the writings of the German-born philosopher, Friedrich Nietzsche, which led him to be critical of all organized religions.

Known as the Sage of Baltimore, Mencken (50) married Sara Haardt, an English professor eighteen years younger. Sara died within five years of their marriage following a short battle with tuberculosis. Twenty years later, H. L. Mencken quietly died in his sleep following a stroke. He was 75.

October 8th

Courage is what it takes to stand up and speak; courage is also what it takes to sit down and listen.

Sir Winston Churchill
Statesman
(1874 - 1965)

Sir Winston Churchill, one of the greatest and most respected wartime leaders, began life as a rebellious student with a speech impediment. Somewhat isolated from his parents, Sir Randolph, a politician from the Spencer aristocratic family, and his American-born socialite mother, Jennie, young Winston turned to his nanny, Elizabeth, for affection and comfort.

Churchill graduated from the Royal Military College in Sandhurst and enlisted in the Queen's Own Hussars as a Second Lieutenant. He distinguished himself during the second Boer War and WWI. The heavily-decorated young Churchill also served as a war correspondent for various British newspapers. He faced front-line combat in British India in 1897. After 34 years as a Member of Parliament Churchill was thrust into the role of wartime Prime Minister during the first months of WWII. Churchill skillfully led his country through the Hitler years all the while facing his share of domestic controversy, including his stance on India and his opposition to the abdication of Edward VIII.

In 1963, President John F. Kennedy named Churchill an honorary citizen of the United States. Sir Churchill died of a stroke at the age of 90.

October 9th

The most important thing to remember is this: to be ready at any moment to give up what you are for what you might become.

W. E. B. Du Bois
Sociologist and Writer
(1868 - 1963)

W. E. B. Du Bois (William Edward Burghardt) was born in Great Barrington, Massachusetts, where he experienced little racism as a child. His mother, Mary (formerly Burghart) Du Bois, came from a Dutch-English-African family of former slaves who had gained their freedom in the late 1700's. William's father, Alfred Du Bois, abandoned the family when his son was two, leaving the young Mary as the sole supporter and parent.

Young William proved to be an excellent student and attended Fisk University in Nashville, Tennessee where he would experience racism for the first time. Du Bois studied at Harvard (Bachelor of History – cum laude) and in 1895, he was the first African American to be awarded a PhD from Harvard. Du Bois became an important intellect within the American black community. In 1909, he was one of the founders of the NAACP (National Association for the Advancement of Colored People). Du Bois championed full civil rights and political representation for all colored people, including Africans and Asians.

Du Bois, along with Booker T. Washington, became an important spokesman for the black community. W.E.B. Du Bois died at the advanced age of 95, one year after the U.S. Civil Rights Act became law.

October 10th

Greatness, generally speaking, is an unusual quantity of a usual quality grafted upon a common man.

William Allen White
Newspaper Editor and Writer
(1868 - 1944)

William Allen White was affectionately known as the 'Sage of Emporia', which is nestled between Topeka and Wichita in the middle of Kansas. During his five-decade newspaper career, the small-town gentleman commanded a national reputation as the editor of the Emporia Gazette. The newspaper was widely perceived as a model of excellence in small-town journalism.

White was born in Emporia but spent most of his childhood in neighboring El Dorado, Kansas. Graduation from the University of Kansas (1892) led to an editorial writer position with the Kansas City Star. Within a few short years, White (27) bought the Emporia Gazette which, after more than a century, remains in the White family with White's great-grandson, Christopher, at the helm. During his day White's pen was feared by opponents and presidents called upon him for his mid-America wisdom. His life-long association with U.S. presidents began with a friendship with President Teddy Roosevelt in the 1890's.

The much-traveled White published twenty-two literary works during his lifetime, including short story collections. William Allen White died in his beloved Emporia at the age of 75.

October 11th

The person who writes for fools is always sure of a large audience.

Arthur Schopenhauer
Philosopher
(1788 - 1860)

Arthur Schopenhauer, a descendant of German wealth from both his parent's families, developed a strong philosophical voice during the first half of the 19th century. His father, Heinrich Schopenhauer, is believed to have taken his life when young Arthur reached his mid-teens. Johanna, his mother, a writer in her own right, moved the family to Weimar, the creative capital of Germany of the day.

At the age of 25 while still a university student, Schopenhauer wrote a dissertation which was published as his first book – *On the Fourfold Root of the Principle of Sufficient Reason*. Five years later he released his most influential work under the title *The World as Will and Representation*. Schopenhauer's analysis of human psychology and the importance of human love would exercise great influence on Sigmund Freud. Schopenhauer was also one of the first modern philosophers to deal with homosexuality.

Schopenhauer, who was devoted to various pets during his lifetime, championed the birth of the Society for the Prevention of Cruelty to Animals. He was a healthy man until the last year of his life.

Arthur Schopenhauer died of heart failure in Frankfurt at the age of 72.

October 12th

*Happiness is a butterfly,
which when pursued,
is always just beyond your grasp,
but which, if you will sit down quietly,
may alight upon you.*

Nathaniel Hawthorne
Writer
(1804 - 1864)

Nathaniel Hawthorne's great-grandfather was one of the judges to preside over the Salem Witch Trials in Massachusetts in 1692 and who later in his life repented for his involvement. Perhaps for that reason, young Nathaniel added the "w" to his last name. His sea captain-father died of yellow fever when Nathaniel was four.

The withdrawn Nathaniel was born in Salem and attended Bowdoin College where he met Henry Wadsworth Longfellow (*Evangeline*), Horatio Bridge and future 14th U.S. president Franklin Pierce. Hawthorne actively participated in Pierce's campaign and was appointed U.S. Consul in Liverpool, England.

Hawthorne published his first novel, *Fanshawe*, at 24. His writing career was interrupted during his 30's while he earned a living in various official positions in Massachusetts. In 1850, he resumed his literary career and produced his most famous novel - *The Scarlet Letter* – followed by *The House of the Seven Gables* (1851), *The Blithedale Romance* (1852) and *The Marble Faun* (1860).

The shy Nathaniel Hawthorne died in Plymouth, New Hampshire, while on a trip with his friend, Franklin Pierce.

October 13th

One hundred percent of the shots you don't take don't go in.

Wayne Gretzky
Professional Hockey Player
(b. 1961)

Wayne Gretzky (Wayne Douglas) has been labeled by sportscasters and fellow players as "the greatest hockey player" to ever play the game. Wayne was born in Brantford, Ontario, Canada, the first of five children of Walter and Phyllis Gretzky. Wayne's ancestry is a combination of English (his mother) and Polish-Ukrainian-Belarusian on his father's side. Wayne learned the basics of hockey from his father on the backyard rink.

Gretzky proved to be an exceptional player in his pre-teen years earning over 500 points in one season. By 14, he was making a name for himself in Junior B hockey. At 18, Gretzky turned professional with a 3 million dollar contract in the newly-formed World Hockey Association joining the National Hockey League a year later. During a 20-year career, Gretzky established a long list of records many of which stand to this day. Along the way, Gretzky contributed to his team winning four Stanley Cups.

Wayne and actress Janet Jones had a fairy-tale wedding in 1988. The couple lives in California and has five children. The Hockey Hall of Famer (1999) served as Executive Director of the Gold Medal winning men's hockey team at the 2002 Winter Olympic Game in Salt Lake City.

October 14th

***It is a wise father
who knows his own child.***

William Shakespeare
Playwright and Poet
(1564 - 1616)

William Shakespeare's date of baptism was recorded as April 26th, 1564, but his precise birth date remains unknown. What is known is Shakespeare's birth place – Stratford-upon-Avon. Records suggest that his parents practiced Catholicism at a time when the practice was forbidden. Shakespeare's private life and his physical appearance were not recorded so much has been left to speculation over the centuries.

At approximately the age of 18, Shakespeare married Ann Hathaway who was eight years his senior. Church records suggest the marriage may have been rushed since the couple became parents to a daughter named Susanna six months following the wedding ceremony. Twins (son Hamnet and daughter Judith) were born two years later. Shakespeare set up his writing career out of London sometime during the late 1580's. He shared his time between London and Stratford-upon-Avon. Scholars continue to debate whether Shakespeare actually authored all 38 plays attributed to him. But no concrete proof suggests differently. The above quote was borrowed from Shakespeare's *The Merchant of Venice* (Act II Scene II) as spoken by Launcelot Gobbo, Shylock's servant.

William Shakespeare died at the early age of 52 in Stratford-upon-Avon survived by his wife, Ann, and two daughters, Susana and Judith.

October 15th

Guard well within yourself that treasure, kindness. Know how to give without hesitation, how to lose without regret, how to acquire without meanness.

George Sand
Writer
(1804 - 1876)

George Sand, born in Paris as Armantine Lucile Dupin in a well-established French family, became a successful 19th century novelist. The Dupin family could trace its ancestral lineage to Augustine II, the King of Poland, and to French royalty. Sand's mother, Sophie, was a commoner and young Armantine was raised by her grandmother at her estate in Berry.

At the age of 19, Sand married the Baron Casimir Dudevant. Two children were born before Sand (27) left her husband eleven years into the marriage. Sand began a life of rebellion engaging in numerous romantic liaisons with various high-profile French society gentlemen, including the great Romantic period composer, Frédéric Chopin. During a brief relationship with Jules Sandeau, Sand discovered her writing talent. In 1832, she published her first solo novel (*Indiana*) under the George Sand pen name. Sand was a very independent woman creating her own style by wearing men's clothing, smoking and practicing her liberal approach to intimate relationships, including with French actress, Maris Dorval.

George Sand died at 71.

October 16th

If you carry your childhood with you, you never become older.

Abraham Sutzkever
Poet
(1913 - 2010)

Abraham Sutzkever (Avrom Sutskever) was born in Smorgon, Russia, which is present-day Belarus. His young life was shaped greatly by the two world wars. When young Avrom was a child his family was forced to flee the German invasion into Siberia. Three years after the war he and his father's death, the family settled in Vilna.

One day before the start of WWII Abraham (26) married a young lady named Freydke. Within twenty-four months Sutzkever, his wife and newborn son as well as his mother were sent to a German camp. His son and his mother were murdered by the Nazis. Sutzkever and Freydke managed to escape and he spent the rest of th war as a member of the underground resistance movement. He eventually settled in Tel Aviv.

Sutzkever pursued his childhood passion for poetry. In pre-war 1939 Russia, he published his first volume of Yiddish poetry – *Lider* (*Songs*). From the end of WWII to his death, Sutzkever established himself as "the greatest poet of the Holocaust".

Abraham Sutzkever enjoyed a long and productive life. He died in Tel Aviv at the age of 96.

October 17th

Alcohol gives you infinite patience for stupidity.

Sammy Davis Jr.
Entertainer
(1925 - 1990)

Sammy Davis Jr. was born into a show business family. His father (Sammy Davis Sr.) and his Cuban mother (Elvera Sanchez) were both vaudeville dancers. Young Sammy was raised by his paternal grandmother during the early years. At the age of 3, he became part of the Will Mastin Trio headed by his uncle Will.

During WWII, Davis came face to face with racism for the first time in his short life. He soon discovered his on-stage talents as a member of an entertainment unit deflected 'some' of the problem. At 29, Davis lost his left eye in a car accident. In the mid-1950's, Davis starred on Broadway in *Mr. Wonderful*. His first adult movie role was in the Rat Pack film *Ocean's Eleven* (1960) starring Frank Sinatra, Dean Martin, Joey Bishop and Peter Lawford.

Davis enjoyed a successful recording career with such hits as *I've Gotta Be Me, In The Ghetto* and the memorable *Candy Man*. The versatile performer also developed an uncanny ability to deliver perfect impressions of many of the days celebrities. His many skills made him a popular star in Las Vegas for decades.

Sammy Davis Jr. died at 64 of throat cancer in Beverly Hills.

October 18th

Faith is a sounder guide than reason. Reason can go only so far, but faith has no limits.

Blaise Pascal
Philosopher and Mathematician
(1623 - 1662)

Blaise Pascal, born in Clermont-Ferrand, France, was home schooled by his father, Etienne Pascal, a commissioner of taxes on behalf of the King of France. Young Blaise developed a profound interest in mathematics and the sciences. Pascal, in his short life, exercised a great influence on the worlds of mathematics and science. He is considered to be one of the most important writer-philosophers of the French Classical period.

At the age of 19, Pascal invented the prototype of the first mechanical calculator with a desire to help his father with the endless tabulations of collected and owed taxes. His scientific inventions included the hydraulic press, the syringe and extensive research in what is known in modern times as the barometer. Pascal the philosopher is considered one of the major theological thinkers of his century with the publishing of *Pensées* (*Thoughts*). *Pensées,* released seven years after his death, is considered to be among the finest writing in the French language.

Blaise Pascal, plagued by illness since his late teens, died at 39 of stomach cancer.

October 19th

The only thing to do with good advice is to pass it on. It is never of any use to oneself.

Oscar Wilde
Writer, Playwright and Poet
(1854 - 1900)

Oscar Wilde grew up in a rather idyllic family setting in mid-19th century Dublin. His father, Sir William, was knighted in 1864 for his exceptional medical service to the poor communities of Dublin. The Wilde household reflected Lady Wilde's love of art and literature. Young Wilde was educated at home studying languages with a French and German tutor.

Wilde attended Trinity College in Dublin where he shared a room with his older brother, William. While on campus, Wilde began to develop the "Wilde legend". He grew his hair unfashionably long and developed a flair for colorful clothing which attracted other issues. He was attacked by four students but he managed to fight off all four convincingly. Following university Wilde returned to his home to discover that love of his life and childhood friend, Florence Balcombe, had married another gentleman.

Wilde's lifestyle eventually led him to serious conflict with the legal authorities which resulted with a two-year confinement in prison. By the time of his release his health had deteriorated. Oscar Wilde died of cerebral meningitis at 46.

October 20th

One can never speak enough of the virtues, the dangers, the powers of shared laughter.

Françoise Sagan
Writer
(1935 - 2004)

Françoise Sagan, born Françoise "Kiki" Quoirez, wrote her most famous and most critically acclaimed novel at the tender age of 19. *Bonjour Tristesse* (*Hello Sadness*) was published in 1954 and immediately gained Sagan international success. The story of her 17-year-old character, Cécile, captured the imagination of a generation.

Sagan was born in Cajarc, France, in a bourgeois family. Her father served as a company director and her mother came from wealthy landowners. Sagan adopted her pen name from one of the characters (la Princesse de Sagan) from Marcel Proust's *In Search of Lost Time*. Sagan proudly lived an extravagant lifestyle and was referred to as "a charming little monster" by writer François Mauriac. Sagan had two short-lived marriages and a life-long relationship with fashion designer, Peggy Roche.

Sagan battled drug and alcohol addictions several times during her life. Her health deteriorated in early 2000. Françoise Sagan died of pulmonary embolism a few months following her 69th birthday.

October 21st

Friendship is an art, and very few persons are born with a natural gift for it.

Kathleen Norris
Writer
(1880 - 1966)

Kathleen Norris (Kathleen Thompson), the highest paid writer of her time, was born in San Francisco during the last decades of the 19th century. Norris was educated at the University of California.

At 29, Norris married writer Charles Norris, brother of novelist Frank Norris. Within a few years Kathleen Norris was producing a large collection of short-stories for major magazines. In 1911, Norris published her first book. The critically-acclaimed *Mother* propelled her into the limelight. Even President Theodore Roosevelt became a fan. A series of popular novels followed – *The Child* (1914), *Heart of Rachel* (1916) and *Martie The Unconquered* (1917). Her 1922 *Certain People of Importance* transformed Norris into a champion of causes, including abolition of capital punishment, anti-nuclear disarmament and women's rights. A number of her works became movies, including 1927's *My Best Girl* with Mary Pickford.

Norris enjoyed a long and productive creative life. Kathleen Norris died at 86.

October 22nd

No duty is more urgent than that of returning thanks.

Saint Ambrose
Religious Leader
(339 - 397)

Saint Ambrose's journey to the important position of Bishop of Milan during the 4th century was as extraordinary a journey as Saint Ambrose was an extraordinary man. Aurelius Ambrosius, born in a Christian family in Trier, Germany, was catapulted in the role as one of the most influential clerics of the century.

Saint Ambrose, raised in a household of intellects, studied law in preparation for a life as a public servant. He rose to the highly respected role as Governor General of Aemilia-Liguria in northern Italy. Then in the year 374 his life changed as the result of a series of events beyond his control. Auxentius, the then Bishop of Milan, suddenly died. Ambrose, in his role as Governor General, attended the election of the new bishop in the hope of easing tension between the Catholics and the Arians. His eloquent speech led to his acclamation as the new Bishop of Milan. He embraced the role by giving all his money and possessions in the name of the poor of Milan.

Saint Ambrose, considered one of the four most important theologians of the Church, died at 58.

October 23rd

The cruelest lies are often told in silence.

Adlai Stevenson
Politician
(1900 - 1965)

Adlai Stevenson, a descendant of an illustrious political family, served his country in various high-profile roles. During his thirties and forties, Stevenson held a number of key positions in Franklin Roosevelt's administration. He quickly attracted the attention of the leaders of the Democratic Party.

Stevenson was born in Los Angeles, California, but grew up in the city of Bloomington, Illinois. His grandfather, Adlai Stevenson I served as Vice President during Grover Cleveland's 1893-1897 presidency and his father, Lewis Stevenson, Secretary of the State of Illinois, was considered a Democratic potential in the late 1920's. But it was his maternal great-grandfather, Jesse Fell, who Stevenson most imitated. Fell was a dear friend and campaign manager for Abraham Lincoln. Jesse Fell had also founded the family business during the mid-1880's – The Daily Pantagraph newspaper.

Stevenson was Governor of Illinois between 1949 and 1953. He ran against and lost to Republican Dwight D. Eisenhower for the presidency in 1953. President Kennedy appointed Stevenson as the U.S. Ambassador to the United Nations serving forcefully during the infamous Bay of Pigs landing on Cuban territory.

Adlai Stevenson died of a heart attack at 65.

October 24th

What is a home without children?
Quiet.

Henny Youngman
Comedian
(1906 - 1998)

Henny Youngman (originally **Juggman**), born in Liverpool, England, grew up in Brooklyn, New York. Youngman's introduction to the world of comedy came when he was hired by a print shop to write one-line gags for comedy greeting cards. A young comic named Milton Berle came across Youngman's writing and tried to talk him into a career in show business.

Youngman made use of the music skills his family encouraged and launched a jazz band. He learned to rely on his own particular brand of humor to hold an audience. Soon he was headlining a stand-up comedy act with his rapid-fire inoffensive one-liners interspersed with some violin playing. By the mid-1930's he was featured on high-profile radio shows which eventually led to television and recording contracts. Youngman's seven-decade career earned him the respect and admiration of audiences and fellow comedians.

Youngman, labeled "The King of One-Liners by columnist Walter Winchell, married the love of his life, Sadie. She died in 1987 following a long illness. He loved making people laugh and rarely took a vacation over his 70 years in the business. Henny Youngman died as the result of pneumonia at the age of 91.

October 25th

***One doesn't have a sense of humor.
It has you.***

Larry Gelbart
Producer/Writer and Playwright
(1928 - 2009)

Larry Gelbart was part of the creative team which produced one of television's landmark comedy series. The Emmy Award-winning *M*A*S*H* starring Alan Alda and a solid cast of actors debuted in the fall of 1972 and ran for eleven seasons. Gelbart and Gene Reynolds co-developed the series based on a the 1968 Richard Hooker novel. They also wrote the pilot script for the series with a Korean War backdrop.

Gelbart was born in Chicago to Jewish immigrant parents. Gelbart's father, Harry, ran a barber shop where entertainer Danny Thomas frequented. When Gelbart was sixteen, his father proudly showed Thomas some of the original material written by his son. A writing career was launched which led to writing for Jack Paar, Danny Thomas and later Bob Hope. Gelbart honed his skills on such television shows as Sid Caesar's *Your Show of Shows*. Along a six-decade career, Gelbart was responsible for such classic stage moments as *A Funny Thing Happened on the Way to the Forum* (1962) and movies' *Oh God!* (1977) and *Tootsie* (1982).

After a short battle with cancer, Larry Gelbart died in Beverly Hills at 81.

October 26th

***Try to learn something about everything
and everything about something.***

Thomas Henry Huxley
Biologist
(1825 - 1895)

Thomas Henry Huxley, a bright boy forced out of school due to his family's financial misfortunes, grew up to become one of the most knowledgeable people of his time. Huxley's thirst for knowledge drove him to educate himself in the most complicated of disciplines. His self-education made him a very celebrated anatomist during the last half of the 19th century.

Huxley was born into a British middle-class family of intellectuals. With only two years of formal schooling, young Huxley taught himself various languages, including German, Latin and Greek. Huxley's "education" continued when he enlisted in the Royal Navy at 20. Based on a competency test he became Assistant Surgeon on board the HMS Rattlesnake. During this period Huxley carried out numerous studies on marine invertebrates. By 25, he was elected a Fellow of the Royal Society. Between the ages of 29 and 60, Huxley, who was nicknamed "Darwin's Bulldog" for his energetic defense of Charles Darwin's theory of evolution, held a number of important teaching positions.

In 1885, Huxley (60) retired from his public duties and devoted his time to writing. Thomas Huxley died of a heart attack following a bout with pneumonia. He was 70.

October 27th

My strength lies solely in my tenacity.

Louis Pasteur
Chemist
(1822 - 1895)

Louis Pasteur is best remembered for his research in the prevention of various diseases which had plagued mankind for centuries. His work established Pasteur as one of key figures in the study of microbiology.

Pasteur was born in Dole, France, to parents who survived in 19th century poverty. His intellect led him to earn degrees in the finest school – the exclusive Ecole Normale Supérieure. During his studies he met and eventually married Marie Laurent, the daughter of the school's rector. The couple had five children losing three before adulthood to typhoid. A grief stricken Pasteur dedicated himself to put an end to pre-mature deaths among children. By 22, Pasteur had gained national attention for his research and was appointed professor of chemistry at the University of Strasbourg. Pasteur's research led to a remarkable reduction in mortality with the vaccines for rabies and anthrax. He is also remembered for creating a method preventing milk and wine from causing illness and death. The method is called pasteurization.

Pasteur has been honored by numerous countries worldwide. Louis Pasteur succumbed to a series of strokes in Paris at the age of 72.

October 28th

I no doubt deserved my enemies, but I don't believe I deserved my friends.

Walt Whitman
Poet
(1819 - 1892)

Walt Whitman was born into a poor family of nine children on Long Island, New York. Walter Sr. and his wife, Louisa, favored the teachings of the Quaker religion. Because of constant financial problems the Whitman family moved a great deal creating an unhappy childhood.

By 11, Whitman, the second oldest child, had been forced to leave school in order to help support the family. For a number of years Whitman held various jobs in printing. During his mid-twenties he became editor of the Brooklyn Eagle and began to further his writing skills with freelance fiction and poetry. In the summer of 1855, Whitman (36) published his masterpiece – *Leaves of Grass*. The collection of poetry, despite being originally labeled as obscene, brought him international fame and was reprinted several times during his lifetime.

Whitman is considered by modern scholars as the "father of free verse" and is recognized as having exercised a great influence on the generations of poets to follow. Walt Whitman died at 72 of pleurisy.

October 29th

You don't choose your family.
They are God's gift to you,
as you are to them.

Desmond Tutu
Spiritual Leader and Activist
(b. 1931)

Desmond Tutu, the young boy from a working-class family, grew up to become one of the key voices in the 20th century battle against apartheid in South Africa. Tutu was elevated by the Anglican Church of South Africa to the important role as the first black South African Bishop of Cape Town.

In his youth Tutu wanted to pursue medicine as a career but his family could not afford such an education. His father was a teacher and his mother was a cook in a school. Tutu followed his father's example and became a teacher until he entered St. Peter's Theology College. By 35, he had earned a Master's degree (1966) in theology from King's College in London. In 1976, the movement against apartheid was born and Tutu argued forcefully for stronger action from the U.S. and Great Britain in the form of an investment boycott. The boycott did eventually take place in 1985 and was successful in forcing the South African government into much-needed reform.

Tutu's battle for human rights brought him international acclaim. In 1984, he was awarded the Nobel Peace Prize. At the age of 66, Tutu was diagnosed with prostate cancer which was arrested with treatment in the U.S. Desmond Tutu retired with the title emeritus Archbishop of Cape Town.

October 30th

***Mix a little foolishness
with your prudence:
it's good to be silly
at the right moment.***

Horace
Philosopher
(65 BC - 8 BC)

Horace, the most influential lyric poet of the Augustine era, was lovingly guided by his former-slave father. Horace's father, a farmer in the ancient town of Venusia, transplanted the family to Rome in order to offer his young son a proper education. Horace eventually studied in Rome and in Athens.

After the assassination of Julius Caesar and following the death of his beloved father, Horace settled in Rome where he grew as a poet alongside Virgil and Lucius Varius Rufus. Over a three-decade period Horace wrote countless poetry based on two main themes – *beatus ille* ("the beauty of the simple life") and *carpe diem* (commonly translated as "seize the day"). Horace's influence can be clearly measured throughout the centuries in the works of such masters as Garcilaso de la Vega, Pierre de Ronsard, Montaigne, Voltaire and Shakespeare.

Ben Jonson and Lord Byron translated Horace's Ars Poetica written in 18 B.C. from the original Greek. Horace died at 57 with no heirs and bequeathed his land to Emperor Augustus. The site remains to this day a pilgrimage for his followers.

October 31st

Love is never outside ourselves;
love is within us.

Louise Hay
Writer and Motivational Speaker
(b. 1926)

Louise Hay is one of the motivational speakers encouraging self healing to emerge out of the last quarter of the 20th century. Hay also authored a number of self-help books and founded a publishing company to represent similar writing projects.

Hay was born in Los Angeles in a poor environment. Her mother eventually married a man who, by Hay's recollections, was a violent person. She also states that she was sexually abused by a neighbor as a small child. In her late twenties she married an English businessman named Andrew Hay. The marriage lasted fourteen years.

At the age of 58, Hay published her first self-help book called *You Can Heal Your Life.* Promotional appearances on *The Oprah Whinfrey Show* sent the book to the New York Times best seller list. In 1984, she launched Hay House Publishing which has served as the publisher for Deepak Chopra and Wayne Dyer.

> ## *"To meet the deadline."*

During the presidential election of 1860, the Republican Party platform aggressively advanced the concept of a gradual extinction of the practice of slavery. Eleven of the southern states immediately declared their session from the United States of America to form the Confederate States of America. Within weeks of assuming the presidency, Abraham Lincoln faced a nation at war with itself. The first shot of the American Civil War was fired April 12th, 1861, at Fort Sumter in South Carolina. By the time the last shot rang out on June 22nd, 1865, a staggering three quarters of a million American men had died in action or later from fatal combat wounds.

The tragedy of the American Civil War extended into the many prisoner-of-war camps on both sides. Within months into the civil war, the Union and Confederate armies faced a harsh reality for which they were simply not prepared – the excessive volume of prisoners. The war had been forced on two unprepared armies. Prisoner-of-war camps had to be hastily assembled and supplied for what turned into hundreds of thousands of detainees. Conditions were harsh – poor nutrition, lack of proper sanitation and untrained and inadequate staffs. The mortality rate was estimated at a staggering seventeen to twenty-three percent of the prison population.

Attempting to control the growing unrest proved to be extremely difficult. In a desperate attempt to prevent massive escapes a line was often drawn in the dirt around the camp or simple wooden rails stretched in place of a high wall. The guards, who called "the dead line", would repeatedly issue warnings to the prisoners not "*to meet the deadline*" or they would be shot.

November 1st

A healthy male adult bore consumes each year one and a half times his own weight in other people's patience.

John Updike
Writer
(1932 - 2009)

John Updike was born in Reading, Pennsylvania, and grew up in a small community within a short distance. Updike was greatly influenced by his mother's repeated attempts to become a published writer. After graduating from Harvard with a degree in English, Updike began a long association with one of the most important literary magazines of the time – The New Yorker.

Updike wrote a total of twenty novels plus more than a dozen short story collections over a writing career which spanned five decades. Early in his career he created a character (Harry "Rabbit" Angstrom) which loyal readers followed through four popular books beginning with *Rabbit, Run*. The literary series earned Updike two Pulitzer Prize for Literature awards. Updike gained international attention by depicting the pain and suffering of the average American.

Updike's distinctive writing style established him as one of the important writers of his time. John Updike lost his battle with lung cancer a few months before his 77th birthday.

November 2nd

Common sense and a sense of humor are the same thing, moving at different speeds. A sense of humor is just common sense, dancing.

William James
Psychologist and Philosopher
(1842 - 1910)

William James grew up in a wealthy household of intellects where a well-rounded world education was encouraged. Family trips to cosmopolitan Europe proved to be beneficial for all the James siblings. William's brother was acclaimed novelist Henry James and his sister, Alice, became a writer in her own right.

James was born in New York City's affluent society to wealthy Henry James Sr. Ralph Waldo Emerson served as godfather to the young William James. James earned a medical degree from Harvard Medical School in 1869 but never set up a medical practice. James turned his attention and passion to a new emerging science – psychology. He was a prolific writer producing *Principles of Psychology* in 1890 to world acclaim.

James was not blessed with a strong constitution and suffered from poor health most of his adult life. He also struggled from bouts of depression. William James retired from his life-long teaching post at Harvard in 1907 and died of heart failure three years later at 68.

November 3rd

Life is a moderately good play with a badly written third act.

Truman Capote
Writer
(1924 - 1984)

Truman Capote perfected his writing skills from the age of eleven forever carrying a dictionary and a notepad. His neighbor and childhood friend in Monroeville, Alabama, was celebrated writer Harper Lee who as a young woman in her 30's would write one of 20th century's best novels – *To Kill A Mockingbird*.

Capote was born Truman Speckfus Persons in New Orleans, Louisiana, the son of 17-year-old Lillie Mae Faulk and Archulus Persons. His parents divorced when he was four and he was shipped to Monroeville to be raised by his mother's relatives. Capote took the name of his mother's second husband, Cuban-born Jose Capote. In 1948, Capote (24) wrote *Other Voices, Other Rooms* which introduced him to the literary world. During the next ten years Capote wrote a collection of popular novels, Broadway plays and screenplays. But Capote hungered for more – he hungered to be a "celebrity". Celebrity status was achieved with the release of his next two novels – *Breakfast at Tiffany's* (1958) and the unforgettable *In Cold Blood* (1966).

Capote, an openly gay person who stood a few inches over five feet, became the "star" he always wished to be. He also became addicted to alcohol and drugs. Truman Capote died at 59 in Los Angeles of liver damage.

November 4th

The real voyage of discovery consists not in seeing new landscapes, but in having new eyes.

Marcel Proust
Writer
(1871 - 1922)

Marcel Proust is often considered by other writers as "the greatest novelist of the 20th century" (Graham Greene) and his literary output as "the greatest fiction" (W. Somerset Maugham). Proust, a sickly child, began to write and be published at a very early age.

Proust was born in Autreuil which is today a district of the city of Paris. His upper-middle class family consisted of his pathologist-father (Archille) and his well-read mother (Jeanne). Despite poor health, Proust received an excellent education. Between 1913 and his death Proust published his greatest literary work in seven eagerly anticipated parts. *À la recherche du temps perdu* (*In Search of Lost Time*), consisting of over 2,000 characters developed in 4,000-plus pages, established Proust as a major figure in French literature.

Proust's battle with chronic asthma began before his 10th birthday and plagued him all his life. Recognizing that his life would be short, Proust more or less barricaded himself in his bedroom to complete his work.

Marcel Proust died of pneumonia at 51.

November 5th

Patience and perseverance have a magical effect before which difficulties disappear and obstacles vanish.

John Quincy Adams
Statesman
(1767 - 1848)

John Quincy Adams, a quiet recluse of a man more comfortable in his reading room than in public, served an astonishing 54 years of his eight-decade life in high-profile public service. Adams, the sixth President of the United States, like Abraham Lincoln, suffered from depression.

Adams, the son of John Adams, one of the Founding Fathers and the second President of the U.S., served his country in various roles as diplomat, senator, congressman and president (1825-1829). Adams has the distinction of having returned to Congress as a member of the House of Representatives following his presidency. He is the only former president to do so. Adam played key roles as a diplomat during important historical moments, including negotiating the Treaty of Ghent which ended the War of 1812 between the U.S. and Great Britain. Adams was a strong opponent to the practice of slavery and predicted a war between the states on the issue.

Louisa Adams, his devoted wife for almost fifty years, helped her husband carry out the social aspects of his diplomatic duties. John Quincy Adams collapsed during a heated debate in the House of Representatives and died two days later. He was 80.

November 6th

*Love knows not its own depth
until the hour of separation.*

Kahlil Gibran
Poet and Artist
(1883 - 1931)

Kahlil Gibran was the world's third best-selling poet behind William Shakespeare and Lao-Tzu. The Lebanese-born writer came to the U.S. as a 12-year-old in the final year of the 19th century with his family. His mother took various jobs to support her family of four all the while encouraging her children to pursue educations and to remember their heritage.

During his early teen years Gibran enrolled in a local art school where he met avant-garde artist Fred Holland Day. Between the ages of 15 and 19, Gibran returned to Lebanon to continue his education. Within a short period, and before his return, tuberculosis took the lives of his younger sister and his brother. His mother died soon after of cancer. Gibran (21) launched his own career as an artist with an exhibition of his work in 1904 in Boston. The exhibition introduced him to Mary Elizabeth Haskell, a respected teacher ten years his senior, who would influence every aspect of his life.

Gibran also died of tuberculosis at the early age of 48. His will left all his possessions to Mary Haskell. Over twenty years of personal letters between the two lovers were donated to the University of North Carolina Chapel Hill Library. Before her death in 1964, Mary Haskell gave her collection of one hundred original Gibran paintings to the Telfair Museum of Art in Savannah, Georgia.

November 7th

A woman is always younger than a man at equal years.

Elizabeth Barrett Browning
Poet
(1806 - 1861)

Elizabeth Barrett Browning is considered one of the most popular and influential poets of the Victorian Era. The style and content of her poetry had an impact on two great American poets – Edgar Allan Poe and Emily Dickinson.

Browning was born Elizabeth Barrett Moulton in a wealthy English family. Both her paternal and maternal grandparents had built their fortunes in part on the slave trade. Elizabeth was the first of twelve children born to Edward and Mary Barrett. Like most young ladies of the period, Elizabeth was home-schooled concentrating on Homer. Her first poem is reported to have been written at the age of six and her first collection published when she was 15 – *Essay on Mind and Other Poems*. The prolific writer who suffered from a lung disease met and married author Robert Browning. One of the most famous romances in literature lasted until her death.

Elizabeth Barrett Browning's health deteriorated after the death of her brother and father. She died in her beloved husband's arms whispering one final word – "Beautiful!"

November 8th

A bank is a place where they lend you an umbrella in fair weather and ask for it back when it begins to rain.

Robert Frost
Poet
(1874 - 1963)

Robert Frost frequently set his poems in rural settings and made use of his uncanny command of American colloquial speech to deal with complex social issues. Frost became one of the most popular and respected poets of the 20th century.

Frost attended Harvard University for a few years but was forced to leave because of illness. He spent a part of his 30's as an English teacher in New Hampshire before transplanting himself and his family to England in 1912. Soon after his arrival in the London area his first collection of poetry, *A Boy's Will* was published. Frost devoted his life to his two loves – poetry and teaching. The prolific writer taught English in Massachusetts and Vermont. During his five-decade writing career, Frost was honored with four Pulitzer Prize recognitions.

Robert Frost, the average man's poet, died from prostate cancer. On his gravestone a line from one of his poems reads – "I had a lover's quarrel with the world."

November 9th

One word frees us of all the weight and pain of life; that word is love.

Sophocles
Playwright and Poet
(496 BC - 406 BC)

Sophocles' father, Sophilus, had acquired great wealth as a manufacturer of combat armor. The highly-educated Sophilus oversaw the education of his artistic son. Sophocles' precise date of birth in Attica was not properly recorded.

Sophocles recorded his artistic victory at the Dionysian theatre competition. Annual drama competitions were the process by which new plays were introduced and judged. Over the decades of competitions Sophocles never placed less than second and ranked first on twenty occasions. Sophocles' innovative approach to the ancient form of playwriting was key in the development of drama during his lifetime. Character development and added character conflict elevated the form to a new respectability.

Historical records report that Sophocles wrote a total of 123 plays but a mere seven have survived the centuries. Sophocles died at the advanced age of 90.

November 10th

Anyone who has never made a mistake has never tried anything new.

Albert Einstein
Physicist
(1879 - 1955)

Albert Einstein, at 36, introduced to the world what undoubtedly is the 20th century's most discussed equation. $E=mc_2$, the theory that small amounts of mass could be converted into greater amounts of energy, was received amongst a great deal of controversy but eventually understood and accepted by the world scientific community.

In 1933, Adolf Hitler rose to power in a changing Germany. While on a lecture tour in the U.S., news reached Einstein describing the mood in Germany and some of the actions taken by the Hitler regime. The new leader passed a law which forbade Jews from holding public office, including at universities. Public book burnings were orchestrated by the government, including the burning of Einstein's writings. As well, the father of physics discovered his name was on a government list marked for assassination. Einstein settled in the U.S. and before the outbreak of the war warned the White House about the possibility Germany had atomic weapons. The word "Einstein" has come to define genius.

The father of modern physics spent the last two decades of his life at the Institute for Advanced Study in Princeton, New Jersey. In the spring of 1955, Einstein suffered an abdominal aortic aneurysm. Albert Einstein died at 96 at the Princeton Hospital with unfinished work by his bedside.

November 11th

What a distressing contrast there is between the radiant intelligence of the child and the feeble mentality of the average adult.

Sigmund Freud
Psychologist and Neurologist
(1856 - 1939)

Sigmund Freud was an outstanding student at high school and at the University of Vienna. His desire to study law soon gave way to his growing interest in medicine. Freud earned his medical degree at the age of 25 and joined the psychiatric clinic in the Vienna General Hospital. Before his 30th birthday, Freud opened his private practice specializing in the care of "nervous disorders".

Beginning with hypnosis as a tool to unlock the subconscious, Freud quickly progressed to the very controversial "talk therapy". Freud established the new discipline of psychoanalysis. In 1938, the detention and interrogation by the Gestapo of his 43-year-old daughter, Anna, convinced Freud it was time to leave his beloved Vienna. With the invaluable help of a sympathetic Nazi official named Anton Sauerwald, the family escaped to London. Sauerwald was imprisoned in 1945 but Anna Freud's intervention gained his release in 1947.

During his later years Freud lived in extreme pain due to a spreading cancer. Freud persuaded his friend, Dr. Max Schur, to help him end his life. Sigmund Freud died in September of 1939 at the age of 83.

November 12th

*It is unwise to be too sure
of one's own wisdom.
It is healthy to be reminded that
the strongest might weaken
and the wisest might err.*

Mahatma Gandhi
Political Leader
(1869 - 1948)

Mahatma Gandhi, the gentle soft-spoken gentleman who preached and lived the concept of "satyagraha" (devotion to truth and non-violent means), died at the hand of a misguided Hindu nationalist. In his lifetime, Gandhi became the most important figure in India's 20th century history.

Mohandas Karamchand Gandhi was born a Hindu in the coastal town of Porbandar, British India. His mother, Putlibai, who was a devote Jain, exercised a great influence on her young son. While he was studying law at the University College in London, his beloved mother died. According to custom thirteen-tear-old Gandhi was wed to Kasturbsa Makhanji (14) in an arranged marriage with the newlyweds continuing to live with their respective parents. The loving couple eventually had four sons and remained together until Ba, as she was affectionately called, died in Gandhi's arms in 1944. As the non-violent leader of the Indian National Congress political movement, Gandhi was imprisoned on several occasions on the way towards winning India's independence.

Gandhi earned the honorary name of Mahatma, which means "Great Soul", during his stay in South Africa fighting for Indian rights and lived to witness India's independence.

November 13th

True friendship is like sound health;
the value of it is seldom known
until it be lost.

Charles Caleb Colton
Cleric and Writer
(1780 - 1832)

Charles Caleb Colton earned a Master of Arts degree from King's College in London in 1804. In 1812, Colton (32) accepted the appointment as Vicar of Kew and Petersham where he apparently performed his clerical duties erratically. At the age of 48, Colton walked away from the church and left England.

Colton traveled across the United Sates before settling in Paris. Over the following few years he accumulated an impressive art collection. Unfortunately he also cultivated a weakness for gambling where he eventually lost his modest fortune.

During his lifetime, the eccentric Colton published a number of books which proved to be popular in 19th century England. Charles Caleb Colton took his own life rather than face life-saving surgery.

November 14th

Discovery consists of seeing what everybody has seen and thinking what nobody has thought.

Albert Szent-Györgyi
Physiologist
(1893 - 1986)

Albert Szent-Györgyi was awarded the Nobel Prize in Physiology in 1937 in recognition for his extensive research leading to the discovery of Vitamin C. Szent-Györgyi donated all the prize money to Finland because the Hungarian Volunteers came to the aid of the country after the Soviet Union invasion of 1939.

Szent-Györgyi was born in Budapest, Hungary, the son of a landowner and an aspiring opera singer. The Szent-Györgyi ancestry boasts three generations of scientists. His pursuit for his medical degree was interrupted by WWI until he eventually earned a PhD in 1917. During the war years, Szent-Györgyi became an active member of the Hungarian resistance movement. His activities were disruptive enough for Adolf Hitler himself to issue a warrant for his arrest sending him into hiding for the last years of the war. He became an elected member of parliament with the goal of running for president of Hungary but communist rule prevented it.

During the late 1940's, **Szent-Györgyi** transplanted himself to the U.S. Albert Szent-Györgyi died one month after his 93rd birthday.

November 15th

Those who make the worst use of their time are the first to complain about its brevity.

Jean de la Bruyère
Playwright and Poet
(1615 - 1696)

Jean de la Bruyère played a minor role both in French literature and in the French court of the mid-to-late 1600's.

Jean de la Bruyère was born in Paris into a middle-class family. De la Bruyère's father served as the controller of finance at city hall. His desires to be counted amongst the French aristocracy led him to alter his family name without permission to de la Bruyère to suggest nobility. He studied law at the University of Orleans. A role in the revenue department in the city of Caen eventually led to the household of Louis, the Prince of Condé and as the tutor to the royal family. The position also gave him a membership to the French Court. In 1688, de la Bruyère (43) wrote a book called *Caractères* (*Characters*) which caused him numerous enemies in the French Court. From his privileged vantage point he wrote about the corruption and hypocrisy within the French Court. De la Bruyère was reluctantly admitted to l'Académie française in 1693.

Jean de la Bruyère's sudden death at the age of 51 a mere few years after the release of *Caractères* led to various scenarios of fowl play. The official cause of death was listed as apoplexy, a term used to define what is today more likely related to heart failure.

November 16th

***It's never too late to be
who you might have been.***

George Eliot
Writer and Journalist
(1819 - 1880)

George Eliot, born Mary Anne Evans in Warwickshire, England, published her first novel, *Amos Barton,* at the age of 39. Over her less than two-decade writing career, Eliot wrote seven novels to establish herself as one of the great writers of the Victorian period.

Eliot believed the use of a male pen name would distinguish her from other female authors of the time who, for the most part, limited their writing style to light romance novels. Eliot's desires to become a novelist were encouraged by the philosopher George Henry Lewes with whom she lived in a very public relationship for over 24 years until his death in 1878 despite his marriage to Agnes Jervis. Eliot's second novel, *Adam Bede*, was such a huge success that the reading public became eager to know the true identity of the writer behind the name George Eliot. She finally stepped out of the shadows to a surprised public. Scholars have often considered *Middlemarch* (1872) to be one of the finest novels of the English language.

In May, 1880, Eliot (61) married John Cross, twenty years her junior, only to become very ill in the fall of the same year. Mary Anne Evans, alias George Eliot, died in late December of 1880.

November 17th

Peace is not absence of conflict, it is the ability to handle conflict by peaceful means.

Ronald Reagan
Actor and Politician
(1911 - 2004)

Ronald Reagan's adult life reads like a Hollywood script – launched a broadcast career in a small Illinois radio station, earned the rank of Captain during WWII, became a popular movie actor, elected governor of one of the largest states in the union and then, at the age of 70, became the 40th president of the United States. Reagan served as president between 1981 and 1989 and is recognized as one of the most popular leaders in modern times.

Reagan was born in Tampico, Illinois, to Jack and Nelle Reagan. He inherited his mother's optimistic faith in the goodness of people. Reagan was featured in a series of movies such as *Santa Fe Trail* (1940) and *King's Row* (1942) but is best remembered as The Gipper in *Knute Rockne, All American*. Regan earned his first political wings as the president of the Screen Actors Guild in 1947. Reagan served two terms as Governor of California – 1967-1975. During the Reagan White House years, he dealt with the end of the Cold War, the 1986 bombing in Libya and the Iran-Contra affair not to mention an assassination attempt.

In 1994, Reagan was diagnosed with Alzheimer's disease. The former president spent the next ten years with his beloved wife, Nancy, by his side. Ronald Reagan died of pneumonia in California at the age of 93.

November 18th

The most wasted of all days is one without laughter.

E. E. Cummings
Writer and Poet
(1894 - 1962)

E. E. Cummings, born Edward Estlin Cummings in Cambridge, Massachusetts, began his lifelong love affair with poetry at an early age. Examples of his writing style were captured in poems written to his beloved father at the age of six. Cummings explored many traditional styles but early in his maturing career he developed his own unique style.

Following graduation from Harvard, Cummings was employed by a local book dealer. By the outbreak of WWI, Cummings (early 20's) and a campus friend joined an ambulance corps in Europe. His eccentric behavior was misinterpreted as espionage and he spent three-plus months in a military prison in Normandy. After the war, Cummings made use of his brief prison experience as the basis of his critically-acclaimed novel – *The Enormous Room* (1922). He capitalized on the literary attention by releasing a collection of poems under the title *Tulips and Chimneys* in 1923. Cummings was often referred to by other writers in lower case letters – e. e. cummings.

The avant-garde poet traveled extensively throughout Europe. E.E. Cummings died as the result of a stroke in September of 1962 just months shy of his 68th birthday.

November 19th

*Forgiveness is
the economy of the heart ...
forgiveness saves,
the expense of anger
The cost of hatred,
the waste of spirits.*

Hannah More
Writer
(1745 - 1833)

Hannah More was the fourth of five daughters born in Bristol, England. Her schoolmaster-father took responsibility of the siblings' education. During their first years of homeschooling the girls were introduced to Latin and French. The close-knit family also encouraged the children to write.

By 17, Hannah More had written her first play – *The Search After Happiness*. During her 20's, More joined the rather elite literary circle in London and met Edmund Burke and Samuel Johnson. Throughout her long life, Hannah More wrote a number of successful plays, including the tragedy *Percy* (1777). More spent the last five decades of her life writing a very long list of extremely popular poems such as *Sacred Dramas* (1782) and *Moral Sketches* (1819).

Following the example of her father, who had founded several schools, More became the key motivator in the establishment of a dozen schools in the rural areas in England. Her sister, Martha, participated. Hannah More died in Wrington, England. She was 88.

November 20th

***You shall judge a man by his foes
as well as his friends.***

Joseph Conrad
Writer
(1857 - 1924)

Joseph Conrad, born Józef Teodor Konrad Korzeniowski of Polish ancestry, did not speak English when he arrived in Great Britain at the age of 21. By his late twenties, the young seaman had been granted British citizenship and had legally changed his name to Joseph Conrad. His sixteen years at sea would serve Conrad, the writer, extremely well.

Conrad, born in what is now Berdychiv, Ukraine, in the mid-19th century, came from Polish nobility. His father, Apollo, was a playwright and translated great literature to Polish, including Victor Hugo and Charles Dickens. Conrad lost both his parents in his early years – his mother to tuberculosis when he was eight and his father four years later. He was raised by an uncle in Krakow. At 16, Conrad began the life of an adventurous seaman until his mid-thirties. For the next three decades Conrad wrote complex novels woven from his sea-going voyages to exotic destinations. A number of films have been based on his works – *Lord Jim* with Peter O'Toole (1965), *The Secret Agent* (1996), and Francis Ford Coppola's *Apocalypse Now* (based on *Heart of Darkness*) starring Marlon Brando, Robert Duvall and Martin Sheen.

The very successful Conrad gathered fame and wealth during his thirty years-plus writing career. He declined a British knighthood because of his own Polish heritage. Joseph Conrad died of a heart attack at 66.

November 21st

The one thing that does not abide by majority rule is a person's conscience.

Harper Lee
Writer
(b. 1926)

 Harper Lee, the self-proclaimed tomboy during her early years in Monroeville, Alabama, wrote one novel in her lifetime. The novel became a best-seller immediately after it was published in July, 1960. Over the past five decades *To Kill A Mockingbird* has sold over 30 million copies and is considered by literary scholars as the best novel of the 20th century.

 Harper Lee was born, raised and lived all her life in Monroeville, Alabama, the setting for *Mockingbird*. Her father, Amasa Coleman Lee, was a lawyer and the model for her character Atticus Finch. Lee's mother, Frances', maiden name was Finch. The autobiographical similarities continue with the fact that Scout, the book's young narrator, was Lee herself in many ways. Scout's childhood friend in the book, Dill, was inspired by Lee's real Monroeville next-door neighbor and friend who was none other than a young Truman Capote. Capote would grow up to give the world some memorable novels – *Breakfast at Tiffany's* and *In Cold Blood*. In 1962, the *To Kill A Mockingbird* movie earned Gregory Peck an Oscar for Best Actor.

 Lee was awarded the 1960 Pulitzer Prize for Literature. Lee turned her back on the life of a celebrity and never wrote another novel. Harper Lee continues to lives in Monroeville, Alabama.

November 22nd

Some people stay longer in an hour than others can in a month.

William Dean Howells
Writer
(1837 - 1920)

William Dean Howells wrote his first novel at the age of 35 (*Their Wedding Journey*) and established his literary reputation ten years later with the release of *A Modern Instance*. His true value to the literary world is likely his influence as the editor of The Atlantic Monthly.

Howells was born in Martinsville, Ohio, (now Martins Ferry) to newspaper editor William Cooper and Mary Dean Howells. At 21, Howells worked at the Ohio State Journal which triggered friendships with various contemporary writers such as Nathanial Hawthorne, Ralph Waldo Emerson and Henry James. In his late 20's, Howells became a member of the editorial staff of The Atlantic Monthly and held the position of editor until 1881. In his position, Howells was instrumental in introducing non-American writers (Émil Zola and Leo Tolstoy among others) to U.S. readers. Howells, often referred to as The Dean of American Literature, also played an important support role for American writers such as Emily Dickinson.

In addition to novels (especially *The Rise of Silas Lapham* – 1885), Howells published a collection of poems in 1895 – *Stops of Various Quills*. William Dean Howells died in Manhattan at the age of 83.

November 23rd

If my doctor told me I had only six minutes to live, I wouldn't brood. I'd type a little faster.

Isaac Asimov
Writer and Biochemist
(1920 - 1992)

Isaac Asimov, a master of the science fiction form of literature, emigrated from his native Russia with his parents when he was three. Considered one of the most prolific writers in literature, Asimov wrote and edited some 500 books, compiled an impressive list of short stories as well as taught biochemistry at Boston University.

Asimov was born Issak Yudovich Ozimov in Petrovichi, Russia, near modern-day Belarus. His orthodox Jewish parents settled in Brooklyn, New York, with young Isaac and his one-year-old younger sister, Manya. A brother, Stanley, was born in the U.S. Asimov (19) had his third short story submitted to and published by Astounding Science Fiction in 1939 (*Marooned Off Vesta*). In 1941, *Night Fall*, considered the best science fiction short story written gave him international recognition. Asimov, the creator of the *Foundation* trilogy and the *Galactic Empire* series, was a member of Mensa International.

At the age of 63, Asimov had triple by-pass surgery. In 1992, his death was reported to be the cause of kidney failure. But it wasn't until 2002 that his wife, Janet, and daughter, Robyn, went public with the fact that Isaac Asimov had actually died from being infected by HIV by a blood transfusion during the 1983 heart operation.

November 24th

*From your parents
you learn love and laughter
and how to put one foot
before the other.
But when books are opened
you discover that you
have wings.*

Helen Hayes
Actress
(1900 - 1993)

Helen Hayes, referred to as the First Lady of the American Theater, launched her performing career early in life. At 10 Hayes was featured in a short film called *Jean and the Calico Doll* (1910). Her active career covered seven decades.

The talented actress was born Helen Brown in Washington, D.C., to Francis and Catherine Estelle. Her mother, Essie, was an aspiring stage actress. Hayes' maternal grandparents fled from Ireland during the potato famine. *The Sin of Madelon Claudet* (1931) starring a young Robert Young in a support role, was Hayes' first sound film and it earned her a Best Actress Oscar. The versatile Hayes also has the rare distinction of having won Tony and Emmy awards as Best Actress plus a Best Actress in a Supporting Role Oscar for 1970's *Airport*. She enjoyed a long and impressive career on stage as well as in motion pictures. Hayes was married to playwright Charles MacArthur and the couple adopted a son, James MacArthur, who starred in television's highly successful *Hawaii Five-0*.

Hayes suffered from asthma and spent her last years fundraising. Helen Hayes died from heart failure at 92.

November 25th

*Do not dwell in the past,
do not dream of the future,
concentrate the mind
on the present moment.*

Buddha
Spiritual Leader
(543 BC - 483 BC)

Buddha, born Siddhārtha Gautama, in what UNESCO believes was Lumbini, in modern-day Nepal, is the founder of Buddhism. The exact dates of Gautama's birth and death were not properly recorded. Buddhism is both a religion and a philosophy which now has more than 500 million followers throughout the world.

Traditional records show that Gautama's ancestry can be traced to Hindu royalty. At the age of 16, his father, King Suddhodana, set a pre-arranged marriage into motion. After 29 years of marriage, Gautama set out on a life-long search for enlightenment giving up all his worldly possessions. Over the next 45 years, he discovered the value of meditation as the path to enlightenment and traveled the known world of the day to share his knowledge.

Buddha means the "Awakened One" and Gautama is considered the Supreme Buddha. At the age of approximately 80, Buddha died in modern-day India.

November 26th

***A person who knows
how to laugh at himself
will never cease to be amused.***

Shirley MacLaine
Actress
(b. 1934)

Shirley MacLaine was born Shirley MacLean Beaty in Richmond, Virginia, to Kathryn and Ira Beaty. MacLaine's father was a psychology professor and her mother (maiden name MacLaine) was a drama teacher from Nova Scotia, Canada. MacLaine also had a younger brother who pursued a career in entertainment as an actor-producer-director – Warren Beatty (adding an extra 't' to his family name) who earned fourteen Oscar nominations.

MacLaine (21) launched her career in a 1955 Alfred Hitchcock movie called *The Trouble with Harry*. She earned a Golden Globe as Best Newcomer and went on to star in a series of impressive titles, including *Around the World in 80 Days* (1956), *The Apartment* (1958) with Jack Lemmon, *The Children's Hour* (1961) co-starring James Garner and *Irma la Douce* (1963). MacLaine won a Best Actress Oscar in James L. Brooks' 1983 *Terms of Endearment* with Jack Nicholson. MacLaine's memorable role of Ouiser Boudreaux in 1989's *Steel Magnolias* won her the admiration of her peers.

Shirley MacLaine is also known for her strong beliefs in New Age spirituality and the occult.

November 27th

***Most of the shadows of this life
are caused by standing
in one's own sunshine.***

Ralph Waldo Emerson
Poet, Essayist and Lecturer
(1803 - 1882)

Ralph Waldo Emerson is considered to be one of the great thinkers of the 19th century. Emerson first gained attention with the publishing of an essay entitled *Nature* (1836) and he quickly established himself as the leader of the Transcendental movement of the 19th century.

Emerson was the second of five sons born to the Rev. William Emerson and his wife, Ruth. Emerson's maternal uncle was named Ralph. Three other Emerson children died in childhood. Young Waldo was raised by his mother with the help of his sister, Mary Moody, after his father died in 1811. Mary Moody had a great influence on the young boy. He was not an outstanding student but did serve as Class Poet at Harvard. Emerson championed individuality and personal freedom and became a key member of the transcendental movement. He followed his father's calling into the Unitarian ministry at 26 but resigned at 29 after the death of his young wife.

During the early 1830's, Emerson launched a very successful career as a lecturer. He delivered well over 1,500 lectures in his lifetime. A major fire in 1867 destroyed the family home which prompted him to end his lecturing career.

Ralph Waldo Emerson died as a result of a battle with pneumonia at 78.

November 28th

***In seeking wisdom thou art wise;
in imagining that thou hast attained it -
thou art a fool.***

Lord Chesterfield
Statesman
(1694 - 1773)

Lord Chesterfield became an important political figure during Great Britain's 18th century. The Earl of Chesterfield was a title created for and bestowed upon Philip Stanhope, the 1st Earl, in 1628.

Lord Chesterfield was born Philip Dormer Stanhope, and educated at Cambridge. At the age of 21, Lord Chesterfield became a member of the House of Commons. He quickly distinguished himself as a gentleman and an exceptional orator. Lord Chesterfield was dispatched to The Hague in 1728 as ambassador and in 1731 negotiated the Treaty of Vienna. He further distinguished himself as the Lord-Lieutenant of Ireland and received great honors on his return to London. Lord Chesterfield was considered a man of letters in his day and counted among his friends the French literary giants, Voltaire and Montesquieu. Lord Chesterfield shared his guidance and aspirations with his illegitimate son, Philip Stanhope, in the form of a series of exceptionally well-written letters spanning his son's life. In 1768, his son suddenly died in his 36th year. His father carried his grief to his own death.

Five years following his son's untimely death, Lord Chesterfield died. He was 79.

November 29th

It is not what we do
but also what we do not do,
for which we are accountable.

Molière
Playwright and Actor
(1622 - 1673)

Molière (Jean-Baptiste Poquelin) is considered by modern literary scholars to have earned the distinction as one of the great masters of the comedy form. Young Jean-Baptiste was born in a wealthy and well-established French family. He was drawn to the less respected life of an actor at an early age. During this period of French history, actors were not even granted burial rights in sacred ground.

Following thirteen years as an actor, Poquelin began his writing career under the name Molière to possibly keep shame from his conservative family. Molière, the playwright, soon became a favorite of the French Court winning the patronage of Philippe I, the brother of King Louis XIV. He frequently tested the patience of the court and the church but proved to be popular with the theatre public. Two of his plays, *Le Misanthrope* and *Le Malade Imaginaire* secured his place in French literature.

While performing the role of the hypochondriac in *Le Malade Imaginaire,* Molière, who suffered from pulmonary disease, collapsed on stage. He died a few hours later. Molière was a few weeks beyond 51. The King permitted the great playwright and actor to be buried in a cemetery.

November 30th

*A wise man gets more use
from his enemies
than a fool from his friends.*

Baltasar Gracian
Clergyman and Writer
(1601 - 1658)

Baltasar Gracian was a Jesuit priest and writer during the first half of the 17th century. He was born in Belmonte, Spain, the son of a medical doctor. Following his uncle who was a priest, young Baltasar was enrolled in a Jesuit school. In 1627, the 26-year-old was ordained and took the vows of the Jesuit Order in 1633.

Gracian became a popular preacher in the eyes of the various congregations but less so by his Jesuit superiors. He was prone to dramatics in the pulpit such as reading "correspondence" directly from hell. The young unorthodox cleric further displeased his superiors by repeatedly publishing literary works without church permission. Eventually, at the age of 56, Gracian was sent to the Spanish village of Graus in the province of Huesca following the publication of his famous literary work – the three volume *Criticón*. The church was less concerned with the content of the allegoric novel as with his on-going defiant behavior.

Baltasar Gracian died at the age of 57. He was buried in Tarazona, Spain.

> **"Wearing your heart on your sleeve."**

During the Middle Ages, the European social structure was divided into three groups – king, lords and lower class. The right to rule over land and people was believed to be the divine right of royalty. The middle and lower classes were expected to pay homage to their king in the form of loyalty and taxes. The feudal system was perfected with one purpose – to control the far-reaching territories of a kingdom.

The role of Knights was an important and high-profile part of the military and social life of a kingdom. Achieving knighthood was a long and arduous journey reserved for very few and began with the chosen male becoming a page. The Code of Chivalry embraced three aspects – military, social and religion. A person would be dubbed a knight for noble deeds rendered on behalf of the kingdom in the midst of a joyful royal celebration.

Knights were closely associated with horsemanship and combat. During periods of peace, knights participated in jousting tournaments in front of royalty and common people. The dangerous "game" of jousting dates back to the 11th century as a form of perfecting combat skills. King Henry II of France died in a jousting match in the summer of 1559. Chivalrous knights might dedicate their match to a particular lady in the royal court. The lady might choose to offer the knight a kerchief representing her colors. The knight would tie the kerchief around his arm to face his foe.

The gesture became known as *"wearing your heart on your sleeve"*.

December 1st

*There are two kinds of light –
the glow that illuminates,
and the glare that obscures.*

James Thurber
Writer and Cartoonist
(1894 - 1961)

James Thurber (James Grover Thurber) suffered an accident as a child which may have contributed to his odd imagination. During a game of "William Tell" with his two brothers he was struck in the eye by an arrow. The science of neurology records a condition called the Charles Bonnet Syndrome where accelerated visual imagination can result from traumatic eyesight loss.

Thurber attended the Ohio State University but was prevented from graduating because he could not participate in the mandatory ROTC course. Following WWI he launched his writing career with the Columbus Dispatch newspaper. During his early 30's, Thurber relocated to New York City where he remained for the rest of his life. In 1927, he became a member of The New Yorker staff. By 1930, his wit found a new creative outlet when some of his drawings were retrieved from a trash can. During his lifetime Thurber also wrote countless short stories and fables. Two of his writing projects became the basis of Hollywood films – *The Male Animal* (1942) starring a young Henry Fonda and *The Secret Life of Walter Mitty* (1947) with Danny Kaye.

James Thurber died of pneumonia in 1961. He was 66.

December 2nd

The biggest problem in the world could have been solved when it was small.

Witter Bynner
Writer and Poet
(1881 - 1968)

Witter Bynner (Harold Witter Bynner), a writer and poet, was born in Brooklyn, New York, but raised in Brookline, Massachusetts. Bynner graduated from Harvard in 1902 and launched his lengthy writing career as a journalist with McClure Magazine. He soon devoted all his energy and time to writing.

Bynner traveled extensively throughout Asia during the 1920's and 30's. While in China he became fascinated with both Chinese literature and the Chinese language. He mastered the language to the point of translating a large number of the Chinese masters. Bynner's fascination with China and Japan greatly influenced his later literary work. During the late 1930's, Bynner and his lifelong partner, Robert Hunt, moved to the creative community in Santa Fe, New Mexico. The two hosted elaborate parties for such people as Robert Frost, Aldous Huxley, Errol Flynn, Rita Hayworth and Thorton Wilder.

Witter Bynner suffered a severe stroke when he was 84. He died three years later in Santa Fe.

December 3rd

Neither a lofty degree of intelligence nor imagination nor both together go to the making of genius. Love, love, love, that is the soul of genius.

> Wolfgang Amadeus Mozart
> Composer
> (1756 - 1791)

Wolfgang Amadeus Mozart, baptized Johannes Chrysostomus Wolfgangus Theophilus Mozart, created over 600 complex music compositions to become one of the world's most popular composers. The extraordinarily gifted Mozart managed to accomplish greatness in a short life. He died of what modern medicine suggests might have been acute rheumatic fever in his mid-thirties.

Mozart was born in Salzburg, Austria. His father, Leopold, a musician and teacher took responsibility for the education of his two children, young Wolfgang and his older sister, Marie Anna. He began to compose music at the age of five and was engaged as a court musician at 17. By the time he reached his mid-20's, Mozart had married and achieved some financial stability. He counted among his friends Johann Sebastian Bach and Friderick Handel.

Some scholars believe Mozart may have suffered from depression in his last years. After he became ill, Mozart was obsessed with completing his *Requiem.* Ten days before his 35th birthday, Wolfgang Amadeus Mozart died leaving his wife, Constanze, and two sons, Karl and Franz.

December 4th

You cannot shake hands with a clenched fist.

Indira Gandhi
Politician
(1917 - 1984)

Indira Gandhi (born Indira Priyadarshini Nehru) grew up in a political family which played an important role in India's struggle for independence. Her grandfather, Motila Nehru, had a strong presence within India's political scene. Jawaharlal Nehru, Gandhi's father, and a key figure in India's journey towards independence, became the country's first Prime Minister.

Gandhi, born in Allahabad, British India, was the only child of Jawaharlal and Kamla Nehru. She studied at Oxford but left the university before graduating. During her university days she met and eventually married a fellow student named Feroze Gandhi. When her father assumed the role of Prime Minister, Gandhi became his personal assistant. After the death of her father, Gandhi (47) earned a seat in the government of Lal Banadur Shastri. In 1966, she was chosen to fill the position of Prime Minister following Shastri's sudden death. Gandhi served for a total of four terms with a brief interruption in 1977 when her party lost the election. Gandhi proved a natural leader on numerous fronts, including the creation of the "Green Revolution" which revolutionized agriculture and reduced to a degree on-going food shortages.

On October 31, 1984, while on her way to an interview for a documentary with actor Peter Ustinov, the Prime Minister of India was shot repeatedly. Indira Gandhi died weeks before her 67th birthday.

December 5th

The optimist proclaims that we live in the best of all possible worlds, and the pessimist fears this is true.

James Branch Cabell
Writer
(1879 - 1958)

James Branch Cabell, a fantasy fiction writer active during the first half of the 20th century, was highly regarded by his contemporaries. His champions included Mark Twain, H.L. Mencken and Sinclair Lewis. His literary output was pure escapism which complimented social behavior of the 1920's.

Cabell came from an old and distinguished Virginia family. He attended one of Virginia's finest campuses at the College of William and Mary during the closing years of the 19th century. In 1919, he was catapulted into the eye of a controversial storm because of his most famous novel – *Jurgen*. The content was considered far too sexually symbolic for the times. The publisher was ultimately placed on trial on obscenity charges but eventually acquitted. The storm established Cabell's reputation with the general public.

Cabell's writings fell out of favor during the 1930's because he failed to grow beyond fantasy fiction. In the early 1970's a number of his novels were reprinted and are still available. James Branch Cabell died in 1958 at 79.

December 6th

The true measure of a man is how he treats someone who can do him absolutely no good.

Samuel Johnson
Writer and Lexicographer
(1709 - 1784)

Samuel Johnson, who failed to earn a university degree, created a practical work of art equaled by no other writer. *The Dictionary of the English Language* (1755) was assembled over the period of nine years and reined over the language until the Oxford English Dictionary was produced in 1928.

Johnson (25) married Elizabeth "Tetty" Porter (46), the widow of his close friend, Harry Porter. Johnson was employed as a contributing writer for a popular periodical called *The Gentleman's Magazine*. In 1746, Johnson was contracted to create a dictionary for a total fee of 1,500 guineas (approximately $2,500U.S in today's currency.). The massive book would boast of well over 40,000 entries. The concept of writers' royalties did not exist and, as a result, Johnson, the sole author, never benefited from the extraordinary success of the dictionary. As a result Johnson frequently found himself distracted from his work due to mounting debts. Johnson later procrastinated over another great achievement. As much as a decade was devoted to editing and assembling in eight volumes *The Plays of Shakespeare* (1765).

At 53 Johnson, still plagued by never-ending debts, was finally awarded an annual pension by King George III which allowed him to live comfortably for the remainder of his life. Johnson died from various health issues at 75.

December 7th

Man is a history-making creature who can neither repeat his past nor leave it behind.

W.H. Auden
Poet and Educator
(1907 - 1973)

W.H. Auden (Wystan Hugh) grew up in Birmingham, England, the last of three sons born to George Augustus, a medical doctor, and Constance, a nurse. Both his grandfathers were members of the Church of England clergy. During his school years, Auden lost his own faith in any organized religion. He graduated from Oxford in 1928 with a degree in English Literature.

Following his stay at Oxford, Auden (23) became a devoted and well-liked schoolmaster at various boys' schools in England and Scotland. In 1930, his first literary work (*Poems*) was published by London's famous Faber and Faber Publishing House. Months prior to the outbreak of WWII, Auden and his partner, writer Christopher Isherwood, left England for the U.S. where he became a citizen in 1946. Auden suffered much criticism for his decision. He wrote over 400 poems, two of which were book length, and hundreds of essays on a myriad of subjects. In the 1940's, Auden returned to the church.

During his later years, the witty and articulate Auden would frequently become lost in his thoughts. W.H. Auden died at his summer home in Vienna at the age of 66.

December 8th

There is a boundary to men's passions when they act from feelings; but none when they are under the influence of imagination.

Edmund Burke
Philosopher and Statesman
(1729 - 1797)

Edmund Burke, born in Dublin, Ireland, was elected to the British House of Commons at 36 and became in his lifetime one of his adopted country's most respected statesmen. He never shied away from championing unpopular positions.

The Burke household was a perfect blend of opposites. Richard Burke, Edmund's lawyer-father, was a strong supporter of the Church of England while his mother, Mary, was from Irish-Catholic ancestry. Burke elected not to follow his father's advice to pursue law but in his early twenties set out on a path to become a professional writer. In time after he settled in England he was drawn into public life. Burke led debates in the House on such unpopular subjects as defending America's right to tax itself, the end of capital punishment and voiced support for Irish Catholic rights. His strong opinions cost him his seat in the House of Commons at times but he always managed to find his way back.

Edmund Burke died as a result of stomach ailments. He was 68.

December 9th

Pick battles big enough to matter, small enough to win.

Jonathan Kozol
Writer and Educator
(b. 1936)

Jonathan Kozol was a non-fiction writer who spent over forty years as an educator in the inner city schools of Massachusetts. He published countless books advocating that the barriers between children of color, children from poor families and the children of the wealthy be eliminated. Kozol called for true integration in schools throughout the United States.

Kozol was born in Boston, Massachusetts, and graduated from Harvard in 1958, *summa cum laude*, with a specialty in English literature. He was granted a Rhodes scholarship to Oxford but left the campus in favor of pursuing a writing career. He devoted time in Paris surrounded by established writers. Kozol returned to the U.S. and joined the Boston School Board. He has been awarded a number of fellowships in his life and he currently sits on the editorial board of the Greater Good Magazine published by the University of California.

Kozol is the author of several books on education, including *Death at an Early Age* (1967). Jonathan Kozol, with the help of the non-profit organization Education Action, continues to influence teachers.

December 10th

Learn to get in touch with the silence within you, know that everything in this life has a purpose.

Elisabeth Kübler-Ross
Psychiatrist
(1926 - 2004)

Elisabeth Kübler-Ross was born in Zürich, Switzerland, the first of triplets and raised in a devout Protestant family. Her two sisters were named Erika and Eva. Kübler-Ross pursued a degree in medicine but her studies were interrupted by the outbreak of WWII. She eventually earned her medical degree from the University of Zürich in 1957 at the age of 31.

After her university studies, Kübler-Ross married a fellow student (Emanuel Ross) and moved to the United States. Over a short period she became aware of the treatment of terminally ill patients by medical staffs in hospitals. Kübler-Ross took on the role of an instructor at the University of Chicago - School of Medicine in the hope of improving the care of dying patients. In 1969, she wrote a ground-breaking book called *On Death and Dying*. The book introduced the concept of the five stages of grief – denial, anger, bargaining, depression and acceptance.

Elisabeth Kübler-Ross died in 2002 after a series of strokes left her paralyzed.

December 11th

Have a heart that never hardens,
a temper that never tires,
a touch that never hurts.

Charles Dickens
Writer
(1812 - 1870)

Charles Dickens, one of literature's most iconic writers released many of his classic works in a popular marketing method for the time. The Dickens novels were released to an eagerly waiting reading public in serial form over, at times, a large part of a year. But Dickens took the process one step further. Unlike other writers of his time, he wrote the new installments as they were serialized in order to keep the content as fresh as possible.

A perfect example of the serialization process was the classic *A Tale of Two Cities*. The 45 chapters were released over a period of 32 weeks between April and November, 1859. The format allowed the writer to create and gauge cliffhangers thereby increasing the readership's appetite for the next installment. The Dickens classic, *A Tale of Two Cities,* has sold more than 200 million copies. Dickens, the philanthropist, was instrumental in helping in the raising of the funds for the founding of the first hospital for children in the English-speaking world – the Great Ormond Hospital in London.

Dickens' 22-year marriage to Catherine Hogarth ended in 1858. The belief is that Dickens and an actress named Ternan spent the last dozen years of his life together. Ternan received a substantial annuity from his final will.

December 12th

*Don't judge each day
by the harvest you reap
but by the seeds that you plant.*

                            Robert Louis Stevenson
                                      Writer
                                 (1850 - 1894)

Robert Louis Stevenson (Robert Louis Balfour Stevenson) achieved greatness in the literary world and ranks among the most translated writers in history. During his lifetime he became a literary celebrity whose genius was admired by other great writers from Rudyard Kipling to Ernest Hemingway, and he accomplished it all within a short but productive life. He died at 44.

Stevenson inherited his predisposition to frail health from his mother's Balfour ancestry. In his twenties, Stevenson gave up the study of engineering in favor of a writer's life. His father negotiated a compromise fearing his son might fail in literature. Stevenson earned a degree in law (1875). During an active writing career which spanned less than two decades, Stevenson gave the world a number of literary classics such as *Treasure Island* (1886), *The Strange Case of Dr. Jekyll and Mr. Hyde* (1886) and *Kidnapped* (1886).

In 1890, Stevenson and his family moved to the Samoa Island in the South Pacific in search of an ideal climate for his failing health. Robert Louis Stevenson collapsed and died four years later. The young 44-year-old writer was buried in Vailima, Samoa.

December 13th

Laughter is the closest distance between two people.

Victor Borge
Entertainer
(1909 - 2000)

Victor Borge, affectionately known as "The Clown Prince of Denmark", was a child prodigy in his birth place of Copenhagen. He gave his first piano recital at the age of eight. Borge studied at the Royal Danish Academy of Music under the great maestros of the day.

Borge, born Børge Rosenbaum, grew up in a Jewish household where both parents were musicians. His father, Bernhard, was a violist with the Royal Danish Orchestra and his mother, Frederikke, was a concert pianist. Borge spent a few years in concert halls before beginning to incorporate humor into what quickly grew into a successful comedy act. At the outbreak of WWII, Borge (30) fled to the U.S. via Finland arriving in New York with a mere few hundred dollars. Within a few years, Borge was starring on various radio programs demonstrating his unique brand of humor. His phonetic punctuation routine became a favorite with audiences worldwide.

His wife (Sarabel) of 47 years died in September of 2000. Victor Borge died in December of the same year a few days shy of his 91st birthday.

December 14th

Sometimes we stare so long at a door that is closing that we see too late the one that is open.

Alexander Graham Bell
Inventor
(1847 - 1922)

Alexander Graham Bell (born Alexander Bell), the inventor of the telephone, was born in Edinburgh, Scotland, but also lived long periods of his life in the U.S. (Washington, D.C.) and in Canada – Brantford, Ontario and later in Nova Scotia. All three countries proudly claim Bell "as their own".

As a precocious young boy, Bell asked his father, Alexander Melville Bell, for a middle name of his own. On his 11th birthday, Bell was permitted to adopt a middle name and he chose "Graham" in honor of a family friend from Canada. Bell's mother's deafness greatly influenced the direction his life took in his adult years. The entire Bell clan moved to Ontario, Canada, in search of a better climate to off-set his failing health. Bell's fascination with sound led him in his twenties to an invention many scholars consider to have had the greatest single impact on modern society – the telephone. His wife, Mabel, whom he married when he was a very successful 30-year-old, was also deaf. As a wedding gift he gave Mabel all his shares in the newly formed company called Bell Telephone Company. Bell, one of the co-founders of The National Geographic Society, spent a great deal of the last three decades of his life at the family home in Cape Breton, Nova Scotia. Alexander Graham Bell died in Nova Scotia. Mabel died the following year.

December 15th

*Life lived for tomorrow
will always be just a day away
from being realized.*

Leo Buscaglia
Writer and Motivational Speaker
(1924 - 1999)

Leo Buscaglia (Felice Leonardo Buscaglia) earned his PhD from the University of Southern California in 1963 and remained on the teaching faculty until his retirement. After his retirement he was granted the distinct honor of being named Professor At Large.

During his popular teaching years, Buscaglia began to appear as a lecturer on PBS. The programs attained such wide popularity that PBS would air them during their high-profile fund-raising periods. Buscaglia's lectures frequently focused on the obstacles which prevented the expression of love. He battled the social and personal barriers preventing the expression of love with his own personal life lessons. The lectures struck an international chord and were he labeled "Dr. Love". By the end of the 1990's, his book sales had reached nearly twenty million in countless languages.

Dr. Love underlined time and time again the value of personal bonds to enrich our lives and reach true fulfillment. Leo Buscaglia died at age 74 of a heart attack at his home near Lake Tahoe, Nevada.

December 16th

The conquering of self is truly greater than were one to conquer many worlds.

Edgar Cayce
Psychic
(1877 - 1945)

Edgar Cayce reluctantly became an early psychic in the ever-expanding practice during the latter part of the 19th century. For some time he refused to accept the content of his own readings during his trances. He felt they were contrary to his religious beliefs as a devout Christian and active member of the Disciples of Christ.

Cayce was born in Hopkinsville, Kentucky, one of six children. His parents, Leslie and Carrie, were poor Kentucky farmers. Cayce's formal education ended with the equivalent of Grade 9 because his family could not afford the expense. In his early twenties, he developed a severe case of laryngitis resulting in a complete loss of speech. Through the intervention of several hypnotists he eventually regained his ability to speak. Because of his own experiences with hypnotic trances, Cayce discovered his paranormal talent as a psychic. He gained fame but refused to be commercialized and used his gift to help those in need.

During his active years, Cayce reportedly conducted well over 20,000 readings. He was both praised and criticized in his lifetime. Edgar Cayce died as a result of a stroke in 1945. He was 67.

December 17th

***By all means, marry.
If you get a good wife,
you'll become happy;
if you get a bad one,
you'll become a philosopher.***

Socrates
Philosopher
(470 BC – 399 BC)

Socrates is considered by most modern scholars as one of the key founders of Western Philosophy despite the fact he left very little in written form. The true importance of his historic value lies in the writings of his disciples, especially Plato.

According to Plato's writings, Socrates was born around 470 BC in Athens. His father, Sophroniscus, was executed later in his life. Sophroniscus married twice – Phaenacrete, Socrates' mother, and later to Xanthide with whom he had three sons. Tradition tells us that Socrates did not work preferring the noble task of discussing philosophy. Despite the fact that he was not employed as a teacher, he did have a large following. He did serve valiantly in the Athenian army where he distinguished himself in several military campaigns. Socrates, based on later accounts, had serious doubts about democracy.

Socrates' disciples left numerous writings referring to and describing the "Socrates Method". The method examined the moral concepts of "Good and Justice". Traditional accounts suggest Socrates died while imprisoned for his political beliefs by drinking a poison. He was approximately 74.

December 18th

*The tragedy of life doesn't lie
in not reaching your goal.
The tragedy lies
in having no goal to reach.*

Benjamin Mays
Minister and Educator
(1894 - 1984)

Benjamin Mays (Elijah), the youngest son of poor southern tenant farmers and former slaves, championed the dignity of all human beings. His life's work underscored the distinct gap between American ideals and social reality. Mays' thinking and writings served on numerous levels as the foundation of what would later become the civil rights movement throughout the U.S.

Mays earned a PhD at the University School of Religion at the age of 41. His education was interrupted numerous times. During his school years young Mays worked at several jobs to cover his expenses, including as a Pullman porter. He co-authored (with Joseph Nicholson) the first sociological study of black churches – *The Negro's Church* (1939). Mays served as Dean of the School of Religion at Howard University for six years. In 1940, he began a 27-year role as president of Morehouse College. Mays was professor and mentor to a young Martin Luther King Jr. and remained close friends until King's assassination. Mays delivered an emotional eulogy at King's funeral.

Benjamin Mays died at the age of 90 in Atlanta.

December 19th

I have failed many times, and that's why I am a success.

Michael Jordan
Athlete
(b. 1963)

Michael Jordan (Michael Jeffrey), considered the greatest basketball player in the history of the game, was considered too short to qualify for his high school basketball team. His second love, baseball, got his full attention.

Jordan was born in Brooklyn, New York. His mother, Deloris, worked in banking and his father, James, was an equipment supervisor. He grew up very close to his father. In his second year at high school he grew four inches and finally earned a spot on the team. He averaged 20 points per game and earned a scholarship to the University of North Carolina at Chapel Hill. According to Jordan his turning point moment was the winning basket for the 1982 NCAA Championship. In 1984, he joined the NBA's Chicago Bulls and quickly proved himself a star on and off the court. His career was interrupted in 1993 when his beloved father was murdered. He returned to the NBA in 1995. Jordan became a popular representative on the endorsement market.

Jordan helped the Bulls win six NBA Championships and was the league's scoring leader in ten of his 15 playing seasons.

December 20th

***Patience and passage of time
do more than strength and fury.***

Jean de la Fontaine
Poet and Fabulist
(1621 - 1695)

Jean de la Fontaine was a widely read poet during the 19th century despite the fact his literary career was not launched until he entered his thirties. His literary output would set the style in the known world.

De la Fontaine was born in the ancient village of Chateau-Thierry north of Paris. His father, Charles, was a minister of forests and water system. Both his father and his mother, Françoise, were from upper-middle class wealthy families. After a short stay at the seminary, de la Fontaine studied law. He was admitted to the French bar. At 28, his family arranged a marriage with the beautiful 16-year-old Marie Héricart. Neither put great effort into the relationship and they lived apart. His first accepted work, *Eunuchus*, was published when he was 33. History remembers him for his most famous literary achievement – *Fables* (1668). Later in life, de la Fontaine (52) fell in love with Madame de la Sablière and they spent the last twenty years of their lives together.

De la Fontaine was part of a group called Rue du Vieux Colombier which included Racine, Boileau and Molière. He became a member of l'Académie française. Jean de la Fontaine died in Paris at 73.

December 21st

I prefer the errors of enthusiasm to the indifference of wisdom.

Anatole France
Poet, Writer and Journalist
(1844 - 1924)

Anatole France began his writing career in 1867 as a 23-year-old journalist in Paris. During his long and distinguished creative life he earned much praise and was considered during his time as the "ideal man of letters" in all of France.

France was born in Paris to the owner of a very successful book store and the young Anatole spent his younger years surrounded by great literature. After graduation he worked with his father in the store. In 1869, his first literary work, *La Part de Madeleine,* was published and introduced him to the literary circles. France's novel, *Le crime de Sylvestre Bonnard* firmly established his reputation as a serious writer. He became deeply involved in the country's mid-19th century political scandal known as the Dreyfus Affair when he openly supported Alfred Dreyfus, a Jewish army officer falsely accused of espionage. France's most acclaimed novel, *La révolte des anges,* in 1914 secured his place in French literature.

France was a member of l'Académie française, the illustrious literary body established in 1635 by Cardinal Richlieu. He also earned the Nobel Prize for Literature in 1921.

Anatole France died at the age of 80.

December 22nd

Courage is the ladder on which all other virtues mount.

Clare Boothe Luce
Politician, Diplomat and Writer
(1903 - 1987)

Clare Boothe Luce was born Ann Clare Boothe in New York City to a professional dancer (Anna Clara Schneider) and violinist Franklin Boothe. Her first ambition as a child was to become an actress and was understudy to Mary Pickford on Broadway at 10.

Four years following graduation, a young 20-year-old Clare married a clothing industry heir named George Tuttle Brokaw. Her husband proved to be an alcoholic by her own admission and the marriage ended within six years. In 1935, Clare (32) married Henry Luce, the publisher of the successful magazines, Life, Time and Fortune. They enjoyed a very successful and high-profile 32-year relationship until his death in 1967 when she was 64. During WWII, she gained a reputation as a Life reporter writing from the European front lines. Beginning in 1943, Luce served two terms as a Republican congresswoman. A fatal car accident in 1944 took the life of her 20-year-old Stanford University daughter The tragedy was devastating and she turned to Bishop J. Fulton Sheen for support eventually leading to her conversion to Catholicism two years later.

Luce earned the Presidential Medal of Freedom in 1983. Clare Boothe Luce died of brain cancer at the age of 84 in her Watergate apartment in Washington, D.C.

December 23rd

Every time we love,
Every time we give,
It's Christmas.

Dale Evans
Actress, Singer and Song Writer
(1912 - 2001)

Dale Evans was born Frances Octavia Smith in Uvalde, Texas, and her adult life began in her early teens. At 14, she eloped with Thomas Fox and gave birth to a son at 15. The relationship ended in divorce at 17. A second marriage lasted six years.

During her twenties, she changed her name to Dale Evans and launched a singing career. Along the way, she married her music arranger, Robert Dale Butts. In 1947, a fourth marriage to actor-singer Roy Rogers lasted over 50 years until his death in 1998. Rogers and Evans had one daughter, Robin Elizabeth, born with Down Syndrome, who died just shy of her second birthday. The couple adopted four girls. Evan's long-lasting entertainment career included a popular television (*The Roy Rogers Show*) and more than 30 western-action movies. In addition, she wrote hundreds of songs, including the popular *Happy Trails* and *The Bible Tells Me So*.

Evans championed the perception of children born with disabilities. Dale Evans died of congestive heart failure at 88.

December 24th

Home is the nicest word there is.
Laura Ingalls Wilder
Writer
(1867 -1957)

Laura Ingalls Wilder, born in Wisconsin during the mid-19th century, grew up to become the author of one of the most widely-read series of books. Her father, Charles, had an adventurous spirit which took the family to various early rugged pioneer settlements before creating a home in De Smet, South Dakota. The family of four siblings struggled through some difficult times. The experiences would prove the basis of some of the most popular literature of the early 20th century.

At the age of 18, Ingalls married a well-respected 28-year-old bachelor named Almanzo Wilder. The new couple faced a number of difficult years dealing with harsh winters, devastating droughts and the loss of their home and barn to a fire. In 1894, Ingalls (27) and Wilder (37) settled in Mansfield, Missouri where they rebuilt their lives. Her daughter, Rose, began pursuing a writing career and encouraged her mother to become a columnist for the Missouri Ruralist. When Ingalls was 64, and with the support of her daughter, the first book in the *Little House on the Prairie* series was published. Her writings offered her and her husband a very comfortable retirement life.

Almanzo died in 1949 at 92. Laura Ingalls died in 1957 a few days after her 90th birthday in her Mansfield, Missouri, home.

December 25th

Blessed is the season which engages the whole world in a conspiracy of love.

Hamilton Wright Mabie
Editor and Writer
(1846 - 1916)

Hamilton Wright Mabie was born in Cold Springs, New York. His mother, Sarah Colwell Mabie, was a descendent of a wealthy Scottish-English family while his father's (Levi Jeremiah Mabie) ancestors were French political exiles. During his early years, the family moved to Buffalo, New York.

Mabie attended Williams College during the 1860's and earned a degree in law from the Columbia Law School in 1869. Mabie (30) married Jeanette Trivett. He had difficulty developing a fondness for law and, at the age of 33, he became a staff writer for the New York-based weekly magazine, The Christian Union (renamed The Outlook in 1893). In 1882, he became a published writer with the release of *Norse Stories*. Between the early 1880's and 1914, Mabie wrote a large number of books, including several children's writing projects. Some of Mabie's writings are still available.

Hamilton Wright Mabie died at the age of 70.

December 26th

***Peace on earth will come to stay,
when we live Christmas every day.***

Helen Steiner Rice
Poet
(1900 - 1981)

Helen Steiner Rice earned the honorary title of "America's inspirational poet laureate" because of her ability to create uplifting poetry.

Rice was born in Lorain, Ohio, in the first year of the 20th century. Her father, a railroad employee, died during the horrific influenza epidemic which engulfed a large part of the world in 1918. Rice achieved success in the business world which was still a rarity for women at the beginning of the century. As manager of advertising for a major company, Rice developed her natural writing skills. At 28, she married a successful banking executive (Franklin Rice) only to lose him to suicide within a few years as the result of the stock market crash. Rice became a very popular writer for the American Greeting Card Company. The Rice verses were often used in dramatic readings on *The Lawrence Welk Show*. Her inspirational verses were published in a series of books which have sold eight million copies.

Helen Steiner Rice died in her beloved Lorain weeks before her 81st birthday.

December 27th

We are more often frightened than hurt; and we suffer more from imagination than from reality.

Lucius Annaeus Seneca
Philosopher and Statesman
(4 BC - 65 AD)

Lucius Annaeus Seneca (often referred to simply as Seneca), the second son of Seneca, the Elder, was born in Cordoba in the south of Spain, but grew up in Rome. Seneca, the Elder, had accumulated some wealth and enjoyed the privileges of Rome's upper-middle class.

Seneca experienced poor health from his early years and was predisposed to various health issues. His reputation as an intellect earned him a position within Rome's elite circles. Emperor Claudius called upon Seneca to tutor his son and the next emperor – Nero. When Nero (25) assumed the role of Emperor following the death of his father in 54 AD, Seneca became special advisor to the young emperor. In the year 65 AD, a plot was devised to assassinate Nero, then 36. Seneca was falsely accused of participating in the plot and ordered by the emperor to end his own life.

Before his 70th birthday, Lucius Annaeus Seneca, already in failing health, took his own life.

December 28th

Do not wait for extraordinary circumstances to do good; try to use ordinary situations.

Jean Paul Richter
Writer
(1763 - 1825)

Jean Paul Richter (born Johann Paul Friedrich Richter) grew up in a religious home with his pastor-father dying when Richter was approximately sixteen. The death of the elder Richter and the financial situation left the family devastated. Richter's mother struggled to keep the family whole.

At 18, Richter enrolled at one of the oldest schools in the world – the University of Leipzig – where he devoted himself to the study of literature. In his early twenties, Richter published two works which failed to draw any attention. But in 1793, Richter (30) released his powerful romance novel, *Die unsicht bare Loge (The Invisible Lodge)* under the pen name of Jean Paul in honor of the French author, Jean-Jacques Rousseau. The critical acclaim encouraged the young writer and he plunged himself into a series of books, including *Hesperus* in 1795 which established him firmly in German literature.

In his late thirties, Richter married Caroline Meyer. The Richters never recovered from the loss of their only son, Max. In 1824, Jean Paul became blind and died within a year.

December 29th

***Every noble work is
at first impossible.***

Thomas Carlyle
Writer and Historian
(1795 - 1881)

Thomas Carlyle grew up in a very devout Calvinist household in Scotland. His parents had plans to have young Thomas enter the clergy but Carlyle underwent a spiritual crisis while at the University of Edinburg. The personal crisis drew him towards a career in literature.

Carlyle became a mathematics professor following his university graduation. His major literary work, *Sartor Resartus*, was serialized in 1833 and 1834 and received with caution because of the complex writing style. At the age 42, Carlyle published a three-volume work called *The French Revolution: A History*. The first volume was accidentally burnt by a maid and Carlyle patiently rewrote the missing first part of his work. *Revolution* established his fame as a writer. Carlyle was one of the few philosophers to monitor the industrial revolution in Europe. His writings stirred a great deal of social controversy.

During his university years Carlyle developed a painful stomach condition which plagued him all his life. He spent his final years in London. Thomas Carlyle died at 85.

December 30th

*__Genius begins great works;
labor alone finishes them.__*

Joseph Joubert
Writer
(1754 - 1824)

Joseph Joubert spent his early years in a religious college in Toulouse, France. Following graduation the young studious Joubert remained in the south of France as a teacher at his alma mater. In his mid-twenties Joubert transplanted himself to Paris.

During his academic career Joubert was given the prestigious role of inspector-general of the university system under Emperor Napoleon Bonaparte. His circle of literary friends in Paris included François-René Chateaubriand, the French writer who launched the Romantic Period. He also counted the great French writer Denis Diderot (1715-1784) as a close friend. Joubert was a prolific writer during his lifetime but published none of his writings. Joubert's philosophy embraced illness as a means of personal growth.

Joubert's health issues were a frequent problem during his adulthood. Joseph Joubert died in Paris three days before his 70th birthday. After his death, his widow turned his writings over to his friend, Chateaubriand, and were published in 1838 - *Recueil des pensées de M. Joubert* (*Collected Thoughts of Mr. Joubert*). Centuries later, and with thanks to Chateaubriand, Joubert is best remembered for *Pensées*.

December 31st

Wise men make proverbs,
but fools repeat them.

Samuel Palmer
Painter and Writer
(1805 -1880)

Samuel Palmer, born in the Newington district of London, England, was raised in a very pious household. His father, Samuel Palmer, Senior, was a bookseller and a dedicated Baptist Minister. Young Samuel received no formal education but developed a natural talent for painting at an early age.

Some of Palmer's greatest works were painted during a prolific period while living in a cottage near Shoreham (1826-1835). He became part of a group of young artists greatly influenced by William Blake. During an art showing of his Shoreham work in 1825, Palmer (20) was the target of some harsh criticism and refused to allow his work to be exposed. In 1837, Palmer (32) married nineteen-year-old Hannah Linnell, and began to teach art in order to support a growing family. During the mid-1860, he returned to his Shoreham style and gained critical success. Palmer was somewhat forgotten by the art world after his death in 1881. Sadly, his surviving son destroyed a great part of his father's artistic output in order to protect him from further humiliation.

Modern scholars consider Palmer a key figure of England's Romanticism period for his exquisite pastoral paintings. Samuel Palmer and his beloved Hannah are buried side by side in Surrey, England.

> **"Let the cat out of the bag."**

During the early centuries, food goods were a direct result of the family farm fields or garden patch. The soil would supply the raw products, mostly vegetables, rye and barley, to build a meal for the peasants. The family mid-day main meal would often consist of a stew. Bread, and bread products, was a mainstay in all homes. The peasants lived mostly on dark, heavy bread because only the wealthy could afford the preferred white bread because wheat required an expensive manure mix in the soil.

Lords could afford to raise livestock which would in time supplement the family diet. Pigs and sheep were popular farm animals. The sheep was a thin creature whose meat was considered less desirable. The pig, on the other hand, became a popular meat supply because of taste and quantity of tasty flesh. Pigs were a relatively easy farm animal to keep since pigs found their own food. The forests were rich with wild creatures, including deer, rabbits and boars but the peasants were forbidden to hunt. Poaching was considered a serious crime and if caught the penalty could be the loss of a hand.

One of the oldest forms of food retailing known to mankind is likely the local market. Throughout the ages people gathered at local markets and fairs to buy livestock, produce and other goods. A merchant would allow the peasant to select the live animal of his choice, mostly pigs, which was then dropped into a cloth bag for easy transporting. Untrustworthy merchants might slip a cat into the bag knowing the purchaser would not discover the ruse until much later when he reached home. The unscrupulous merchant relied on the fact that the purchaser would not *"let the cat out of the bag"* before leaving the marketplace.

Index of Sources

Abba Eban . . . Sept 13
Abraham Lincoln . . . Jan 15 Apr 28
Abraham Sutskever . . . Oct 16
Adlai Stevenson . . . Oct 23
Aeschylus . . . July 21
Aesop . . . May 28
Albert Camus . . . Jan 3 Aug 13
Albert Einstein . . . Apr 29 Aug 12 Nov 10
Albert Schweitzer . . . Feb 23 Aug 26
Albert Szent-Gyorgi . . . Nov 14
Aldous Huxley . . . June 30
Alexander Dumas . . . May 26
Alexander Graham Bell . . . Dec 14
Alexander Pope . . . Mar 24
Alfred Lord Tennyson . . . Sept 4
Ambrose Bierce . . . July 18
Anatole France . . . Dec 21
Andy Rooney . . . Mar 25
Ann Sullivan . . . May 6
Anthony Powell . . . Mar 4
Antoine de Saint-Exupéry . . . Jan 5 July 28
Anton Chekhov . . . June 26
Anwar Sadat . . . Feb 16
Aristotle . . . Mar 8
Arthur Schopenhauer . . . Oct 11
Audrey Hepburn . . . Aug 19
Ben Johnson . . . Jan 20 May 11
Baltasar Gracian . . . Nov 30
Ben Stein . . . Mar 28
Benjamin Disraeli . . . Jan 12
Benjamin Franklin . . . Sept 25
Benjamin Mays . . . Dec 18
Bernard Meltzer . . . May 31
Bertrand Russell . . . Mar 21 Aug 1

Bill Cosby . . . David Starr Jordan

    Bill Cosby . . . Aug 2
    Bill Gates . . . Sept 8
    Billy Graham . . . June 22
    Bishop Fulton J. Sheen . . . May 4
    Blaise Pascal . . . Oct 18
    Brigham Young . . . May 7
    Buckminster Fuller . . . Sept 22
    Buddha . . . Nov 25
    Carl Rogers . . . Apr 5
    Carl Sagan . . . May 12
    Carl Sandburg . . . July 24
    Catherine the Great . . . Jan 24
    Cesare Pavese . . . Oct 3
    Charles Baudelaire . . . Apr 21
    Charles Caleb Colton . . . Nov 13
    Charles Dickens . . . Apr 20 Aug 9 Dec 11
    Charles-Louis Montesquieu . . . May 22
    Charlie Chaplin . . . Mar 11
    Che Guevara . . . July 30
    Chief Dan George . . . Aug 24
    Cicero . . . Jan 2
    Clare Boothe Luce . . . Dec 22
    Clarence Darrow . . . Jan 11
    Claude Levi-Strauss . . . July 13
    Comte De Bussy-Rabutin . . . Feb 15
    Confucius . . . Jan 25 Aug 27
    Dag Hammerarskjold . . . Sept 5
    Dale Carnegie . . . Sept 6
    Dale Evans . . . Dec 23
    Dali Lama . . . Jan 27 May 30
    Daniel Enright . . . Jan 1 Aug 6
    Danny Kaye . . . Apr 1
    David Brinkley . . . Apr 27
    David Starr Jordan . . . July 26

| Deepak Chopra . . . Frank Scully |

Deepak Chopra . . . July 3
Derek Walcott . . . Feb 12
Desiderius Eramus . . . Jan 22   June 23
Desmond Tutu . . . Oct 29
Dolly Parton . . . Aug 11
Dorothy Canfield Fisher . . . July 10
Dr. Seuss . . . June 5
E. E. Cummings . . . Nov 18
Earl Wilson . . . July 27
Eckhart Tolle . . . Mar 13
Edgar Allan Poe . . . May 20
Edgar Cayce . . . Dec 16
Edmond Burke . . . Apr 14 Aug 28 Dec 8
Edna Buchanan . . . Mar 7
Edward Everett Hale . . . June 20
Edward R. Murrow . . . June 8
Elbert Hubbard . . . Feb 21
Elie Wiesel . . . Apr 15
Elisabeth Barrett Browning . . . Nov 7
Elizabeth Stanton . . . Apr 2
Elizabeth Kübler-Ross . . . Dec 10
Emile Zola . . . Feb 2
Emily Dickinson . . . Apr 9
Epictetus . . . Apr 24
Epicurus . . . Sept 11
Erma Bombeck . . . Jan 23
Ernest Hemingway . . . Jan 18
Eugene Ionesco . . . May 5
Father James Keller . . . Jan 6
Francis Bacon . . . Feb 27   June 18
Florence Nightingale . . . June 25
François de la Rochefoucauld . . . July 5
Françoise Sagan . . . Oct 20
Frank Scully . . . Mar 6

Frank Tyger . . .   Isaac Asimov

    Frank Tyger . . . Mar 9
    Franklin D. Roosevelt . . . Aug 31
    Franklin P. Jones . . . June 21
    Fred Allen . . . Jan 30
    Frederick Douglass . . . May 18
    G. K Chesterton . . . Feb 7   Aug 22
    Garison Keillor . . . Mar 30
    George Bernard Shaw . . . May 17 Sept 24
    George Carlin . . . May 8
    George Eliot . . . Feb 5   Nov 16
    George Sand . . . Oct 15
    George Santayana . . . Oct 6
    George Washington Carver . . . Feb 4
    George Jessel . . . Mar 19
    Groucho Marx . . . Aug 4
    H. L. Mencken . . . Oct 7
    Hamilton Wright Mabi . . . Dec 25
    Hannah More . . . Nov 19
    Harper Lee . . . Nov 21
    Helen Hayes . . . Nov 24
    Helen Keller . . . Apr 16   Aug 14
    Helen Steiner Rice . . . Dec 26
    Henny Youngman . . . Oct 24
    Henri Frédéric Amiel . . . June 6
    Henry Ford . . . Aug 10   Sept 21
    Henry James . . . May 2
    Henry Kissinger . . . Aug 17
    Henry Miller . . . Sept 3
    Honoré de Balzac . . . Sept 9
    Horace . . . June 1   Oct 30
    Horace Greeley . . . July 24
    Indira Gandhi . . . Dec 4
    Irene C. Kassorla . . . Sept 27
    Isaac Asimov . . . Nov 23

| J.R.R. Tolkien . . . Joseph Conrad |

J.R.R. Tolkien . . . May 13
Jack Lemmon . . . Apr 11
Jack London . . . May 14 Oct 2
James Baldwin . . . Feb 6 May 25
James Branch Cabell . . . Dec 5
James M. Barrie . . . Apr 8
James Thurber . . . Dec 1
Jean de la Bruyère . . . Nov 15
Jean de la Fontaine . . . Dec 20
Jean-Jacques Rousseau . . . Jan 26
Jean-Paul Richter . . . Jan 16 Dec 28
Jean-Paul Sartre . . . Mar 14
Jesse Jackson . . . June 10
Jimmy Durante . . . Feb 9
Johann Schiller . . . Apr 10
Johann von Goethe . . . July 25 Aug 30
John Buchan . . . July 2
John C. Maxwell . . . Apr 4
John Dryden . . . July 8
John F. Kennedy . . . Aug 20
John Galsworthy . . . Mar 10
John Gray . . . Aug 16
John Kenneth Galbraith . . . Oct 1
John Lennon . . . May 21
John Newton . . . Mar 1
John Quincy Adams . . . Nov 5
John Ruskin . . . June 17
John Sheffield . . . June 15
John Steinbeck . . . Sept 18
John Updike . . . Nov 1
John W. Gardner . . . Sept 14
Jonathan Kozel . . . Dec 9
Jonathan Swift May 24
Jonathan Winters . . . Aug 7
Josef Albers . . . July 19
Joseph Conrad . . . Nov 20

A Year in Quotes - Book One

Joseph Joubert . . . Marie Dressler

Joseph Joubert . . . Dec 30
Josh Billings . . . June 28
Jules Renard . . . June 16
Karl Menninger . . . June 19
Khalil Gibran . . . Sept 26 Nov 6
Katharine Hepburn . . . Feb 26
Kathleen Norris . . . Oct 21
Kin Hubbard . . . Mar 27
Kurt Cobain . . . Mar 23
Lady Montagu . . . Feb 19
Laura Ingalls . . . Dec 24
Lao Tzu . . . Mar 2
Larry Gelbart . . . Oct 25
Lauren Bacall . . . Jan 31
Leo Aikman . . . May 23
Leo Buscaglia . . . June 29 Dec 15
Leo Tolstoy . . . Feb 20
Leonardo Da Vinci . . . June 4
Leroy 'Satchel' Page . . . May 15
Les Brown . . . Aug 29
Les Miz . . . Jan 21
Lewis Carroll . . . Mar 20
Lord Chesterfield . . . Nov 28
Louise Hay . . . Oct 31
Louis Pasteur . . . Oct 27
Lucius Annaceas Seneca . . . Dec 27
Mahatma Gandhi . . . Nov 12
Malcolm Forbes . . . Sept 17
Marcel Pagnol . . . Sept 12
Marcel Proust . . . Nov 4
Marcus Aurelius . . . July 4
Margaret Mead . . . Sept 23
Marie Dressler . . . July 31

A Year in Quotes - Book One

Mark Twain . . . Pythagores

Mark Twain   . . . Jan 8   Mar 17   Aug 18
Marlene Dietrich   . . . Feb 22
Marquis De Sade   . . . June 7
Martin Luther   . . . July 1
Martin Luther King   . . . Feb 25
Maya Angelou   . . . Jan 7   July 14
Michael Jordon   . . . Dec 19
Michel de Montaigne   . . . Mar 22   Sept 30
Michelangelo   . . . Oct 5
Mignon McLaughlin   . . . Mar 26
Miguel de Cervantes   . . . Apr 13
Molière   . . . Nov 29
Mother Teresa   . . . Feb 8   Apr 7
Napoleon Bonaparte . . . Feb 3
Nathaniel Hawthorne . . . Oct 12
Nelson Mandela   . . . Feb 29
Norman Cousins . . .   Apr 22
Norman Vincent Peale   . . . June 3
Ogden Nash . . . May 10
Oliver Wendell Holmes . . . Apr 30
Oprah Winfrey . . .   Apr 23
Orville Wright   . . . May 9
Osbert Lancaster   . . . Sept 19
Oscar Levant . . . Jan 9
Oscar Wilde   . . . Jan 4   June 9   Oct 19
P. T. Barnum   . . . Mar 31
Pablo Picasso . . . Aug 8
Paul Valery   . . . Mar 12
Peter de Vries   . . . June 27
Peter Drucker   . . . May 27   Sept 2
Peter Ustinov   . . . Feb 10   June 2
Plato . . . Apr 19   Aug 25
Price Cobb . . . Sept 16
Publilius Syrus . . . July 13
Pythagores . . . Jan 19

Rabbi Kushner . . . Thomas Carlyle

Rabbi Kushner . . . Feb 11
Rabindranath Tagore . . . Oct 4
Rainer Maria Rilke . . . Mar 15
Ralph Waldo Emerson . . . Apr 3   Nov 27
René Descartes . . . July 11
Renoir . . . Jan 17
Robert Frost . . . Apr 12   Nov 8
Robert H. Schuller . . . May 16
Robert Louis Stevenson . . . Feb 14   Dec 12
Rodney Dangerfield . . . Mar 18
Ronald Reagan . . . Nov 17
Rumi . . . May 3   June 12
Saint Ambrose . . . Oct 22
Saint Augustine . . . May 1
Saint Francis of Assisi . . . Feb 1   Aug 15
Sammy Davis Jr. . . . Oct 17
Samuel Johnson . . . June 11   Dec 6
Samuel Palmer . . . Dec 31
Shana Alexander . . . Sept 15
Shirley MacLaine . . . Nov 26
Sigmund Freud . . . Apr 25   Nov 11
Socrates . . . Dec 17
Sophocles . . . Nov 9
Soren Kierkegaard . . . July 6
Stephen Hawking . . . May 29
Stephen King . . . July 23
Sun Tzu . . . Sept 7
T. S. Eliot . . . Mar 16
Tallulah Bankhead . . . Sept 28
Tennessee Williams . . . Feb 18
Terry Moore . . . Dec 29
Theodore N. Vail . . . Sept 20
Thomas Campbell . . . July 9
Thomas Carlyle . . . Dec 29

A Year in Quotes - Book One

Thomas de Quincey . . . Zig Ziglar

Thomas de Quincey . . . June 14
Thomas Edison . . . Mar 5 Aug 23
Thomas Henry Huxley . . . Oct 26
Thomas Jefferson . . . Feb 28
Tim Cahill . . . Aug 5
Tom Bodett . . . July 22
Truman Capote . . . Nov 3
Unknown . . . Jan 14 Feb 24 Apr 6
Victor Borge . . . Dec 13
Victor Hugo . . . Mar 3 July 17
Voltaire . . . Jan 13 Aug 3
W. E. B. Du Bois . . . Oct 9
W. H. Auden . . . Dec 7
W. Somerset Maugham . . . Feb 17 Aug 21
Walt Disney . . . Apr 18
Walt Whitman . . . Oct 28
Walter Winchell . . . July 20
Warren Buffett . . . July 12
Wayne Dyer . . . Mar 29
Wayne Gretzky . . . Oct 13
Wilferd A. Peterson . . . Sept 10
Will Rogers . . . Apr 17
William Allen White . . . Oct 10
William B. Prescott . . . Sept 29
William Butler Yeates . . . July 15
William Dean Howells . . . Nov 22
William James . . . Nov 2
William Shakespeare . . . July 7 Oct 14
William Shedd . . . Feb 13
William Wordsworth . . . July 29
Wilson Miger . . . Jan 28
Winston Churchill . . . May 19 Sept 1 Oct 8
Witter Bynner . . . Dec 2
Wolfganf Amadeus Mozart . . . Dec 3
Xenocrates . . . July 16
Yogi Berra . . . Jan 10
Zig Ziglar . . . Jan 29

*"**A life paved with selfless kind deeds allows one to eventually grow to heaven."***

Jerry Appleton

Jerry Appleton

Photo by Diane Schryver

Jerry Appleton is a retired Canadian broadcaster having served in both the creative and executive segments of the industry for over four decades. He was part of the original Global Television Network launch team in Canada and worked with Rogers Broadcasting Ltd. Jerry started his career at CHCH-TV (Hamilton, Ontario) where he worked as a studio director involved in such television classics as *Don Messer's Jubilee*, *The Hilarious House of Frightenstein* and *Party Game* with Jack Duffy, Dinah Christie and funny-man, Billy Van. Jerry was also the founding-president of Venture Entertainment Group - a Toronto-based production-distribution company.

Over the years, he took on the role of Executive Producer of a number of television projects, including the first years of the popular *SCTV* comedy series, the Jack Silberman/Gillian Darling-produced *Island of Whales* documentary narrated by Mr. Gregory Peck and countless other television projects. He also served as Executive Producer on behalf of Global with Gladys Rackmil on the award-winning Nederlander Productions-Global made-for-tv movie, *A Case of Libel*, starring Ed Asner, Daniel J Travanti and Gordon Pinsent. During the early 1980's, Monty Hall convinced Jerry to participate in the *Variety Club of America* and, with great pride, he executive produced over 20 annual telethons raising countless millions for special children.

Jerry currently shares his time between two homes – Ontario, Canada and Paradise Village near Puerto Vallarta, Mexico.

www.ingramcontent.com/pod-product-compliance
Lightning Source LLC
Chambersburg PA
CBHW032057090426
42743CB00007B/157